THE LIFE OF ROBERT OWEN

Robert Owen

A Sketch by J. Comerford

Taken at the request of A.H.R.

THE LIFE OF
ROBERT OWEN

By G. D. H. COLE

Author of "The Life of William Cobbett,"
"The World of Labour," etc.

MACMILLAN AND CO., LIMITED
ST. MARTIN'S STREET, LONDON
1930

PREFACE TO SECOND EDITION

I have taken the occasion of this new edition both to correct a few errors in the text, and to attempt in a revised opening chapter, a modified evaluation of Owen's position in the development of Socialist thought. Otherwise, I have made only minor changes.

G. D. H. C.

HAMPSTEAD,
February, 1930.

PREFACE TO FIRST EDITION

I have not tried to make this book an absolutely full life of Owen, much less a full account of the Owenite movement. Thus, I have touched very lightly on the various Owenite communities and societies, and have not dealt at all with those in which Owen took no personal part. Nor have I reproduced the mass of detail contained in Podmore's *Life of Robert Owen;* for that remains accessible to the student. But I think I have given the salient facts of Owen's life and influence, and connected them with the various social and economic movements which his doctrines vitally affected.

The material contained in Chapter VIII I used some time ago for an article on "Owen's Educational Ideas," which appeared in the *Hibbert Journal.*

I have to thank a number of friends who have helped me with the book. Mr. Joseph Trask has given me great help with the bibliography; Mr. W. R. Straker and Mr. R. W. Postgate have lent me rare books which I do not possess. Professor Hall and the Co-operative Union kindly allowed me to consult the valuable collection of Owen's letters and papers at Holyoake House, Manchester. To these and to many others I tender my best thanks.

G. D. H. COLE.

HAMPSTEAD,
   April, 1925.

CONTENTS

CONTENTS

LIST OF ILLUSTRATIONS

ROBERT OWEN

CHAPTER I

ROBERT OWEN AND HIS TIMES

The name "Industrial Revolution" is modern; but the idea is as old as the events which it describes. The men who lived through the period of decisive economic change that links the eighteenth and nineteenth centuries together had no doubts about its revolutionary character. The revolution in industry was not, to be sure, of the same order as the contemporary Revolution in France. It was marked by no one overmastering incident; nor was its achievement crammed into a few years of violent catastrophe and turmoil. By comparison with the fall of the *ancien régime*, it moved slowly and by steps each in itself insignificant. At no one moment did those who passed through it become conscious that they were living in a new world. It created rather a need for constant piecemeal adjustments, now here, now there, as one part after another of the life of the nation fell under its destroying and creative force. Nor was it, like the French Revolution, by a definite date finished and complete, so that men could take stock of it as a chain of past events. The Industrial Revolution never ended. It is not over

B   I

now: indeed, in our own day it is entering upon a new and deeply significant phase.

There is a second difference. The Revolution in France, whatever economic and social causes lay behind it, appeared to contemporaries above all as a product of human wills. Men had made it, appealing in the consciousness of their wrongs to ultimate and compelling notions of human right. It was, in the minds of its supporters, the triumph of human reason made actual through the General Will of the sovereign people, and, in the minds of its opponents, a disaster and a crime born of men's overweening belief in reason as against tradition, in popular will as against the principle of authority in the State. Both views regarded it as essentially man-made, as the outcome of a certain spirit and attitude in the minds of men.

The Industrial Revolution, by sharp contrast, appeared primarily as the product of forces outside men's control. Men, doubtless, were making the individual inventions by means of which it advanced; and this man's enterprise and that man's "abstinence" were the necessary conditions of its successful development. But the new entrepreneurs and capitalists, and even the inventors, whatever importance might be attributed to their individual contributions to the stream of economic progress, were conscious of swimming in the wave of opportunity. The movement, they felt, was bigger than they: their very enterprise was a sign of the times, and the outcome of forces which they did not make, but only answered.

Still more were the theorists of the movement conscious of this impersonal quality. In their view

2

the Industrial Revolution appeared above all as a great emission of powers inherent in a natural economic order. From Adam Smith to Ricardo, the elder Mill and M'Culloch this attitude dominates the new science of Political Economy. The French Physiocrats, in the true spirit of the eighteenth century enlightenment, had conceived the right art of government as consisting in the adjustment of the social system to an underlying natural order, ready and waiting to come to man's aid if he would but throw down the artificial barriers he had wantonly placed in its way. *"Laissez-faire, laissez-passer,"* they said, bidding men and Governments stand out of nature's path. The English economists, from Adam Smith onwards, took up the cry. They bade Governments make an end of monopolies, privileges, tariffs, of all artificial restraints on the free natural enterprise of mankind. And, in this spirit, when the new industrialism arose without the aid of Governments, and began ruthlessly pushing its way through the obstruction which law and custom had set in its path, its advance seemed to them the assertion of a natural force that was bent on bringing the world to wealth and happiness of its own motion. Men could collaborate with this force, as the husbandman can work with nature to increase the fertility of the land. But the force itself was conceived as a force of nature, and not as a product of the human will.

It is a familiar paradox that men tend to act most vigorously when they proclaim that they are only doing what the order of the universe bids them do, and will achieve even in their despite. Undoubtedly, this sense of acting with nature lent

power and energy both to the actions of the entrepreneurs of the Industrial Revolution and to the
theorists who set out to formulate and interpret its
laws. These new capitalists and the new Political
Economists were alike very positive—very much
assured of their own rightness and of the un-
answerable logic of their demands. They had,
above all, the ruthlessness that goes with this assurance. They were not unconscious that the new industrialism was being born in the travail of the
society that was its mother. But they were possessed
by a secure faith in its ultimate rightness; and beside this the sufferings, the unrest and the destruc-
tion that accompanied it seemed to them matters
of little account. They were on the side of progress; and he who opposed the advance of the new
order was standing blindly in the way of a resistless
natural force.

Robert Owen, the subject of this book, had much
in common with these apostles of the new economic
order. He became himself a great industrialist, and
he was never for a moment in doubt about the triumph of the machine and of large-scale production
based upon the new sources and instruments of
power. But his interpretation of the needs of the
time was widely different from that of his fellow-
capitalists and fellow-economists; for he insisted
above all on the need for controlling and organising the vast new forces which had been let loose
upon the world. Even more than Ricardo or
M'Culloch, he regarded these forces as natural, as
things given to man rather than made by his creative
power; for in Owen's view man was ever the creature
of his environment. But, so far from drawing the

4

moral that men should leave these forces of nature to operate free and uncontrolled, Owen held that their emergence demanded conscious and deliberate regulation in the common interest. The new forces, he insisted, were not individual but social forces; they were replacing the individual producer, making a thing with the work of his own hands, by a collaborating group of producers, who must work together in designed harmony in order to achieve a good result. Competition was of the essence of the old order, and not of the new. The vital principle of the new industrialism must be Co-operation.

In this above all else Owen's significance lies. It is the idea that unifies all his varied activities. Whether he is pleading for a Factory Act to protect the helpless servants of the new machines, or for a universal system of liberating education, or for Trade Unions, or for his own scheme of Co-operative communities, the dominant idea in his mind is the need for the social control of the new productive power. Nature has put this power at the disposal of men; but it is men's business to see that it is used aright, and to make of nature's new fertility not a jungle, but an ordered garden.

Both interpretations—Owen's and that of his fellow-industrialists and economists—were possible inferences from the facts on which they were based. And the interpretation which Owen rejected was, in the circumstances of his own day, by far the easier to endorse, except for those upon whom the new economic system fell with the impact of calamity. For the forces which he wished to control were arising under conditions which made their control an exceedingly difficult thing. They developed fast, but sporadically, springing up now here and now there unpredictably, and appearing as the individual acts of the particular entrepreneurs who were first to exploit them. The machinery of State, devised for quite different ends and in the hands of a narrow class which had for the most part little understanding of the new economic forces, was singularly ill-adapted for directing them aright, or indeed at all. Each entrepreneur was too busy with the abundant tasks and opportunities that lay ready to his hand to be disposed to give much thought to the wider problems of the new order, or to join with his fellows in thinking out a concerted plan of development. The mass of the people, unenfranchised and unorganised, was dragged along helplessly behind the new Juggernaut, and was the more impotent to control its course in that it was confronted with a power that it did not even begin to understand. There was no man, no class, no force at all in Society strong enough to exercise the control which Owen demanded. But that he saw the necessity of it, long before the means of achieving it had come to exist, and that he spent the best part of his life in struggling to bring these means into existence, are the secrets of Owen's greatness.

In our own day, this is not difficult to appreciate; for the history of the past hundred years is made up largely of the gradual devising—still far from complete—by Society of the means of controlling the new forces that were let loose by the Industrial Revolution. Nowadays, men may still regard Owen's ideal as wrong; but they can no longer dismiss it as merely visionary or impracticable. Owen was the pioneer of British Socialism, and, like most pioneers, had a far surer grasp of ends than of means. Since his day, Socialism has become a power and, short of Socialism, a good deal of the social control for which he pleaded in vain has become an accomplished fact. His dreams are coming true, though not as he dreamed them; for within his larger prescience, the individual figures and fancies of his dreaming were drawn inevitably from his own time and not from ours. He could see the need for Socialism and social control arising out of the conditions of the machine age that must be men's master until they would learn to control it by their united power; but he could not see the painful stages by which humanity would have to learn its lesson.

Herein Owen's Utopianism lies. His own vision of the needs of the new age was so clear that he asked men to proceed directly to their full realisation. But men were still utterly unprepared for the way of living that he prescribed. Not only were they personally unready: they were above all without the collective means of making themselves ready; and the organisation needed for this purpose could not be improvised in a day or a year. It had to be built up gradually and with many pains of growth. Owen was indeed aware that the men he saw around him were unfit to live according to the laws of the "new moral world" of his ideal; but, attributing their unfitness solely to the defects of their environment, he supposed that if this could but be changed all would be well. His Co-operative communities were attempts to change men's hearts and minds by placing them in a new environment better adjusted to the needs of the new social conditions. They failed, partly because his conception of these needs was defective, but even more because the minds of men could not be changed so easily as he supposed.

These experiments in community-making belong to the later years of Owen's life, when he had lost much of his earlier balance and been forced into impossible attempts by his sense of the urgency of the need for practical demonstration of his ideal. He began with a far more realistic sense of what could and could not be done. There is a good deal to be said for the view that throughout the latter part of his life Owen was at least a little mad. His idea—and he was always a man of one idea—had run away with him, and he had lost his sense of the relation of means to ends. Earlier, at the great cotton mills at New Lanark, which made his name famous throughout the world, he had been content to begin building up from the foundations. At that stage of his career, he had the good sense to see that men could not be made suddenly to live according to the new moral law of a totally unfamiliar environment. At New Lanark, accordingly, he began with the children, and made his system of education—startlingly modern in its essential features and ideas—the cornerstone of his constructive work. But later he grew too impatient to wait upon the slow results of educational advance. He was drawn into a working-class movement of revolt that was crying out for leadership in its crusade for liberation from the tyranny of the machine. The active spirits in this movement found in his ideas the inspiration that they sought. Owenism was for them

8

the hope of mastery over the new industrialism that was bearing them down; and Owen, when they cried out to him to be their leader, was not able to resist their appeal. He was swept along upon the swift current of their hopes, fain to believe in the impossible because the possible offered neither present release from affliction nor assured hope for a future within the range of common imagination.

Thus Socialism passed from being a moral ideal to become for a few years the slogan of a national economic movement. For those few years Owen, the great employer, became the recognised leader of Trade Unionism and of the British working class. But he was never at home in this leadership. He had been too much used, as an employer, to playing the benevolent autocrat and ordering men about for their good to be at ease in the leadership of an essentially democratic movement. He wanted the Trade Unions to submit, as readily as his employees at New Lanark had submitted, to his benevolent despotism. The cause was, in his eyes, essentially a crusade for the moral regeneration of Society as a whole, and not a war of class against class. The struggle to achieve a wage advance here, or to resist a wage reduction there, did not interest him; for to his mind Trade Unionism and Co-operation were of account only as means to the establishment of the "New Moral World." He and his followers were therefore constantly at cross purposes. They might need his ideal to buoy them up with hope in the day-to-day struggle; but for the many the immediate incidents of the struggle for better conditions were necessarily of more importance and urgency than the ideal itself. This divergence of atti-

9

tude made Owen an impossible leader; and as soon as it was realised, consciously or half-consciously, on both sides, Owen and the main body of the working-class movement parted company by common consent. For the years immediately preceding the collapse of the Grand National Consolidated Trades Union in 1834, Owen was the generally acknowledged leader of the Trade Union world. After 1834 Owenism became the name of a sect of moral reformers, and in the larger movements of the working class during the remaining twenty years of his life, Owen played no part. Co-operation, which owed to him its ideas and its initial momentum, grew up without his aid. The Trade Unions almost forgot that he had ever been their leader. Socialism ceased, in Great Britain, to count as an economic or political creed.

Owen's practical connection with the working-class movement was, indeed, only an episode, forced on him by circumstances over which he had no real control. His effective contribution consists not in this, but in the idea of Socialism as the collective control of the new forces generated in the Industrial Revolution. He himself would perhaps have stated the case in a different way; for the essence of his message, as he conceived it, lay in his repudiation of men's individual responsibility for their actions, and in his assertion of the overmastering influence of environment upon character. "Men's character," he was never weary of saying, "is made for, and not by, them"—place them in the right social environment, and they will develop the right moral ideas, and order their lives in the right way. But this half-truth is in reality only the

negative aspect of Owen's teaching; for, even if
his contention be accepted, it remains to settle
what is the right environment and what are the
right ideas and ways of living to put into men's
minds. The filling of this void by the idea of social
co-operation is Owen's practical and positive contribution; and it is in reality this that in every
aspect of his activity forms the solid basis of his
achievement.

With it goes a second idea, less wide in scope but
hardly less important. Owen is the first person, in
Great Britain at any rate (for Fourier was pro-
claiming the same idea independently in France),
to assert plainly the vital influence on the character
of men and of Society of the actual conditions of
labour. He saw the key to the problems of morals
and politics alike in the right organisation of the
economic life of Society. So preoccupied was he
with this aspect of human affairs that the great
political and intellectual upheaval of the French
Revolution appears to have exerted upon him
literally no influence at all. The challenging proclamation of the political "Rights of Man" left
him utterly unmoved because he conceived of the
world of politics as no more than an emanation
from the real world of economic relationships. In
this, though he proclaimed no Materialist Conception of History, he essentially anticipated Marx.
Political movements, as such, seemed to him merely
superficial, unless they were firmly grounded in
economic realities. This attitude, doubtless, came
to him largely from his upbringing; but it is at the
roots of his thought. Unlike Marx in that he never
sought to build up a political party upon an

economic foundation, he is essentially at one with
Marx in discerning the foundations of Socialism in
the inherent logic of the economic order.

Owen began life, as we shall see, with few advantages. He was born at Newtown, Montgomeryshire, a remote little town of central Wales, far
from the bustle of the great commercial centres.
His father was a tradesman in the town, and most
of his relatives were farmers or tradesmen. He received only the ordinary education of the village
school, from a master who could teach him little
beyond the rudiments of reading and writing. At
seven he became usher in his school; at nine he left
school and went to work. But the spirit of adventure stirred in him. At ten he left Newtown, and
came to London in search of fortune. From ten to
eighteen he was shop-boy or assistant, first in Stamford, then in London, and last in Manchester. At
eighteen, with a borrowed hundred pounds for his
capital, he set up in business for himself as a manufacturer of the new textile machinery. Fortune and
his personal qualities favoured him, and at twenty-
nine he became the head of the great cotton mills
at New Lanark, already among the biggest and
best equipped in Great Britain.

Owen's career up to this point is a typical ro-
mance of commerce—an adventure of the Industrial Revolution after the hearts of the apostles of
self-help and capitalist abstinence, well fitted to
point a Victorian moral or adorn an economic
tract. One expects it to end with Owen amassing a
vast fortune, dying a baronet at least, and founding
a great "house," with probably a seat in the Lords
and a prescriptive right to order other folk about.

But, in fact, Owen has never been a favourite theme of the economic tract-makers. For the story goes on in quite the wrong way. Owen made a fortune at New Lanark; but he valued his position there, not as a means to money-making, for which he cared hardly at all, but as the chance of his life for putting into practice certain ideas which from boyhood had been developing in his mind. He saw everywhere around him the miseries and cruelties which attended the Industrial Revolution, especially in its earlier stages. He saw men, women and children maimed, stunted and demoralised by the slavery of the new factories, condemned to work impossibly long hours under incredibly vile and unhealthy conditions, treated not as human beings, but as mere instruments for the accumulation of riches. This whole bad business seemed to him not only wrong and indefensible in itself, but also quite unnecessary even as a means to money-making. "I can make manufacturing pay," he said to himself, and was soon to say to others, "without reducing those whom I employ to misery and moral degradation."

Owen's career as a public man began with his acquisition of the New Lanark mills. And Owenism, as a social system, also began at New Lanark. Owen was like some other great employers of the time, in that he set out to create, not so much a factory, as an industrial community—a whole social system based on a productive unit. This, indeed, was largely forced upon him by the circumstances of the time; for he had to bring the labourers to the factory, to house them and feed them, and to undertake the care of their social life as well as of their work as producers. But Owen went far beyond other employers who built up industrial villages centred round their works. He held already the view, on which all his practice was based, that man is a creature of his environment, and that, according as his material and moral surroundings are good or bad, so will his nature and character be good or bad. Out of this theory of human nature arose both his extraordinarily successful experiment at New Lanark and his later and more artificial essays in community-building. Out of it arose too, from the very first, his intense interest in education; for he recognised clearly that the years of childhood are the most formative period of a man's life, and that, if character is to be made for men by their environment, as he insisted it must be, the making must begin at that stage. Hence the schools for the children at New Lanark, to which visitors thronged from all over Europe and America; and hence the constant concern of Owen and his disciples with the problems of education and educational freedom.

Owen's educational methods would make a big book, where I can give them only a single chapter. In many respects he was a pioneer of teaching methods which are only now slowly getting widespread recognition. He knew the limitations of books, and the value of a direct appeal to the eye in any scheme of education. And he believed, above all, in basing education, not on any learning by rote or any system of material or moral coercion, but on a direct appeal to the interests and aptitudes of the child. Far less than justice has been done to Owen as an educational pioneer. When, as "Owen the Socialist," he dropped out of respectable society, his services to the cause of education were largely forgotten by the wider public, though his disciples long kept his tradition alive, and handed it on to the various movements into which Owenism finally broke up. Every Owenite Society made education one of its principal objects, and gave eager thought to the education of children as well as adults. The schools were always the best-conducted part of the various Owenite communities in this country and America. The ill-fated Birmingham Guildhall of 1834 was designed to contain premises for an Owenite school for the members' children, and schools conducted on Owenite principles, in some cases, long survived the collapse of the wider movement.

New Lanark, as the great world saw it in the days of its glory, appeared as an astonishingly successful experiment in philanthropy and capitalist enlightenment. Owen was commonly described as "Mr. Owen the Philanthropist"; and the royal and other distinguished visitors who went to New Lanark found, in the earlier years, no shadow of reason for suspecting him of a desire to subvert the social order. Indeed, he might himself have disclaimed such a desire; for he certainly had no faith in a political uprising of the many against the few. The new system to which he looked forward, holding New Lanark a mere pale foreshadowing of a few of its features, was to be created by a purely moral and intellectual revolution—a change in the minds of men leading to a universal change of practice, based on the common agreement of all well-intentioned men. There was no hint at this stage of an appeal to the poor to turn the rich off their backs, no suggestion

15

that the rich need become poorer by the enrichment of the poor man's life. Owen's appeal was to Governments and persons in high authority to realise that all he had done at New Lanark, and far more, might be done by the general application of his methods and precepts. He was not a leader of revolt, but a moral reformer; and he commanded a more than respectful hearing from men who would have stopped their ears at the first breath of Jacobin doctrine or levelling desires.

So far, then, Owen is a great pioneer, but a pioneer strictly, on the surface at least, within the limits of philanthropic reform. From the standpoint of the world at large, he was chiefly demonstrating that philanthropy could be made to pay. It must not be supposed, because the evils of the new factory system were allowed to develop practically unchecked, that no one was conscious of them as evils, save those who suffered directly under them. The old aristocracy, still firmly entrenched in political power, included many, even among the foremost in repressing any popular movement of revolt, who saw the inhumanity of the new industrial order, and would willingly, up to a point, have put its abuses right. These aristocrats had no love for the uncouth "cotton lords" of the rising north, whose claims to a share in political power they saw already as a menace to their own monopoly and to the great and glorious Constitution. Sidmouth, who as Home Secretary was among the most persistent persecutors of Trade Unions and radical associations, listened sympathetically to Owen's plans of factory reform and moral regeneration. The ugliness of the exploited poor repelled the aristocratic rich; if Owen could make them prettier and more polite he would have the gratitude of the fastidious.

But there were strict limits to aristocratic philanthropy. The old families had many connections by marriage, or even direct descent into trade, with the world of commerce; and the rich traders, though largely a class distinct from the manufacturing employers, were closely involved in the development of industrialism, and had no mind for anything that would restrict its free scope for exploitation. Moreover—an even more important consideration in the minds of many—the country was at war, and the struggle was plainly one between Napoleon's armies and military genius and the money-bags of Great Britain. Pitt and his successors were the paymasters of Europe in the long conflict, and every penny that could be raised was wanted to sustain the burdens of war and European alliances. In the national interest, it was argued, the country must make money, and then more money; and any sacrifice of life or enjoyment by the workers was justified by the national need.

The appeal, then, of Owen's schemes to the governing classes was that he seemed to have shown how to reconcile philanthropy with exploitation. He made money at New Lanark, both for his successive partners and for himself. The rate of profit was high, despite the fact that Owen steadily put money back into the business, seemingly for quite unproductive purposes. Visitors came from far and near to see how the thing was done—how all the capitalists of the world could grow rich without feeling a twinge of conscience. At New Lanark the trick appeared to work; but Owen's fellow-manu-

facturers remained sceptical and aloof. His admirers were drawn from the non-industrial sections
of the rich—an uneasy generation seeking for a sign.

In a sense, the manufacturers were right. For
though the New Lanark mills made money fast,
they certainly made, under Owen's management,
far less than if he had run them with a sole view to
profit. Owen was an extraordinarily good organiser and business man; and he made his mills a
model of business efficiency. But money-making
was not his object; and, as fast as profits were
made, he wanted to apply them to the service of
his great experiment. This was the cause of his
severance from one group of partners after another.
They wanted the money; he wanted a demonstration in social science. Until he formed, in 1813, his
final partnership with William Allen, Jeremy Bentham, and other fellow-philanthropists, he had
never a free hand. His earlier associates were men
who wanted not merely a moderate return on their
money, but the largest return that could be ex-
tracted in those halcyon days of low wages, long
hours, high profits, and rapid accumulation of capital. Even his last partners, who were content with
a fixed rate of interest, were far more interested
than he in the commercial success of the business,
besides the fact that their views of "philanthropy"
failed on many points to agree with his.

If Owen had stopped short at this point, and
done no more than make New Lanark the world's
model factory, he would have been a great pioneer;
but neither Socialism nor Co-operation would have
any title to claim him among its prophets. But his
development from an enlightened employer seeking

to correct the evils of the factory system into an enemy of capitalism was proceeding during the course of the New Lanark experiment. It was a gradual process. Owen began by proving that a factory need not be the hideous nightmare that most factories were in his day. From re-creating his own factory he passed to urging other employers to follow his example, and to pressing Governments for factory legislation when direct appeals proved fruitless. But the real change came with the end of the long war. The Peace of 1815 destroyed "the nation's best customer." Disbanded soldiers and discharged operatives competed for jobs with agricultural labourers driven off the land by the cessation of the war demand for food supplies. Work was scarce, and hands were many; for in face of a falling infant mortality rate, due largely to the improvement of medical science, and under the impulse of the new industrial conditions, population had rapidly increased. The poor rates soared high, despite drastic reductions in the standard allowed for relief. Falling prices hugely augmented the real burden of the war debt. The debt charge and poor relief together held out the promise of crushing taxation in a time of bad trade. Commissions and committees, official and unofficial, were created to report upon the distress, and to prescribe remedies for it. Any suggestion that promised to relieve the rich of the burden of the poor was certain of respectful consideration.

At this stage in the nation's affairs, Owen came forward with his famous "Plan" for the employment of the poor. Let the State, he urged, or, failing the State, local authorities or groups of private philanthropists, find work for the poor, under a system which would at once take the charge off the poor rates, set the workers again to useful production under good conditions, and provide for their moral and material regeneration. The "Villages of Co-operation" of which Owen recommended the establishment were based on his own experience at New Lanark in all that concerned their methods of government and administration. But, unlike New Lanark, they were to be primarily agricultural communities, carrying on factory work only as an auxiliary employment. Judging mainly by his personal experience of the increased productivity brought about by machinery in the cotton industry, Owen made the most sanguine estimates of the productive capacity of his proposed communities, and applied to agriculture, of which he knew little, calculations based on factory conditions. His colonies would be self-supporting, and more than self-supporting, though no one would work too hard, the standard of life would be good, and the fullest provision would be made for recreation as well as education. The world would soon see how far superior were his "Villages of Co-operation" to the conditions of the old system. All classes would throng into them; society would be transmuted by a peaceful revolution of reason.

Owen's advice was not taken. All the statesmen, Churchmen and aristocrats who gave him a sympathetic hearing founded not one "Village of Co-operation." But, for a time at least, his Plan was seriously considered. He was still in favour with large sections of the governing classes; and the newspapers gave him an excellent show. In Parliament and before the various commissions which were considering remedies for the distress, his plan was freely discussed.

Indeed, there was much to recommend it to men's minds. Poor Law reform was in the air. The Speenhamland system of relief in aid of wages, which had pauperised a large proportion of the whole people, clearly could not last; but, until expanding industry made room for all comers, it could not be abolished unless an alternative could be found. Owen was, indeed, by this time openly denouncing the evils of capitalist competition, and accounting for the hostility of the manufacturers to his plans by the demoralising nature of their occupation as employers. But this did not shock the aristocrats, who were quite pleased to hear the manufacturers told a few home truths by one of their own kind. It was not necessary to hold with Owen's views about a complete change of system in order to be in favour of experimenting with his plan for employing the poor at useful work. Church dignitaries and aristocrats joined Owen's Committee for the furtherance of his scheme; *The Times* and other newspapers wrote encouragingly about it.

But little by little Owen's meaning became plainer. As he gained confidence, his Plan developed in his own mind. He stressed more and more its ulterior result, in an entire change of social system. Respectable people began to shake their heads, and dismiss Owen as a philanthropic visionary, whose good intentions had run away with his judgment. And then, at a critical moment for his Plan, Owen suddenly launched an attack on established religion, and made it an integral part of his

campaign. The Churches, he said in his famous
Address of 1817, were one and all teaching gross
errors, belief in which was the most potent source
of human misery and of human impotence in face
of miseries and abuses.

The crucial error, common, as Owen thought, to
all established religions, was the preaching of the
doctrine of human responsibility. Men in the
mass, he held, were the creatures of environment. The Churches, however, taught that men
made their own characters, and sought to promote good character by the doctrine of rewards and
punishments, whereas the only sound way of making men good was to give them a good material and
moral environment. They would then become good
automatically. But there could not be a good moral
environment if the Church were permitted to teach
its erroneous and immoral doctrine of punishment
hereafter. The moral education, which would be a
vital part of the system in his "Villages of Co-operation," must be wholly free from the contagion of
this pernicious doctrine.

Thus Owen, who had already, in his denuncia-
tions of the effects of commercialism on character,
declared intellectual war on capitalism, now ranked
the Church also among his intellectual enemies.
The second offence was far more serious, because
its tendency was more easily understood, and because it attacked a vital part of the established order
of Church and State, and not merely the rising, but
still uncanonised, generation of industrial mag-
nates. Horrified prelates, who had listened approv-
ingly to earlier expositions of "Mr. Owen's Plan,"
now perceived his real drift, and began to denounce

him as a dangerous infidel. Not in a day, as he was apt to suggest at a later date, but gradually, his aristocratic and influential supporters fell away. Tories called him a subverter of the established order; and as yet the Radicals knew him only as "Mr. Owen the Philanthropist," the friend of Sidmouth and the Duke of Kent, a great manufacturer with a bent for benevolence. For the time, they were no more disposed than the Tories to pay attention to his schemes.

Owen was always quite positive that he was right, and quite undeterred by opposition or neglect. Unmoved by the failure of his efforts to get his Plan taken up by the Tory Government in England, he steered a new course. He called in the New World to redress the balance of the Old. By chance, the occasion offered to buy in the United States the entire lands and buildings of one of those religious, semi-Communistic societies which had sought religious freedom and the moral life through colonisation. Owen bought Harmony from the Rappites. Leaving behind him little societies of disciples in England, Scotland and Ireland, he passed over to America, there to launch, as a private venture on the grand scale, the first Co-operative Community based on his principles. New Harmony was to be for the world a stirring example of the new social system at work.

From 1824 to 1829 Owen spent most of his time in America, paying only brief visits to Great Britain in order to look after his factory at New Lanark. He was thus absent from this country during a time most critical from both an economic and a political standpoint. Great Britain, by the date of his return, had vitally changed. The crisis which followed the Peace of 1815 had been, on the whole, liquidated; and the Industrial Revolution had resumed its swift advance under the new conditions of a country at peace. Tendencies latent during the war, and scarcely emerging during the years of crisis after the war, had become clear and conscious. Both employers and workers had had time to take stock of their position, and to organise their forces in the light of the changed conditions. There was a swift fermenting of thought, the prelude to the decisive events of the next few years. It is almost true to say that Owen had left an England only just emerging from the eighteenth century: he came back to find himself in the new world of the nineteenth.

His own influence in this new world had not merely increased, but essentially changed its character. When he left for America, his disciples were busy with plans for the formation of Communities or "Villages of Co-operation." Orbiston, in Scotland, was formed and broke up while he was away. The more successful experiment at Ralahine, in Ireland, was projected during his absence, though it was not actually started till after his return. But far more important than these abortive Communities was the growth of Owen's influence among the working class. Even before his departure, and while he himself was directly addressing himself to the rich and influential, his essential doctrines had begun to strike roots in the more congenial soil of the rapidly growing class of urban workers. The middle-class Radicals, intent on political reform and largely expressing the mind of the manufacturing class, had naturally no use for Owen's chal-

24

lenge to the whole policy of capitalist individualism and *laissez-faire;* and even those working-class Radicals who, like Cobbett, put their faith in political change and were blind to the economic meaning of the Industrial Revolution, found nothing to attract them in Owen's ideal of a Co-operative system based on the social control of the new powers of production. But among the younger workmen especially, Owenism made its appeal as a gospel of hope, offering both an acceptable ideal and the essentials of a constructive economic policy.

British Socialism, as a working-class movement based on the idea of collective action for the control of the means of production, dates from the years following the Peace of 1815. Out of the distress of the years after the Peace there gradually grew up an organised movement of revolt. The new proletarian forces created by the Industrial Revolution had been long repressed by the war; they now began to express themselves not only in strikes and unrest, but also in the active formulation and spreading of economic and social theories. Thomas Hodgskin, the follower of Godwin, and William Thompson, the interpreter of Owenism in terms of economics, developed the claim, already made by Owen, for a reward to labour corresponding to its rôle as the "sole creator of value." Working-class societies sprang up apace; there was an ardent quest for ideas to justify, and plans of action to further, the struggle of the property-less classes.

Owenism was well fitted to meet at this stage the need of the new working-class movement for a gospel of hope. Against the dominant doctrine of the blessings of capitalist competition, Owen preached

a gospel of social co-operation and of society organised as a Co-operative Commonwealth of producers. Although Owen had appealed to the upper
classes to create the new system for the poor, his
proposals naturally suggested to the workers that
there was no good reason against their taking action on their own behalf. If the rich would do
nothing, the poor must do what they could without
their help. They might not have the resources
wherewith to establish Communities such as Owen
had advocated; but could they not make a start on
a less ambitious scale? The workers gave their own
interpretation to Owenism. Instead of "Villages of
Co-operation," they began to organise little Co-
operative Societies and Stores, partly for propaganda and partly for the buying and selling, on a
mutual basis, of goods of everyday use. They began
to "co-operate" in a small way, not because they
were satisfied with the mere buying and selling of
groceries, but because they wanted to make a practical start and because this buying and selling could
be used as a means of accumulating a common
fund, which could later be applied to more ambitious experiments—perhaps even to the foundation
of working-class Communities based on Owen's
plan.

Both Owenite ideas and, in close connection with
them, Co-operative experiments had developed
considerably among the workers by the time of
Owen's return from America, where New Harmony, after a long struggle against overwhelming
difficulties, had failed and swept away the bulk of
its founder's fortune. Owen, after his return, had
to find himself, and to define his attitude, in rela-

tion to the new movement which had grown up during his absence. It was not a development he had either planned or contemplated, and at first he did not quite know how to take it. There were two reasons for his hesitation. In the first place, the little Co-operative Stores seemed to him very poor and insignificant things beside his vision of a new social order, and he was for a time inclined to look down on them as unworthy embodiments of his great idea. But the second reason was far the stronger. Owen's attitude towards the workers had been hitherto patriarchal; he had planned things for them, but he had not expected them to plan things for themselves. Indeed, according to his theory, external circumstances had so degraded their characters that they were incapable of planning aright. They must, indeed, be led and not driven; but it was not theirs to lead. He had to conquer his own patriarchal instincts in order to accept the new movement. He did not conquer them completely; but before long he got the sense of the new forces that were at work, and placed himself at the head of the first great revolt of the British proletariat.

Thus, almost before he had made any direct appeal to the working class, and certainly without preaching any doctrine of class-struggle or political antagonism, Owen, almost in his own despite, found himself at the head of a considerable movement among the workers. For a short time his influence still flowed apart from the main stream. The great mass of the workers had been swung into the struggle for parliamentary reform, now at length nearing its culmination in the Reform Act of 1832. In this struggle the workers and the bulk of the middle classes were temporarily in alliance. But already discordant notes were being struck. The Whigs were willing enough to assume the leadership of the manufacturing interest; but they had no intention of granting the demand for Manhood Suffrage, or of enfranchising the workers in country or town. Working-class groups, such as the National Union of the Working Classes, were well aware of this, and conscious that their antagonism was as deep to the manufacturers as to the landed aristocracy. The majority backed the Reform Bill, as a first step towards more radical reform; but there were already not a few who declared plainly against any alliance with the manufacturing interest, and some who were ready even to oppose the Reform Bill as an essentially middle-class measure.

Many of Owen's working-class followers were active in these controversies; but Owen himself had practically no part in them. He was no politician, and he did not believe in parliamentary reform—moderate or radical—as a cure for ills essentially social and economic. While the reform agitation continued, Owenism advanced fast indeed, but within a comparatively narrow circle. It did not command the attention of the many, whose minds were concentrated on the political struggle.

But in 1832, after two years of excitement, the House of Lords at last yielded to threats, and the Reform Act became law. The middle classes won their place in political authority; their working-class allies, who had borne a large share in the struggle, were left voteless and unrepresented. Then came the chance of Owenism, transmuted into an appeal to the workers to do, by their own direct action, what political agitation had failed to achieve. Co-operation became the popular working-class gospel: everywhere groups of workers became active, organising Co-operative Societies, Equitable Labour Exchanges, Trade Unions, designed not merely as instruments of collective bargaining, but also as means to the establishment of a Co-operative system. The New Society was to be based, said these pioneers, on the free association of producers in guilds and manufacturing societies strong enough to dispense with employers and with the exploitation of labour for private profit.

Of this new movement Owen was the unquestioned leader. In 1832 he started the National Equitable Labour Exchange, as a mart where the various societies of producers formed by the Trade Unions could market and exchange their goods. In the following year he inspired the Grand National Guild of Builders—an ambitious attempt of the powerful Builders' Union to take over, by direct economic action, the control of the building industry. A little later, he formed the Grand National Consolidated Trades Union, a body seeking to include all producers within its scope, and by the threat of a general strike to enforce, first a universal eight hours' day, and soon a complete transformation of the industrial system.

It may seem, at this day, extraordinary that Owen should have become so easily the head and forefront of the great industrial movements of the years following the Reform Act. He had been a great and successful manufacturer; and, although he had already retired from business in order to devote himself wholly to the work of agitation, it may be thought that his status as an employer would have made him suspect among those whom he came to lead. But he had by this time broken thoroughly both with the governing classes and with the manufacturers; his social and educational work at New Lanark had given him an immense prestige; and he was a man of unlimited energy and devotion in a time when the workers had much ado to find national leaders among themselves.

Moreover, the times were in Owen's favour. The poorer classes, shaken out of their old ways of living by the enclosures in the countryside and the rapid growth of the factory system, were in a condition of acute unrest and maladjustment to the new industrial order. They hated the factories, and the lords of the factories, with the deep resentment of a peasantry uprooted by main force from the traditional ways of living. They were ready to follow any leadership that appeared to promise an escape from the misery and the daily grind of the squalid new factory towns. It is no wonder they were swept off their feet by Owen's gospel, which appeared to make the ending of all their tribulations merely a matter of a few months of organisation for a totally new order of society.

Thus, Owen found himself accepted by large masses of men seeking for a sign as the pioneer of a new gospel of economic freedom and universal brotherhood. Thus he became, almost without exercise of his own will, the leader of the great Trade Union revolt of the eighteen-thirties. The young leaders of the rising working class accepted his influence and sat at his feet. Owenite Societies sprang up throughout the country; Owenism and "Socialism," a new word just coming into use to describe the social aspirations of the workers, were convertible terms. The gospel of "the benevolent Mr. Owen" became a creed commanding passionate loyalty and passionate opposition. Owen had set out to found ideal Communities as a way of regenerating society. He succeeded in founding the modern Trade Union movement and in preparing the way for the other great working-class movement of Co-operation.

But for the time his dreams and the hopes of his followers were to be rudely broken. The millennium was not to be won so easily as Owen prophesied. The manufacturers, now securely allied through the Reformed Parliament with the older governing classes, were in the first flush of their success and triumphant strength. Easily they shattered Owen's great Trades Union in the struggle of 1834; and after a year of strikes, lock-outs and prosecutions, among which the savage sentence on the Dorchester labourers stands out, only scattered fragments were left of the great industrial army of Labour. The Co-operative movement fell with the Trades Union. For the time, it was almost annihilated; and, when it rose again ten years later in the Rochdale Pioneers, it took an independent course very different from Owen's plans, and he had no share in its rapid development. Trade Unionism, reviving a few years later in the new "Amalgamated Societies," knew him no more. He passed out of the main stream of working-class agitation as swiftly as he had entered it.

After the collapse of 1834, the main body of the workers had swung back from industrial to political agitation. From 1836 to 1848 Chartism—a political movement inspired chiefly by economic forces and aiming at the use of political agitation for economic ends—ran its course, and many of the Owenites were absorbed by it. But Owen himself, and the more orthodox Owenites, were as distrustful as ever of political methods, and he played no part in the Chartist movement. Owenism, however, was by no means dead. Amid the collapse of Trade Unions and Co-operative Societies, the little Owenite Associations held together, and soon began again to gather strength. They turned back once more to their original plans, and essayed anew the formation of a model Owenite Community. Harmony Hall, or Queenwood, their final abortive experiment in community-making, was started in 1839, and lasted until 1846.

But, as a social gospel, Owenism was rapidly changing its form. Owen himself was already more than sixty-three years old at the time of the collapse of 1834. From that time onwards he ceased to be an industrial leader, and became primarily a religious teacher—making his social doctrines the basis of a "Rational Religion" of humanity. The Owenite Societies, without dropping their social ideas, laid the stress more and more on their ethical and religious or anti-religious teaching. By successive changes of name and function, the main Owenite body turned from "the Association of the Industrious Classes" into the "Society of Rational Religionists," and gave birth to the modern Secularist and Ethical movements. Owen, in his old age, continued ceaselessly to proclaim the advent of the "New Moral World," but more and more his preaching became merely apocalyptic. After 1834 he had no close contacts with any large section of the working-class movement. He lived nearly twenty-four years longer; but his day was over. At length, in his dotage at eighty-two years old, he turned Spiritualist, and moved for his last five years among table-rappers and mediums. He died at last in 1858, eighty-seven years old, in a world which had largely forgotten both him and his message—a world that had passed from the strains and stresses of the Industrial Revolution into the triumphant complacency of mid-Victorian capitalism. The "Old Immoral World" seemed then securely entrenched in its stronghold of prosperity; the "New Moral World" seemed further off than ever. Owen had long outlived the scenes and days in which he was an actor of renown.

I shall pass over very lightly in this book the last twenty years of Owen's life. A man must be judged by the doings of his manhood, not by the follies of his dotage. Owen's claim to be remembered depends on what he did and wrote between 1800, when he assumed the control of New Lanark, and 1834, when the Grand National Consolidated Trades Union came to an untimely end. In these years he did very much that is memorable. No man has been forerunner and patron-saint of so many movements as he. New Lanark at once suggests the pioneer of popular education and factory reform; the events of 1830–1834 recall the leading figure in the first broad concerted movement of the working class. Socialism and Co-operation alike found in him their first systematic exponent in Great Britain. Secularism and Rationalism, too, took shape under his guidance.

And yet this is not the whole story. Owen carried everywhere with him the prestige of his own commercial success. He was supposed to be a great business man, apt in financial affairs and the conduct of large enterprises. In fact, he was an excellent organiser and manager, with a remarkable power of getting on with his subordinates, but no man ever had less sense of the value of money. He was a great spender; but he could never pause to count the cost of his experiments, or find patience to analyse their financial results. New Lanark paid, but, as long as he could lay his hands on money to go on with it, Owen would not have cared, or perhaps even realised, how much it might lose. Money simply did not interest him: his interest was in his plans for the speedy regeneration of the human race. And, therefore, when he had to work with the scanty resources collected by his followers, he always overspent and got into difficulties, which he realised only when it was too late. The millennium was, for him, always just round the next corner. He was running so fast towards it that he had no time to notice the pitfalls in the way.

Owen's Socialism has often been called "Utopian" and distinguished by that label from the "scientific" Socialism of later times. The description is largely true. Owen's view of human character, extraordinarily valuable as a corrective to the prevailing tendencies of his time, in that it emphasised the influence of environment against those who imputed misery to the poor as a crime, he pushed sometimes to the length of supposing

34

instant regeneration to be the certain result of a change in environment. He was wrong; but he was not stating a falsehood, but overstating a truth. Again, in his emphasis on the associative basis of Socialism, and the necessity of building up the Socialist faith as a consciousness of co-operative capacity among the workers, he made a contribution to Socialist thought which, long lost to sight, is only now being again appreciated. As a writer, he was long-winded, and often prosy; as a man of action he made so many mistakes that his great successes have been largely forgotten. But in the realm of ideas he was immensely the greatest figure in the early development of British Socialism, and, I think, in the whole of British Socialist history. It is easy to laugh at Owen's foibles, such as his relapse into Spiritualism in his old age; but it is quite impossible not to recognise him as a great pioneer of the faith which, all the world over, the workers are still struggling to make the basis of a new social system.

CHAPTER II

THE CHILD

Robert Owen, pioneer of many movements, was born in 1771. At that time, although commerce was rapidly advancing and riches accumulating in the hands of the growing merchant class, Great Britain was still an agricultural country. The one great manufacture—that of woollen goods—both depended directly on agriculture and was carried on in close connection with agriculture, as a small town and village industry, still largely, though not exclusively, organised on the domestic system. Factories existed, indeed; but establishments of any size were still quite exceptional. The great revolution in productive power which we call "the Industrial Revolution" had barely begun. The epoch of the great inventions, of the application of machinery and steam power to industry, was already on its way; but there had not yet been time for it to produce any marked social effect. Arkwright's water-frame had been invented but two years; Hargreaves had taken out his patent for the spinning-jenny only the year before; Crompton's mule and Cartwright's power-loom were still to come. James Watt had patented his steam-engine two years before Owen's birth. The revolution in the iron trade was just entering upon its critical phase; scientific road improvement had

36

begun, and canal construction was just beginning on an extensive scale. In short, the great discoveries which made the Industrial Revolution were gathering that momentum which, in the next half-century, was to transform England into "the workshop of the world."

But, at the time of Owen's birth, few or none realised the magnitude of the changes that had already occurred, still less the combined force which they were about to exert, not merely on industry, but on the whole life of the nation. Adam Smith's *Wealth of Nations*, the great textbook of the transition, did not appear until four years later. Economic thinking was still mercantilist; the trader still dominated the minds of statesmen, and the industrial employer was of little account. Politically, although John Wilkes and his followers had made a tiny ripple on the smooth surface of the Whig ascendancy, there existed no serious movement of revolt or even of reform. The county movement for reform had hardly begun to take shape as a national agitation. The struggle with the American colonies was still in its earliest phase; two years were still to pass before the incident of Boston Harbour, and five before the American Declaration of Independence. The old landed aristocracy, recruited to some extent by intermarriage and fusion with the richer members of the financial and merchant classes, seemed not merely safe in its tenure of power, but practically unchallenged. Land was still the basis of the social and political system, the key to political power and social consideration. Enclosure was already proceeding fast, and was soon to proceed much faster. The yeomanry and the peasantry were being ousted from their old-time status; and the class of "free wage-labourers" was being prepared in readiness for the new factory system. But the mass of the people still lived either by direct labour on the land or by scattered industries carried on in close connection with agriculture. Save on the Tyne and Tees, mining was in its infancy; and the iron industry, though it was growing fast, was still mainly an affair of small concerns. In short, the Industrial Revolution had begun; but the old order was not yet conscious of its challenge.

Young Owen, moreover, passed his childhood amid scenes and men unaffected by the great change. He was born at Newtown, Montgomeryshire, then as now a very small market town of the Welsh border. His father was a saddler and ironmonger, and was also the local postmaster. The lad, sixth of seven children, was evidently precocious. "I was before seven years of age fond of reading all books which came in my way, and thinking of their contents."[1] He read omnivorously, with all the private libraries of the neighbourhood at his disposal, novels, history, poetry, but especially books of religious controversy. For, though this was before the season of political awakening which followed the revolutions in America and France, religious thinking had been awakened by Wesley, Whitefield and Williams, and, especially in Wales, theological controversy was the most natural means of sharpening the wits of a young and ardent seeker after knowledge.

[1] *The Life of Robert Owen*, vol. i. Second Introductory Dialogue.

Three Methodist ladies who had come to live in the neighbourhood ministered to young Owen's awakening. They lent him books, and encouraged him to read and think for himself. His mind either had from the first, or was given during these early years, a strong religious bent. Robert Owen was, from first to last, a deeply religious person, not least when he was denouncing all the creeds, and earning the reputation of an infidel and a materialist. This must be understood if his life is to be understood as a plain and coherent whole.

Methodism and rival religious doctrines and ways of life had, however, as they reached young Owen in his early days, no social or political significance. Though Methodists and other dissenters—above all the Unitarians—played a most important part in the upbuilding of movements of reform, it was not in this guise that they appeared to him. Religious controversies caused him, indeed, at an extraordinarily early age, to begin reflecting about the world and man's place in the world; but, just as his surroundings at Newtown were natural and enduring and did not plainly raise any economic or social issue, so the religious problems to which his mind was drawn were of all time—problems of the individual conscience, and of man's relationship rather to the universe than to his immediate surroundings. He meditated, as it were, even in extreme youth, *sub specie æternitatis*.

To the reader of to-day, all this suggests, maybe, a false impression—that young Owen was a little prig, meddling with things not fit for his age and devoid of the high spirits and capacity for enjoyment that we regard as proper to boyhood. This is true only in part. Boys grew up and concerned themselves with the things of manhood earlier in those days; and Owen was, undoubtedly, possessed with a precocious spirit of inquiry. But the evidence is clear that he had also a strong capacity for enjoyment. He was good at football, the best runner and leaper in his school, very fond of dancing, a keen player on the clarionet, and exceptionally popular both with his fellows and with his elders. He was, he tells us, not strong, but quick and agile—and this was true of his mental as well as his bodily qualities.

His precociousness in thinking about high matters is, therefore, a sign of the times as well as of his individual character. The age which conceived the Lancaster system of education, making the child teach the child, was an age in which children matured quickly, and were thrust out to earn an independent living at a season when with us they are scarcely half-way up the elementary school.

Robert Owen's schoolmaster at Newtown was a Mr. Thickness, whose attainments were apparently not high. "In schools in these small towns it was considered a good education if one could read fluently, write a legible hand, and understand the four first rules of arithmetic. And this, I have reason to believe, was the extent of Mr. Thickness's qualification for a schoolmaster—because when I had acquired these small rudiments of learning, at the age of seven, he applied to my father for permission that I should become his assistant and usher, as from that time I was called while I remained at school. And thenceforward

my schooling was to be repaid by my ushership."[1]
Owen goes on to say that the two years he spent
at school after this change were "lost" to him,
"except that I thus early acquired the habit of
teaching others what I knew." There could hardly
be a more comprehensive exception, in view of his
subsequent career.

Owen's great doctrine in later years was to be
that the greatest influence in forming man's
character is found in his early environment. It
seems plain that these early years at Newtown
exerted a decisive influence on the bent of his
mind. He acquired the itch to learn and still more
the itch to teach. But, ill taught at school and
from an early age scarcely taught at all, he was
driven back on his own resources of acquisition.
He read very widely, but on no system; he thought
keenly, but under no discipline. He passed ideas
into his mind, transmuted them, and made them
his own, without regard for authorities or pre-
cedents. In the purest sense of the term, he began
life as a "free-thinker," for his parents seem from
an early stage to have let him alone, and even
encouraged him to form an independent judgment. This early freedom, or licence, of thinking
greatly influenced his development. No man ever
had less respect or use for authority in intellectual
matters; none more completely used the thoughts
of others as crude raw material for the formation
of his own judgments. The importance of this
will appear when we come to consider the growth
of Owen's heterodox opinions in his years of
manhood.

[1] *Life* (Bell's edition), p. 3.

The eighteenth-century father was, I believe, much behind his Victorian successor in finding the whole duty of parents in the frequent application of the rod. At all events, young Robert Owen was beaten but once, in circumstances best told in his own words, which, written by the old man of eighty-six, yet bring vividly before us the boy out of whom the man had grown. The incident occurred when Owen was scarcely seven years old.

"I was always desirous to meet the wishes of both my parents, and never refused to do whatever they asked me to do. One day my mother indistinctly said something to me to which I supposed the proper answer was 'No,' and in my usual way I said 'No,' supposing I was meeting her wishes. Not understanding me, and supposing that I refused her request, she immediately, and to me rather sharply—for her custom was to speak kindly to me—said: 'What! Won't you?' Having said 'No,' I thought if I said 'Yes, I will,' I should be contradicting myself, and should be expressing a falsehood, and I said again 'No,' but without any idea of disobeying her. If she had then patiently and calmly inquired what my thoughts and feelings were, a proper understanding would have arisen, and everything would have proceeded as usual. But my mother, not comprehending my thoughts and feelings, spoke still more sharply and angrily—for I had never previously disobeyed her, and she was no doubt greatly surprised and annoyed when I repeated that I would not. My mother never chastised any of us—this was left for my father to do, and my brothers and sisters occasionally felt a whip which was kept to maintain order among the children, but I had never previously been touched with it. My father was called in, and my refusal stated. I was again asked if I would do what my mother required, and I said firmly 'No' and I then felt the whip every time after I refused when asked if I would yield and do what was required. I said 'No' every time I was so asked, and at length said quietly but firmly, 'You may kill me, but I will not do it,' and this decided the contest. There was no attempt ever afterwards to correct me; but this difference was soon made up on both sides, and I continued to be the favourite I had always been."[1]

Again, probably, the reader's first instinct may be to exclaim that Owen was a little prig, but, I think, wrongly. He was only a boy of very strong natural power of will, practising its use. The incident profited him later, when he addressed himself to the education of the children at the New Lanark mills.

Owen's *Autobiography*, written towards the very end of his long life, relates many incidents of his childhood at Newtown. Most of these the reader must be left to seek for himself in a book which makes the best of reading, and gives a very good idea of the manner of boy and man he was. It is coloured, of course, by the events of his later life, and he is too apt to attribute to himself in youth clearly formulated ideas and doctrines which he can hardly have matured until later. But these are readily distinguished, and the book, as a whole, is both alive and extraordinarily sincere—as, indeed, was all that Owen did.

[1] *Life*, p. 14.

He enjoyed his childhood, and had evidently from the first the knack of making friends. IIis memories were nearly all pleasant memories: he was happy at home and happy among his associates. His relatives in the neighbourhood were mostly farmers, and he spent pleasant times visiting them and rambling about the country. With one boy cousin he became very intimate, and he also struck up a close friendship with a University student, James Donne, who came to stay and study at Newtown one summer. Owen was eight or nine, and Donne about nineteen; but the two went long walks together, and talked of many things. This friendship, which was maintained in later life, did much, Owen held, to broaden both his understanding and his strong love of nature. He was to carry this love of natural beauty with him into the grimy surroundings of the factory settlement, and to base on it one of the chief features of his system of education at New Lanark.

But not for long was young Owen free to range at will. At nine years of age he left school, after two years as usher, and at once he was given an employment. Next door to the Owens lived the Misses Tilsley, who kept a draper's and grocer's shop. He had helped them on busy days while he was still at school; but in 1780 he passed into their regular employment, and remained there for a year, still living, of course, at home.

One of Owen's brothers had, before this, gone to London in search of a living, and become assistant to a saddler in High Holborn. His employer died, and he married the widow and took over the shop. Young Robert became eager to follow his example

44

and to push his fortune in the larger world. At length he was promised that, when his tenth birthday came, he should be allowed to go to his brother in London, and try to find a job in some draper's shop. The day came, and he took leave of all his fellow-townsmen, paying a round of visits and receiving many parting gifts. His father accompanied him to Welshpool, whence he went to Shrewsbury, the nearest point from which there were coaches direct to London. With forty shillings for his fortune and his brother's house for a temporary home, he was launched upon the great world.

Owen's father had friends in London, to whom he wrote about the boy. Within six weeks one of these, Mr. Heptinstall, lace-dealer, of Ludgate Hill, procured him the offer of a place with a big draper in business at Stamford, in Lincolnshire. The boy was to be apprenticed "for three years— the first without pay, the second with a salary of eight pounds, and the third with ten pounds, with board, lodging and washing in the house." "These terms," Owen writes, "I accepted, and being well found with clothes to serve me more than a year, I, from that period, ten years of age, maintained myself without ever applying to my parents for any additional aid."[1]

[1] *Life*, p. 16.

CHAPTER III

THE SHOP-BOY

Stamford was described by Defoe in his *Tours* as "a very fair, well-built, and wealthy town." It was a corporate town, with a scot and lot franchise, about 500 voters, and a population of between three and four thousand. It was, moreover, a trading centre, important for its markets and fairs, including a special fair each year for the sale of haberdashery. Mr. McGuffog, Owen's employer, had an excellent standing among the tradesmen of the town. His business was, indeed, chiefly with the county families, whose seats were scattered plentifully in the neighbouring regions of Lincolnshire, Northamptonshire, and Rutland. McGuffog was a Scotsman, who had begun business as a hawker, with a capital of half a crown. Gradually he had worked up an extensive connection, and, at length, had opened shop in Stamford as a convenient centre. He was, according to Owen, "thoroughly honest, and a good man of business— very methodical, kind, and liberal, and much respected by his neighbours and customers, and also, for his punctuality and good sense, by those from whom he purchased his goods for sale."[1] "I was fortunate," Owen writes, "in obtaining such a man for my first master."

[1] *Life*, p. 16.

McGuffog was fairly wealthy. He made all his purchases for cash, and insisted on trading only at what he regarded as a fair margin over cost. He lived in a "respectable and comfortable" house, and "had married a daughter of a well-doing, middle-class person." "They appeared," says Owen, "to live on very good terms with each other, and both were industrious, always attending to their business, yet respectable at all times in their persons, and altogether superior as retail trades-people, being quite the aristocracy of that class, without its usual weak vanities."[1]

Owen lived with the McGuffogs, who had no children, but only a nephew and niece of their own, and was treated, he says, "more like their own child than as a stranger come from afar." The business was well managed, and he got an excellent and thoroughly methodical training in all its branches. "I suppose," he writes, "I was considered industrious and attentive to my instructions, for I was seldom found fault with or unpleasantly spoken to by either Mr. or Mrs. McGuffog—the latter often attending to the business."[2]

The house had a good library, and the work was not hard; for the chief business was between ten in the morning and four in the afternoon, and Owen found time on the average for five hours' reading a day during the three years he remained at Stamford. He continued, among other reading, his study of religious books. Mr. McGuffog was a Presbyterian, his wife of the Church of England. The pair, taking Owen with them, attended the

[1] *Life*, p. 17.   [2] *Ibid.*, p. 17.

service of the one in the morning and the other in the afternoon. The contending sermons stimulated Owen's thinking, and he set himself to study the beliefs, not only of the various Christian sects, but also of other bodies of believers. According to his own account, which there is no reason to distrust, he came, at about the age of thirteen, to the conclusion that all the contending sects were wrong, and that the differences of belief were due, not to the individual wills of those who held them, but to the influence of social institutions. "My reason taught me that I could not have made one of my own qualities—that they were forced upon me by Nature; that my language, religion, and habits were forced upon me by society; and that I was entirely the child of Nature and society—that Nature gave the qualities, and society directed them. Thus was I forced, through seeing the error of their foundation, to abandon all belief in every religion which had been taught to man. But my religious feelings were immediately replaced by the spirit of universal charity—not for a sect or a party, or for a country or a colour—but for the human race, and with a real and ardent desire to do them good."[1]

This sounds, no doubt, abominably precocious; and there is, doubtless, in the way it is stated much that is rather the thought of the old man recollecting than of the boy he tries to recollect. But, phrasing apart, there is no doubt that it fairly represents what was taking place in young Owen's mind. Reared in a religious atmosphere, and brought early into contact with sectarian differ-

[1] *Life*, p. 22.

ences, he turned away from all the sects at an age when most youngsters are still quite content to take on trust the theology of their parents and guardians. And he turned the more vigorously away, because he had been before of an exceptionally religious inclination.

Several stories of his youth bear witness to this. Even before he left Newtown he had earned for himself the nickname of "the little parson," and had written, he tells us, three sermons, which he kept until, years later, he read those of Sterne, and found among them three so like in idea that he feared to be thought a plagiarist and destroyed them.[1] At Stamford he gave further evidence of his juvenile pietism. He became shocked at the prevalent disregard of the Sabbath—"and it came into my head, at the age of twelve or thirteen, to write upon the subject to Mr. Pitt, who was then Prime Minister.[2] In my letter I stated the desecration which was going forward in Stamford, and expressed a hope that Government would adopt some measures to enforce a better observance of the Sabbath. . . . In about eight or ten days afterwards, Mr. McGuffog bought a London newspaper, and said to me, 'Here is an answer to your letter to Mr. Pitt.' I expected no answer, and was taken by surprise, and blushed very much. I asked what was the answer. He said it was a long proclamation from the Government, recommending all parties to keep the Sabbath more strictly."[3]

At the time, Owen thought his letter had pro-

---

[1] *Life*, p. 4.
[2] Pitt became Prime Minister at the end of 1783.
[3] *Life*, p. 22.

duced this response; later he saw that it was a mere coincidence. In any case, it was not long before his views changed, and the observance of the Sabbath ceased to be a matter of interest to him.

The three years of his apprenticeship at Stamford soon passed by. McGuffog asked him to remain as an assistant, and pressed him with a good deal of warmth. But Owen was determined to make his way. He had learned all he could in McGuffog's shop; and he wanted a wider sphere of action. He therefore regretfully refused his employer's invitation, and returned to his brother in London in order to look out for a new situation.

During these three years he had seen no member of his family; but now he went from London back to Newtown, stayed awhile with his parents, and paid a round of other visits in the neighbourhood. Meanwhile, his late employer was active on his behalf, and on his recommendation Owen was taken on as assistant by the London drapery house of Flint and Palmer, an old-established business of good repute. The shop was on old London Bridge, and the trade very different in character from McGuffog's connection at Stamford. There the chief business had been with the county families, and in the highest qualities of goods. There had been a well-established routine of politeness, and nothing had been done in a hurry. Flint and Palmer's, on the other hand, was a cash business—"a house established, and I believe the first, to sell at a small profit for ready money only." Owen at once realised the difference. "The customers were of an inferior class—they were treated differently. Not much time was allowed for bargaining, a price being fixed for everything, and, compared with other houses, cheap. If any demur was made, or much hesitation, the article asked for was withdrawn, and, as the shop was generally full from morning till late in the evening, another customer was attended to."[1] In short, Owen had stepped from the old-world manners of Stamford into the bustle of the developing metropolis.

He was very hard worked. "To the assistants in this busy establishment the duties were very onerous. They were up and had breakfasted and were dressed to receive customers in the shop at eight o'clock; and dressing then was no slight affair. Boy as I was then, I had to wait my turn for the hairdresser to powder and pomatum and curl my hair, for I had two large curls on each side, and a stiff pigtail, and until this was very nicely and systematically done, no one would think of appearing before a customer. Between eight and nine the shop began to fill with purchasers, and their number increased until it was crowded to excess, although a large apartment, and this continued until late in the evening; usually until ten, or half past ten, during all the spring months. Dinner and tea were hastily taken—two or three, sometimes only one, escaping at a time to take what he or she could the most easily swallow, and returning to take the places of others who were serving. The only regular meals at this season were our breakfasts, except on Sundays, on which days a good dinner was always provided, and was much enjoyed. But when the purchasers left at ten, or half past ten, before the shop could be quite clear a new part of

[1] *Life*, p. 25.

the business was to be commenced. The articles dealt in as haberdashery were innumerable, and these, when exposed to the customers, were tossed and tumbled and unfolded in the utmost confusion and disorder, and there was no time or space to put anything right and in order during the day. This was a work to be performed with closed doors after the customers had been shut out at eleven o'clock; and it was often two o'clock in the morning before the goods in the shop had been put in order and replaced to be ready for the next day's similar proceedings. Frequently at two o'clock in the morning, after being actively engaged on foot all day from eight o'clock in the morning, I have scarcely been able, with the aid of the banisters, to go upstairs to bed. And thus I had about five hours for sleep."[1] The factory children were not the only slaves of the economic revolution in the eighteenth century.

These conditions were maintained fully only during the spring rush; but this lasted for several months. In the summer business slackened off, and Owen was able to take his meals in some comfort, and get to bed by midnight. But before this time came he had taken steps to escape his slavery, by asking his friends to seek for him a better job. Soon an offer came. His old befriender, Mr. Heptinstall, secured for him the offer of a good post in Manchester, from a Mr. Satterfield, wholesale and retail draper. "It was a first-rate house, and he offered me, besides board, lodging, and washing, in his house, forty pounds a year."[2] This seemed opulence: Owen accepted.

[1] *Life*, p. 26.   [2] *Ibid.*, p. 27.

But, by the time the offer came, he was sorry to leave Flint and Palmer's. Mr. Flint had died before his coming, and the business was carried on by three brothers Palmer, of whom the youngest was about Owen's age. They became great friends, spending their Sundays in various excursions together, and, as the shop became less busy, occupying their leisure with walks and common reading. It was a wrench for Owen to part from his friend, and once more seek fortune, at the age of fifteen or sixteen, in a place where he had not even a single acquaintance.

Satterfield's, Owen found, was not much as a wholesale workhouse, but excellent as a retail shop, with a good business among the wives and families of the well-to-do Manchester merchants and manufacturers. Again he lived in the family, and was well treated and cared for. The work was not hard, and once more he found plenty of time for reading. Mr. Satterfield, Owen writes, was an excellent salesman, but an indifferent buyer, and for this reason, although he did a good trade, he accumulated no fortune. McGuffog was able, in middle age, to retire and take to hunting with the county gentlemen; he bought for cash, and left his widow a thousand pounds a year when he died. But Satterfield had to buy on credit, and was only able to pay his way. The job, however, suited Owen well; and with Satterfield he remained until he was eighteen years old.

By this time, he had got a good experience of the various branches of the retail trade, and had become an excellent judge of fabrics. The three firms for which he had worked had specialised each in different classes of goods; so that he had acquired a very useful all-round training, which was soon to serve him well. He had also, especially from his first employer, learned good habits of nicety and careful book-keeping, while his manners had been polished, and he had read and studied widely. From being a boy he had reached manhood. At eighteen, he was ready to launch out on a new and daring adventure.

CHAPTER IV

A ROMANCE OF BUSINESS

1789 was the year of the French Revolution;
but the event finds no record in Robert Owen's
annals. He was eighteen—an impressionable age.
His contemporaries — Wordsworth, Coleridge,
Southey and a host of young men of all classes—
were soon to be swept off their feet by the new gospel
that blew across the Channel from France. But we
have no evidence that the new doctrines at this time
moved or even interested Owen. His adventures so
far seem to have roused in him no political reactions.
He had thought deeply about religion, and had
begun already to formulate his theory of human
character and its formation; but no political
application of his thoughts had apparently even
begun to suggest itself to him. As we shall see later,
the Jacobin gospel and the principle of political
democracy never did appeal to his mind. He
reached his conclusions about society by an
altogether different route.

1789 stands, indeed, in Robert Owen's history,
as a critical date. But, in connection with him, it
has nothing to do with politics. It is the year in
which, with the spirit of self-help and adventure
strong within him, he launched out boldly on his
own as an employer of labour.

For a boy of eighteen to become an employer seems a startling enough event. But it was not quite so startling then as it would be to-day. In times of great and rapid change such things happen. During the get-rich-quick years of the Great War, there were boys as young who founded munition firms or became shipowners on a sudden. The torrent of economic change opens the career alike to legitimate and to illegitimate talents.

Manchester, in 1789, was in the full flood of the rapid changes which were making the cotton trade the greatest commercial enterprise in the world, and the key industry of the developing capitalist system. The woollen trade, which for centuries past had been the chief industry of the country, and had occupied the minds of many generations of commercial statesmen, was being seriously challenged by its new rival. Lancashire was rivalling the West Riding of Yorkshire as a centre of economic development, and Manchester was becoming the great commercial city of the North, and beginning to adopt those characteristic doctrines which were soon to impress themselves on the whole country as the irresistible business logic of the new order.

In 1700 the whole population of the townships of Manchester and Salford was probably less than 10,000. A rapid increase began early in the eighteenth century; and in 1773–74, when a local census was taken, the township of Manchester had 22,500 and the township of Salford just under 5,000 inhabitants. In addition, the suburbs and neighbouring districts included in the parish of

Manchester had a population of nearly 14,000. But this rapid increase was entirely eclipsed by the growth of the following period. By the time of the first national census, taken in 1801, this total of 41,000 had increased to 95,000. At the fourth census, in 1831, the total was nearly 238,000. In other words, the population of Manchester trebled itself in the first three quarters of the eighteenth century, much more than doubled itself again in each of the next periods of thirty years, and, in the sixty years from 1770 to 1830, multiplied itself by nearly six.[1]

By far the greatest part of this enormous increase was, of course, due to the growth of the cotton trade. That trade did not, indeed, begin with the Industrial Revolution. Long before the coming of the "new machines" and the factory system, there was a small but thriving trade in "Manchester fustians" and other goods in which cotton was employed. "Cotton wool," as raw cotton was then usually called, was imported on a small scale in the seventeenth century and was a regular article of trade with both India and the West Indies in the early eighteenth century. But up to about 1770 the cotton trade in England was of relatively small dimensions, and most, if not all, of the goods that were called "cottons" contained an admixture of other materials. Linen was frequently used as the warp, and "cotton wool" was also regularly mixed with both silk and woollen yarn. It needed the coming of the new machines to enable piece goods to be largely made of cotton alone, and to sweep away the obstacles which did something to hamper

[1] See Wheeler, *History of Manchester*, p. 249 ff.

the growth of the trade in the earlier eighteenth century.

Still, from about the middle of the eighteenth century, the imports of raw cotton grew steadily, and home-made cotton goods came increasingly into favour. In 1700 the imports of raw cotton were under 2,000,000 pounds weight. There was no increase until 1748, when, probably as a direct result of the first important inventions affecting the industry, the imports took a sudden leap forward. In 1751 3,000,000 pounds were imported, and in 1764 nearly 4,000,000. Then came a more rapid advance. By 1780 imports had risen to 6,700,000 pounds. The next decade, however, was really the first that showed the results of the new machinery. 31,500,000 pounds of raw cotton were imported in 1790, and in 1800, despite war conditions, 56,000,000 pounds. By 1830 the annual quantity imported was over 300,000,000 pounds. Similarly the value of cotton exports advanced from £23,000 in 1701 to £355,000 in 1780, £1,662,000 in 1790, £5,406,000 in 1800, and over £18,000,000 in 1830. The increase in the quantity of piece goods exported was, of course, much greater; for the changed methods of production due to machinery brought with them a huge reduction in prices.[1]

The increasing use of cotton goods naturally led to conflicts with the interests concerned in other textile trades. The wool industry was not only the greatest in the country, occupying by far the largest number of workers and by far the greatest

[1] For the above figures, see Baines, *History of the Cotton Manufacture*, Mann, *Cotton Trade Tables*, and Porter, *The Progress of the Nation*, p. 369.

amount of capital: it was also very closely connected with the interests of the governing class. For, whereas the whole of the raw material of the cotton trade, as soon as it used cotton unmixed with other substances, had to be drawn from abroad, the greater part of the material used in the wool industry was produced at home, and prosperity in the wool trade helped to swell the rentrolls of the landowning classes, still firmly entrenched in their practical monopoly of political power. Wool was, indeed, being imported in growing quantities; but this was only to make up a positive shortage in the home supply. It was a very different matter when an alternative raw material, regarded as a new sort of wool and a very much cheaper substitute, began to compete with the dominant trade, and to use more efficient methods of production against it.

The rise of the cotton trade was, therefore, regarded with considerable hostility. At first, before the home industry assumed importance, the opposition was rather to the importation of finished cotton goods from the East. Special legislation against printed calicoes, whether printed abroad or at home, was passed in 1720, and remained in force till 1770, when the industry in Lancashire was at the beginning of its rapid growth. But Manchester fustians and certain other established Lancashire cotton products were specifically exempted from the scope of this Act; and, though attempts were made to use it against the rising industry, they met with no great success. The law was largely evaded, and in 1770 the cotton-trade interest had already grown strong enough to procure its repeal. Thereafter, apart from disputes during the war concerning the taxation of its raw material, the cotton industry was free to develop unchecked. Indeed, it had all the more freedom because it had arisen since the old Tudor legislation which still in part governed its rivals, and because it grew up mainly outside the jurisdiction of the old incorporated towns.

Undoubtedly, one great reason why the cotton industry was allowed to grow is that it soon appeared likely, not so much to compete with the woollen trade, as to open up vast new markets for British goods. It was a perpetual source of lamentation in the eighteenth century that neither India nor the English colonies in America afforded at all a good market for woollen goods, which are naturally in little demand in the hotter climates. Nor was there the prospect of rapidly extending markets elsewhere; for the developed countries had all their own wool industries and largely consumed their own wool. Moreover, even if there had been a rapid increase in demand, it was not easy to see whence it could be supplied; for the output of raw wool could not be easily expanded at home, and there were no large supplies abroad that could be drawn upon.

As the conquest of India proceeded, and the trade with the West Indies and tropical America also developed, it became clear that there were big advantages in the possession of an article of export suited to those countries' needs. The native Indian cotton industry at first stood in the way; but, as the machines developed, this was undermined, and Lancashire began to send her piece goods East and West in ever-increasing quantities. There was no limit to the raw material; for, though the import of raw cotton from India fell off, supplies came in readily, first from Central and South America, and then, with the growth of the slave trade, from the North American continent as well. Only a few years after the close of the War of Independence, the position of the United States as the supplier of Lancashire's raw material began to be firmly established, until American cotton reached in the British market the dominant position it has kept ever since. By 1815 Lancashire was drawing more than half its supply of cotton from the United States.

In 1789 these changes were only on the way; for the new machines which made possible the vast development of the cotton trade were only just being widely introduced. Kay had, indeed, invented his flying-shuttle as far back as 1733, and this, by doubling the output of the weaver, had altered the technical basis of the industry, and set inventors busy seeking means of increasing the supply of yarn by some mechanical improvement in the processes of spinning. But Hargreaves did not perfect his spinning-jenny until 1767, and the water-frame, first commercially developed by Richard Arkwright, made its appearance at about the same time. Arkwright's second patent, which linked up the preliminary process of carding with the subsequent processes of roving and spinning, followed in 1775, and four years later Crompton invented the spinning-mule.

The vital change in the cotton industry was due,

not to the inventions of Kay and Hargreaves, which could still be operated by the worker in his own home, under what is called the "domestic system," but to the new machines introduced by Arkwright and Crompton. These, designed from the first to be operated by power, necessarily involved the introduction of the factory system. Until Boulton and Watt's steam engines came into general use, the power was supplied by water; but the concentration of the workers into factories was none the less the inevitable sequel to the coming of the new machines.

I have used above the names attached by tradition to the various machines as the names of their "inventors." But, in fact, almost every invention was the result, not of an original and complete idea in the mind of one man, but of a gradual accretion of improvements on ideas previously developed to some extent. Usually the credit went to the man who completed the process; but in the outstanding case of Richard Arkwright it has been seriously questioned whether he really invented anything at all, or did not merely combine the work of several earlier discoverers. The point is important chiefly because it afforded a ground for challenging the patents with which Arkwright had sought to protect his monopoly of the new processes. The story of this great dispute, in order to fight which the Manchester employers formed a solid alliance and spent money freely, cannot be told here. It must be enough to say that in 1785 Arkwright's patents were annulled, and all who cared became free to use the new machines.

During the next few years there was, naturally,

a rush of aspirants eager to take advantage of the new opportunities for cheap and profitable production. In and round Manchester, there was a huge outburst of energy in the building and equipping of new factories to operate the new machines. The water-frame had just solved the problem of producing a cotton thread strong enough to be used for the warp; and the mule had enabled the new technique to be applied to the production of fine cotton yarn, as well as of the coarser counts. The road lay open for a great development of the cotton trade on lines of complete independence of any other British industry. For men who could get control even of a little capital, and were prompt in getting to work with the new methods, there was the prospect of high profits and sustained economic prosperity. No wonder there were soon many competitors in the field.

Owen had come to Manchester just at the most critical point of this development. He knew, indeed, nothing at all about machinery; but his varied experience as a salesman had made him an excellent judge of textile fabrics, and especially of the new British-made cotton goods which were then coming into fashion. At Stamford he had first met with Samuel Oldknow's British muslins, which that enterprising manufacturer began to make soon after 1780. Oldknow's muslin sold then for half a guinea a yard, and was reckoned extraordinarily fine, though, towards the end of Owen's life, a much better quality, he tells us, could be bought for twopence a yard.[1] Oldknow was the pioneer; but already, in 1789, a host of other

_____
[1] *Life*, p. 35.

manufacturers was following in his footsteps, and invention was rapidly revolutionising the types of fabric produced by the new machines.

Among the goods dealt in by Satterfield's were wire frames for ladies' bonnets. These were made for the firm by a mechanic of the name of Ernest Jones. This Jones began to talk to Owen about the wonderful new spinning-machines that were being introduced, and to hint to him that there was money to be made by their manufacture. Jones, however, had no capital; but he said that if he had only a hundred pounds it would be enough to serve as the foundation for an excellent business. At length he proposed that Owen should join him in partnership, contributing one hundred pounds in capital while he contributed his mechanical knowledge. They were to share equally in the profits. Attracted by the prospect, Owen wrote to his brother in London, and succeeded in borrowing from him the amount required. He then gave Mr. Satterfield notice, and went definitely into partnership with Jones. A Manchester builder agreed to erect them a workshop, and let it them at a yearly rental, and by the time Owen's notice expired the place was ready. "We had shortly about forty men at work to make machines, and we obtained wood, iron, and brass, for their construction, upon credit."[1]

Thus Owen began his career as an employer. But all did not go smoothly with the new partnership. Jones, though a good enough mechanic, was no business man, and no hand at factory management. Both the commercial control of the business

[1] *Life*, p. 31.

and the management of the workers fell wholly on Owen's shoulders. "I looked very wisely at the men in their different departments, although I really knew nothing. But by intensely observing everything, I maintained order and regularity throughout the establishment, which proceeded under such circumstances far better than I had anticipated. We made what are technically called 'mules' for spinning cotton, sold them, and appeared to be carrying on a good business; while, having discovered the want of business capacity in my partner, I proceeded with fear and trembling."[1]

The whole affair, however, lasted only a few months. At the end of that time, Jones received an offer from a man who had adequate capital and desired to join him in the business. He then thought that he had no further use for Owen, and, with his new partner, offered to buy him out. Owen was to receive as his share six mule machines made by the firm, a reel, and a making-up machine for packing the finished yarn in bundles for sale. Eager to escape from his connection with Jones, he accepted the terms, though he found out afterwards that they would have offered more. "I had now, when about nineteen years of age, to begin the world on my own account, having the promise of the machinery named to commence with."[2]

While Owen was still in partnership with Jones, he received from his old employer, McGuffog, a very flattering offer. McGuffog asked Owen to join him at Stamford, proposing to supply all the capital, give him a half share of profits at once, and

[1] *Life*, pp. 31–2.　　　[2] *Ibid.*, p. 32.

the whole business in a few years' time. This was a very liberal offer; but Owen, for some reason that is not very clear, felt obliged to decline it, possibly because he conceived himself tied to his arrangement with Jones. Had he accepted, he says, he would probably have married McGuffog's niece, whom he found many years later to have been attached to him. "I should most probably have lived and died a rich Stamford linen-draper."[1] One is tempted to doubt whether, under any conditions, Owen would have settled down to so humdrum a way of life.

He refused McGuffog's offer and, on leaving Jones, set up for himself. He succeeded in renting a large new factory in Ancoats Lane, subletting enough of it to have the use of his own portion rent-free. Here he set up his machines; but only three of the promised six mules, with the other two machines, were ever handed over to him by his late partner, whose business soon after came to grief. With these machines and three employees he began work, spinning yarn from rovings which he bought from two young Scotsmen named McConnell and Kennedy, who afterwards rose to be one of the big spinning firms of Manchester. At this stage they had no machinery for spinning, and he none to make rovings, the preparatory process. But by collaboration they were able to do well out of the business.

Soon Owen was making a profit of about six pounds a week, finding no difficulty in disposing of what he produced. He paid twelve shillings a pound for rovings, and sold thread at twenty-two

[1] *Life*, p. 33.

shillings a pound, finding this a comfortable margin. On leaving Satterfield's, he had gone to lodge with a widow in St. Ann's Square, paying half a guinea a week for a bedroom to himself, a sitting-room shared with two other lodgers, and all found. "I found the house clean, the attendance good—tea or coffee, etc., for breakfast—a hot joint, well-cooked, and a pudding or pie daily for dinner—tea in the afternoon—and good bread and cheese and butter, and a glass of ale at supper—and I do not recollect ever living, as mere living, better, or more to my satisfaction. But how this old widow continued thus to supply us and to get her own living out of us, I could never understand. Perhaps the house was her own; and provisions were then (1789–1790) cheap, and manufacturing luxury had not commenced. The widow always appeared cheerful and satisfied."[1] After leaving Jones, however, Owen quitted St. Ann's Square, and went to lodge with the builder from whom he rented his factory.

If Owen had been left to build up his business on his own account, from the small foundations with which he began, he might in time have become a great employer; for profits were large, and capital could be accumulated rapidly out of earnings. But he had been only about a year on his own when a bigger opportunity presented itself. Among the big new spinning mills which had been built in Manchester to work the new machines was one for fine spinning, erected by Mr. Drinkwater, a rich Manchester merchant largely engaged in foreign trade. Drinkwater knew nothing of machin-

[1] *Life*, p. 32.

ery or cotton manufacture. He had relied for the technical control of the mill on a Mr. George Lee, a mechanical expert, who superintended the building and installation, and was to manage the mill for him. But before the plant was fully installed, Lee received and accepted a more advantageous offer, entering into partnership with Sir George Philips of Salford to erect another big mill. Drinkwater was left in a difficulty, for the processes involved were new, and it was not easy to find a man with the necessary technical knowledge to replace Mr. Lee. He advertised the post in the Manchester papers, and, seeing the advertisement, Owen decided on the impulse of the moment to apply. He was nearly twenty, and Drinkwater's mill employed about five hundred workers.

"Without saying a word I put on my hat, and proceeded straight to Mr. Drinkwater's counting-house, and boy and inexperienced as I was, I asked him for the situation which he had advertised. The circumstances which now occurred made a lasting impression upon me, because they led to important future consequences. He said immediately, 'You are too young,' and at that time, being fresh-coloured, I looked younger than I was. I said, 'That was an objection made to me four or five years ago, but I did not expect it would be made to me now.' 'How old are you?' 'Twenty in May this year,' was my reply. 'How often do you get drunk in the week?' (This was a common habit with almost all persons in Manchester and Lancashire at that period.) 'I was never,' I said, 'drunk in my life,' blushing scarlet at this unexpected question. My answer and the manner of it made, I suppose, a favourable impression; for the next question was, 'What salary do you ask?' 'Three hundred a year,' was my reply. 'What?' Mr. Drinkwater said, with some surprise, repeating the words, 'three hundred a year! I have had this morning I know not how many seeking the situation, and I do not think that all their askings together would amount to what you require.' 'I cannot be governed by what others ask,' said I, 'and I cannot take less. I am now making that sum by my own business.' 'Can you prove that to me?' 'Yes, I will show you the business and my books.' 'Then I will go with you, and let me see them,' said Mr. Drinkwater. We went to my factory. I explained the nature of my business, opened the books, and proved my statement to his satisfaction. He then said, 'What reference as to past character can you give?' I referred him to Mr. Satterfield, Messrs. Flint and Palmer, and Mr. McGuffog. 'Come to me on such a day, and you shall have my answer.' This was to give him time to make his inquiries."[1]

When the day came Owen was engaged, and his own machinery taken over at cost price. In this astonishing fashion he became manager over five hundred workers at a salary very high for those days, when he was barely twenty years old. He took up his duties at once. He knew little about the new machinery he was to control, and the mill was not yet in full running order when he took charge. His predecessor had left the day before, and he got no help from Drinkwater, who did not

[1] *Life*, p. 37.

even go down to the mill to introduce him. "Thus, uninstructed, I had to take the management of the concern. I had to purchase the raw material, to make the machines—for the mill was not nearly filled with machinery—to manufacture the cotton into yarn, to sell it, and to keep the accounts, pay the wages, and, in fact, to take the whole responsibility of the first fine cotton-spinning establishment by machinery that had ever been erected, commenced by one of the most scientific men of his day."[1]

Owen faced this trial as he had faced a similar ordeal when he set up with Jones. "I looked grave, inspected everything very minutely, examined the drawings and calculations of the machinery as left by Mr. Lee, and these were of great use to me. I was with the first in the morning, and I locked up the premises at night. I continued this silent inspection and superintendence day by day for six weeks, saying merely yes or no to the questions of what was to be done or otherwise, and during that period I did not give one direct order about anything. But at the end of that time I felt myself so much master of my position as to be ready to give directions in every department."[1]

However the thing was done, Owen made a great success of the mill. Not content with following out his predecessor's plans, he succeeded in greatly improving the quality of the yarn produced, so that before long the yarn made under his management was much finer, and was fetching a much higher price than the stocks left from Mr. Lee's time. Drinkwater had been much laughed at for engaging a boy to manage his mill; but

[1] *Life*, p. 39.

opinion soon came round when the results became apparent. Owen attended both to the mechanical and to the human efficiency of the business. He rearranged and improved the machinery, and he also bettered the conditions of the workers, who, he says, were well satisfied, and over whom he soon acquired a powerful influence. He attributed his success to his habits of exactness and to his knowledge of human nature; already his theories about the formation of character were developing strongly in his mind. He believed that, if men were to do good work, it was necessary to give them a good physical and moral environment.

Owen was left entirely to himself. Drinkwater never entered the mill during the first six months of his management, and in all he visited it only three times during the four years Owen was in charge, and then only to conduct a distinguished visitor. But he kept himself informed of what went on, and at the end of six months asked Owen to visit him at his country residence. Expressing himself much pleased with Owen's work, he offered him, if he would remain as manager, £400 for the second year, £500 for the third year, and then a fourth share in the business with himself and his two sons. Owen naturally accepted this offer, and a deed of agreement was duly signed. He was further allowed, after this, to have his name printed as manager on the packages of yarn made under his control, and his reputation thus spread to a wider circle among the manufacturers in both England and Scotland, where the mill had many customers.

Owen mentions that, up to this time, the raw cotton used in England for machine spinning came from the West Indies, from South America, and from the French island of Bourbon (now known as Réunion). The machines then used in England could not spin the North American cotton, which is now, of course, the chief source of supply. It fell to his lot, while he was manager to Drinkwater, to make the first experiments with the Sea Island cotton, which has ever since been regarded as among the best for fine spinning. This was an accidental success; but his yarns were so good that they fetched 10 per cent. over the current list prices, and were always in great demand. Reliable yarns were not easy to get with the new machinery still largely in the experimental stage. Soon Owen was able to increase the fineness from 120 to 300 hanks in the pound, and to sell his yarns readily at 50 per cent. above the list prices.

In 1792, mainly in consequence of the European War, there was a serious crisis in the cotton trade, and many firms were hard hit. Drinkwater, however, had plenty of capital, and his business did not greatly suffer. In addition to Bank Top Mill, he had another factory at Northwich, employed in water-spinning or machine warp making. Owen was now placed in charge of this mill as well, the previous manager remaining under his general control.

Indirectly, however, the crisis of 1792 had a great effect on Owen's prospects. Samuel Old-know, the Marple muslin manufacturer, has been mentioned already.[1] Oldknow had made, at his big factory at Marple, an establishment which in

[1] See p. 63. For a full account of Oldknow and his interesting career, see *Samuel Oldknow and the Arkwrights*, edited by Prof. G. Unwin.

some respects foreshadows Owen's achievements at New Lanark. He had created what was rather an industrial community than merely a mill, combining agriculture and quarrying with cotton manufacture, and building a village as well as factory accommodation for his workers. Tradition says that he was a model employer for his time, and the records recently unearthed by Professor Unwin and his colleagues seem to bear out this view. Very possibly Oldknow's work had an influence on Owen's later plans, and was in his mind when he created the community of New Lanark.

Oldknow, however, after 1792, was in financial difficulties. He had spent heavily in equipping his establishment and he had not capital enough to stand the strain. He was heavily in debt, we know, to Arkwright, and about this time he began to pay his addresses to Drinkwater's daughter. Owen suggests that his motive was partly, at least, that of getting Drinkwater's capital behind him. Miss Drinkwater, who had another admirer, did not at first receive with pleasure the advances of a man very much older than herself. But Oldknow stood high, and her father was urgent for the match. At length it was arranged.

And now the matter came to affect Owen. Oldknow was anxious to make a firm alliance between his own and Drinkwater's interests and to get both entirely under their united control. The deed of partnership between Drinkwater and Owen stood in the way of this. Oldknow wanted Owen to remain as manager; but he did not want him to become a partner. Finally, he talked his prospective father-in-law round. Drinkwater sent for Owen, and asked him on what terms he would consent to remain as manager, and to rescind the agreement for a partnership.

Owen had suspected what was in the wind, and, on his visit to Drinkwater, he took the deed of partnership with him in his pocket. When Drinkwater put his proposition, his manager's reply was as characteristic as it was decisive. "I have brought the agreement with me," said Owen, "and here it is, and I now put it into the fire, because I never will connect myself with any parties who are not desirous to be united with me; but under these circumstances I cannot remain your manager with any salary you can give."[1]

Drinkwater did his best to dissuade his impulsive colleague, very loth to lose a manager who had done so well for the business. Owen agreed to remain until a competent man could be found to take his place; but his mind was made up. His act, he says, was "an act of feeling, and not of judgment." He gave up, with no certain prospects, not merely an excellent salary, but an agreement of considerable monetary value. He was about twenty-four when this event occurred.

In the end the projected marriage was broken off, and there was no union of the Oldknow-Drinkwater interests. But before this occurred Owen had entered into other arrangements. He remained for nearly a year longer at Bank Top Mill; but other offers were speedily made to him. Samuel Marsland, the great spinner, had with others recently purchased for development the Chorlton estate, and he now offered Owen partnership, with a third of the profits, in a big mill which

[1] *Life*, p. 57.

he proposed to erect. Marsland was to find all the capital. "This was a very liberal proposal, but as he did not offer me *half* of the profits, my feelings induced me to decline it."[1] At a later stage, Owen thought he had been wrong, as an offer which he subsequently accepted was far less favourable.

This was a partnership with two inexperienced young men, who had capital. But before this had been completed, another offer came Owen's way, and he joined with two rich and old-established houses, Messrs. Borrodale and Atkinson, of London, and Messrs. Barton, of Manchester, to form the Chorlton Twist Company. The new mills which he was building on the Chorlton estate were to be under his management, assisted by Mr. Thomas Atkinson, brother of the head of the London firm. He left Drinkwater in 1794 or early in 1795; but it was between two and three years later before the new Chorlton mills were at work. Owen refused to use the new factory for making products which would compete with his old employer's. He specialised at Chorlton on yarns for cloth meant for printing, or for muslins which would not bring him into competition with Drinkwater. Drinkwater, he writes, "had always been kind and liberal to me, except in not being firm in maintaining his engagement with me, and, therefore, I had no wish to injure him."[2] There is not, I think, a single incident in Owen's whole career in which he tried to injure, or even showed himself angry with, any human being. His philosophy, as we shall see, did not permit of anger or injury, and he was singular in acting up to what he believed.

[1] *Life*, p. 58.   [2] *Ibid*, p. 59.

CHAPTER V

MANCHESTER—MARRIAGE

Manchester, though it had become in the eighteenth century one of the most important towns in England, did not become a borough until 1838, or secure any representation in Parliament until 1832. Not till 1792 did it secure even a Commission of Police, or any form of local government other than the feudal jurisdiction of the Court Leet and the Lord of the Manor, whose rights were only extinguished finally in 1846 by their purchase by the town. But already in the eighteenth century the place was a centre of keen intellectual life. Wesley had a strong following, and Unitarianism was vigorously preached from the pulpit of the famous Cross Street Chapel. Dr. Baines, the head of Manchester New College, the Unitarian training centre, was a vigorous personality, and on his staff was the famous chemist, John Dalton, originator of the atomic theory. Dr. Percival, the inspiring genius of the Manchester Board of Health, had founded in 1781 the Manchester Literary and Philosophic Society, of which the two Henrys, Dalton, and Robert Owen, were among the distinguished members. Rich merchants abounded, and De Quincey, in his *Autobiographic Sketches*, bears witness to the high degree of comfort and refinement which prevailed among them.

In short, the city was growing cultured as well as rich before its rapid transformation under the influence of the new machines. John Byrom's diaries reveal it as a pleasant place to live in during the earlier half of the century, while it was still almost untouched by the new conditions. In Owen's day it was already changing. The bustle of life was increasing; factory buildings were rising and mean dwellings spreading over the once pleasant outskirts. The new generation which Owen represented took over the inheritance of its older culture but made of it a new thing—more aggressive, more practical, and above all, more in a hurry.

Owen himself came to Manchester at a time when the new attitude was rapidly displacing the old, but had not yet banished it or made it merely a dead tradition. He played his part in the work of transformation; but he also learnt something from the old order that was passing away. He watched the processes of change at work, and drew his firm conclusions from what he saw with his own eyes.

The years Owen spent at Manchester brought out his latent powers, and completed his development to self-reliant manhood. They also accustomed him to good and intellectual society. He has left an account of himself as he was when Drinkwater first made him the offer of partnership. "I was yet," he writes, "but an ill-educated awkward youth, strongly sensitive to my defects of education, speaking ungrammatically, a kind of Welsh English, in consequence of the imperfect language spoken at Newtown, which was an imperfect mixture of both languages; and I had yet only had the society attainable by a retail assistant. I was also

77

so sensitive as among strangers to feel and to act awkwardly, and I was never satisfied with my own speaking and acting, and was subject painfully to blushing, which, with all my strongest efforts, I could not prevent. In fact, I felt the possession of ideas superior to my powers of expressing them, and this always embarrassed me with strangers, and especially when in company with those who had been systematically well educated, according to existing notions of education."[1]

Before long, however, Owen began to make good friends. His first intimates included John Dalton, the chemist, who had recently become teacher of mathematics at the Unitarian New College at Manchester.[2] In his room at the College Owen and a few others used to meet regularly for discussion. They discussed moral and religious questions and the recent discoveries in chemistry and other sciences, and at one of these meetings, Owen tells us, Dalton first broached his atomic theory. On several occasions young Samuel Taylor Coleridge visited the group, and fell into a high controversy with Owen. "Mr. Coleridge had a great fluency of words, and he could well put them together in high-sounding sentences; but my few words, directly to the point, generally told well; and although the eloquence and learning were with him, the strength of the argument was generally admitted to be on my side."[3] It is a pity we do not know what the contention was about; for Coleridge was at this time still under the spell of the French Revolution, and it may well be that their argu-

[1] *Life*, p. 43.
[2] Now Manchester College, Oxford.   [3] *Life*, p. 49.

78

ment had to do with the fundamentals of political policy.

At these meetings Owen's intelligence and power of expression broadened out. New College was a Unitarian College, and John Dalton was a Quaker; but Owen gave full vent to his anti-sectarian religious opinions. By-and-by the College authorities became nervous, and Dr. Baines, the Principal, asked that they should be held less often on College premises. The group then moved elsewhere, and Owen acquired the name of "the reasoning machine," "because they said I made man a mere reasoning machine, made to be so by nature and society."[1]

Soon Owen found a wider field for the exercise of his intellectual powers. In 1793 he was elected to the Manchester Literary and Philosophical Society, then, under the presidency of its founder, the physician Dr. Percival, the chief haunt of the Manchester intellectuals. Soon afterwards he proposed Dalton for membership, and he was speedily chosen a member of the committee. It was presumably before this that, the subject of the cotton trade coming under discussion, he was called on by Dr. Percival to make his first speech in public. "I had never spoken in the Society, nor ever heard my own voice in public, nor had I the slightest desire ever to hear it. I was too diffident and sensitive to feel any such inclination. . . . I blushed, and stammered out some few incoherent sentences, and felt quite annoyed at my ignorance and awkwardness being thus exposed."[2] However, Owen followed up his speech by writing a paper for the

[1] *Life*, p. 50.   [2] *Ibid.*, p. 51.

Society on the cotton trade. This was in November, 1793, and at later dates Owen contributed three further papers to the Society's proceedings.[1]

Another friendship of Owen's Manchester period was with Robert Fulton, the American pioneer of steam navigation, with whom he was a fellow-lodger for a time in 1794. Fulton had an extra-ordinary career, very characteristic of the times. The child of poor parents, he was apprenticed to a jeweller; but he conceived the desire of becoming a landscape and portrait painter, and came to England to study. Becoming acquainted with James Watt and the Duke of Bridgewater, he again changed his plans, and turned to civil engineering and invention. In 1794 he was busy with an invention for the machine excavation of canals, and in securing a patent for this he had exhausted all his funds. Owen advanced him money, and the two entered into a deed of partnership. This was just after Owen had left Drinkwater, and before he had become a partner in the Chorlton Twist Company. When Owen joined this firm, his partnership with Fulton was apparently cancelled, and the money he had advanced—about £100—was treated as a debt. Their relations continued, on a friendly footing, till 1797, when £60 was repaid. Fulton had, meanwhile, gone to live in France, where he was experimenting with torpedoes for submarine warfare, and Owen heard no more of him either from Paris or after his return to America. Owen

[1] Podmore, vol. i. p. 58. The subjects were, "The Utility of Learning," "The Connection between Universal Happiness and Practical Mechanics," and "The Origin of Opinions with a View to the Improvement of the Social Virtues"—plain foreshadowings of his later theories.

was well pleased in later years to have helped Fulton at a critical period in his career, and, above all, to have been the means of his visiting Glasgow, where he saw Henry Bell's pioneer attempts to make a steamboat,[1] and got the germ of the idea which he afterwards developed in America into a practicable means of steam navigation.[2]

By this time Owen's diffidence had worn off, and he was mixing more freely with Manchester society. He remained shy with women, and did not readily make women friends; but he had a knack of making and keeping men friends. He was, more-over, although he is said to have been an ugly man, apparently attractive to women. At least one beautiful and accomplished young woman seems to have been so attracted as to think of him as a possible husband; but Owen did not realise this until long after. He wrote curiously of the episode when he was old. "That connexion, which I might have obtained had I then possessed sufficient know-ledge of the world and sufficient self-confidence to have sought it, would have been well adapted to have met and satisfied all the feelings of my nature. But it was not to be—circumstances were opposed to it, and another destiny was awaiting me."[3] He tells us that he wanted a wife; but, though he was attracted to the young lady, he was apparently too shy to propose.

At this time Owen was living, or lodging, in Chorlton Hall, the old mansion of the estate on

---

[1] This must have been a very early attempt of Bell's. His "Comet" was not launched until 1812.

[2] For Owen's relations with Fulton, see *Life*, p. 89.

[3] *Life*, p. 67.

which he was building his new factory. A little later, in 1797, he moved to a big house called Greenheys, which had been erected by "a rich Manchester merchant who died before he could occupy it." This merchant, I believe, was no other than the father of Thomas De Quincey, whose *Autobiographic Sketches* contain many references to Greenheys. The De Quinceys did actually live there for some time, and Thomas De Quincey was born at Greenheys in 1790. On the father's death, Owen and a friend and business associate named Marshall bought the house, and converted it into two private residences. Here he lived for two years as a bachelor, with an elderly married couple to look after him. Every day he would order for dinner an apple dumpling—which his housekeeper made excellently—and leave the rest to her. Is it a curious case of heredity that Owen's son, Robert Dale, records in his own autobiography that he used his first freedom in the choice of food to demand an unvarying diet of this same delicacy?[1]

As the Chorlton Twist Company began to get into working order, it became necessary for Owen to bestir himself in establishing business connections. He began to pay regular visits to the Lancashire manufacturing towns and, a little later, to Scotland also. On one visit to Blackburn he had his sole experience of the hunting field. Asked if he would hunt, he said he had no horse save a hired hack. He was at once offered an excellent mount, and did not see how to refuse, though he knew nothing of hunting, and felt no desire for the sport. However, by leaving all to the sagacity of his horse, he cleared all obstacles, and was in at every death.

[1] R. D. Owen, *Threading My Way*, p. 100.

He acquired the reputation of a fine horseman; but he never hunted again.

Owen paid his first visit to Scotland in company with a manufacturer from Preston. It took them two nights and three days of incessant travel to get from Manchester to Glasgow, over roads which were "in a deplorable condition." Mail-coaches had not yet started running, and there was still little intercourse between north and south. Visiting Scotland was like travelling to a strange foreign country. "I then little imagined that I should become so interested in this locality as I afterwards was."[1]

One day, walking in Glasgow, Owen met the sister of one of his Manchester friends, the Robert Spear who had first induced him to take up the spinning of Sea Island cotton. Miss Spear was on a visit to her friend, Anne Caroline Dale, daughter of David Dale, the well-known Glasgow banker and religious leader. They were introduced, and Miss Dale suggested that Owen should pay a visit to her father's big cotton mills at New Lanark. The establishment "then consisted of a primitive manu-facturing Scotch village and four mills for spinning cotton."[2] The visit was arranged; and Owen was much impressed with the situation. "Of all places I have yet seen," he said to his friend, who had accompanied him, "I should prefer this in order to try an experiment I have long contemplated, and have wished to have an opportunity to put in practice."[2] Little did he think, he adds in record-ing the incident, that there was the remotest chance of his wish being gratified.

Out of the chance introduction to Miss Dale

[1] *Life*, p. 62.   [2] *Ibid.*, p. 63.

soon sprang a pleasant intimacy. Miss Dale and her sisters were in the habit of walking in the mornings by the banks of the Clyde, and on several occasions during his visit Owen was their companion. When he left Glasgow Miss Dale asked him to visit her again when he returned to the neighbourhood. Before long he was back, bearing a letter to Miss Dale from her friend Miss Spear. "Letters at that time," he writes, "were rather an expensive luxury between friends residing at a distance. The penny postage had not then been thought of, and there was much private letter-carrying between friends."[1]

The walks by the Clyde were resumed on this visit, and the intimacy grew. "This second visit to Glasgow I found was beginning to create other feelings than mere business."[1] But he made no declaration. Miss Dale's father, who was very often absent on business, he had not yet even met.

Owen, as we have seen, was diffident with women; and it was left for Miss Spear to urge him on. When they met after his second visit, she told him a story of Miss Dale's behaviour after their first meeting. Miss Dale had asked many questions about Owen, and had ended by saying, "I do not know how it is, but if ever I marry, that is to be my husband."[2] With such encouragement to back his own inclination, Owen could hardly hold back. On his third visit he again walked with Miss Dale, and this time asked her permission to become her suitor. Miss Dale gave him to understand that she loved him, without a direct avowal; but she also made it plain that she would not marry without her father's consent, which she deemed unlikely; for

[1] *Life*, p. 65. [2] *Ibid.*, p. 69.

David Dale did not like Englishmen, or Welshmen, and his religious views were exceedingly strict.

David Dale was at this time one of the leading business men of Glasgow. His father had been a grocer at Stewarton in Ayrshire, where David was born in 1739. He was first apprenticed to a weaver in Paisley, and then became clerk to a silk mercer. Before long he started on his own in the linen trade. Accumulating wealth, he added banking to his other concerns, and became one of the principal men in the Royal Bank of Scotland. In 1783 Richard Arkwright visited Glasgow in furtherance of his schemes for the development of the cotton industry, and Dale entered into partnership with the great entrepreneur. The result was the building of the New Lanark mills; but very soon his connection with Arkwright was ended by a quarrel,[1] and New Lanark, which began operations in 1784, passed entirely into his own hands. During the next few years he started, or joined with others in starting, a considerable number of spinning, weaving, and dyeing factories in various parts of Scotland.

But David Dale was not only a big figure in Glasgow business circles, he was also the real head of a very strict Presbyterian sect known as the "Old Scotch Independents," which had split from the parent Church in his youth. This sect employed no paid ministers, its pastors making their living as laymen. Dale was himself both pastor of

[1] For an amusing account of the quarrel, see R. D. Owen, *Threading My Way*, p. 9. According to him, the whole substance of the quarrel was the placing of the wooden cupola on which the factory bell was hung. The two men had an æsthetic difference about it, and agreed to part.

an important church of the sect in Glasgow and a sort of visiting moderator for the sect as a whole. Owen, in the light of later knowledge, paid warm tribute to his character and liberality, but at the outset a man professing Owen's unorthodox religious views, and not a Scotsman, was unlikely to be well received by the leader of the strictest of Scottish sects. Dale was, moreover, a strong Tory; and Owen, however one might classify his political views, was certainly not that.[1] Moreover, there was the difficulty that, intimate as he had become with the daughter, he had not even met the father.

Something had to be done; and once more Owen acted on impulse. He heard a rumour that Dale was anxious to restrict his enterprises, and, among other things, was considering the sale of the New Lanark mills. Acting on this hint, he called on Dale, and asked him on what terms he would be prepared to sell. He was coldly and, as he thought, suspiciously received. "I was now about twenty-seven years of age, and young-looking for my years, and he said, yet looking suspiciously, 'You cannot want to purchase them; you are too young for such a task!' "[2] Owen explained that he was in partner-ship with older men of large capital, and it was at length arranged that he should go to New Lanark and inspect the mills thoroughly, and then return to Manchester to report to his partners. Dale agreed to this; but Owen believed he did not take the proposal seriously.

He lost no time, however, in acting on the per-mission he had received. He posted from Glasgow

[1] See A. Liddell, *Memoir of David Dale*, 1854. Also refer-ences in Podmore and R. D. Owen's *Threading My Way*.

[2] *Life*, p. 71.

to New Lanark. On the journey of under thirty miles he had to pass three toll-gates. Owen had no change, and at the first he presented a half-guinea. At this time gold coins were not in use in Scotland, and the toll-man had never seen one before. He turned it over and over, and finally refused to take it, preferring to let Owen owe the money to accepting an unknown coin. At each of the other gates the same thing occurred. "I concluded," he writes, "I had come to a very primitive district."[1]

Having thoroughly examined the mills, Owen returned to Manchester, and reported strongly in their favour to his partners, two of whom at once set off with him to visit them. Before their arrival in Glasgow Miss Dale had told her father of her relations with Owen, and found him very hostile to the match. Owen, he said, was a stranger and a *land-louper*, and he would not hear of it. Miss Dale told him this bad news, and reaffirmed her determination not to marry without her father's consent.

This was the situation when Owen and his partners, much to David Dale's surprise, waited on him and expressed their real desire to treat for the New Lanark mills. After the necessary inquiries had been made, Dale affirmed his willingness to sell. It remained to fix the price. Dale said that he did not really know how much the place was worth. "But," he added, "Mr. Owen knows better than I do the value of such property at this period, and I wish that he would name what he would consider a fair price between honest buyers and sellers." Owen was somewhat taken aback by this request; but, after consideration, he suggested a

[1] *Life*, p. 72.

price of £60,000, payable at the rate of £3,000 a year for twenty years. Mr. Dale, to the surprise of Owen and his partners, at once said that he would accept these terms, and asked Owen's partners if they agreed. They did so; "and thus, in these few words, passed the establishment of New Lanark from Mr. Dale into the hands of the Chorlton Twist Company."[1]

This clinched the business transition, and in a sufficiently remarkable manner; but it did not at once remove Dale's objections to Owen's union with his daughter. At this time Miss Dale and her sisters were staying at a house in New Lanark, where they often spent part of the summer. This house passed, with the rest of the property, to the new owners, and the Dales proposed to leave at once. At Owen's request, however, they stayed on, and he took up his residence at the Clydesdale Hotel in Old Lanark. He had thus frequent opportunities for meeting Miss Dale, and after a time, on this account, her father insisted on her return to Glasgow. Before long, however, Dale got to know Owen better, and began to like him. He found, too, that his daughter was very much in love; and at length his objections were withdrawn. In the autumn of 1799 Robert Owen and Anne Caroline Dale were married in David Dale's house, according to the usage of the sect to which he belonged. They were married, however, by a regular minister of the Scottish Church. "Mr. Balfour requested Miss Dale and me to stand up, and asked each of us if we were willing to take the other for husband or wife, and, each simply nodding assent, he said, without one word more, 'Then

[1] *Life*, p. 73.

you are married, and you may sit down,' and the ceremony was all over."[1]

Mr. and Mrs. Owen shortly set out for Manchester, where it was their intention to reside. But within a few months things began to go wrong at New Lanark, where the old managers, who had been taken over, were not making a success of the business. It was decided that Owen should leave his partner Atkinson in charge at Manchester, and move to Scotland to assume direct control of the New Lanark mills. Accordingly, at the beginning of January, 1800, Owen entered on his new kingdom, thereafter to be lastingly associated with his name, as resident managing director of the establishment at New Lanark.

[1] *Life*, p. 76.

CHAPTER VI

NEW LANARK, 1800–1813

New Lanark Mills, as we have seen, were founded in 1782 by David Dale, in partnership with Richard Arkwright. But the preliminary work was hardly completed when, two years later, the partnership was dissolved, and the mills passed into Dale's exclusive ownership. Dale meant to be a benevolent employer, and certain features of the system which Owen subsequently developed were started while he was in control. For example, when one of the mills was burnt down in 1786, he paid the work-people their wages until work could be resumed. He made some provision for the education of the children, who were employed in large numbers, and he started, on a small scale, the practice of supplying goods through a store which he established in the village. But David Dale himself took little part in the management of New Lanark, and apparently seldom visited it, though his family spent part of the year at a house in the village. Control on the spot was left to others; at the time when Owen and his partners bought New Lanark it was in the hands of Dale's half-brother, James Dale, and another paid manager.

Owen, although he was the manager and part-owner of the establishment, had not a free hand. His fortune at this time amounted only to £3,000, and, in addition to the interest, he received £1,000 as manager. As the place had been bought for £60,000, and a great deal of money had to be spent on improving it, he was only a junior partner, with a comparatively small holding. His operations were therefore from the first restricted to what he could get his richer partners to accept. Up to a point, they were willing to give him a free hand; but their power of overriding his judgment always imposed limits on what he could do. For his partners were business men, concerned to make as much profit as they could with due regard to the current conventions of factory management. They had bought New Lanark as a business speculation, and not as the field for a social experiment. Owen had other views; but to a great extent he had to keep these views to himself.

He had, however, a great advantage. He was on the spot, and his partners were far away. So far, then, as the actual methods of management were concerned, he could do as he liked, if only he did not make what his partners considered undue calls for money. Moreover, he had tried out in Manchester certain experiments based on his theories, though by no means completely embodying them; and his Manchester businesses had paid handsome dividends. It appears that, during the first years of what he called his "government" at New Lanark, he was given a reasonably free hand.

"I say 'government,' " he wrote many years later, in speaking of his assumption of control, "for my intention was not to be a mere manager of cotton mills, as such mills were at this time generally managed, but to introduce principles in the conduct of the people which I had successfully commenced with the work-people in Mr. Drinkwater's factory, and to change the conditions of the people who, I saw, were surrounded by circumstances having an injurious influence upon the character of the entire population of New Lanark. I had now, by a course of events not under my control, the groundwork on which to try an experiment long wished for, but little expected ever to be in my power to carry into execution."[1] In this spirit Owen took up his task of "government." He meant to make New Lanark not merely a success as a factory, but the laboratory for a great series of social experiments in education and moral and physical reform.

The difficulties which Owen met with at New Lanark are in many respects typical of the time. The rapid expansion of the factory system involved an intensely keen demand for labour. But the factories were unpopular, and few went to work in them save under some sort of compulsion. To a large extent, this compulsion was applied by the forcible breaking-up of the old village life. The enclosures of common and arable land, and the conversion of arable to stock farming, drove many of the villagers out of their native districts to seek employment in the towns. The Speenhamland system of poor relief in aid of wages stimulated the growth of population by making the amount of earnings depend on the size of the family. But even these abundant sources of factory labour were not adequate to supply the clamant needs of the new system. Women and children were extensively employed at very low wages, as the arts of domestic spinning and weaving gave way before the growth of large-scale production. Pauper children, under

[1] *Life*, p. 78.

the name of "parish apprentices," were sent in droves by the Poor Law authorities to work in the factories under conditions of virtual slavery. Moreover, labourers were sought for among the starving peasantry of Ireland, and in the Highlands of Scotland, where the crofters were being driven off the land in thousands for the making of sheep-runs and deer forests for the rich.[1]

In the Lowlands of Scotland, where the New Lanark factory was situated, the condition of the agricultural population was relatively good, and it proved nearly impossible to recruit factory labour from this source. Accordingly, both David Dale and Owen had to get the great majority of their workers from a distance. "It was most difficult," Owen wrote in describing the conditions when he first assumed control, "to induce any sober, well-doing family to leave their home to go into cotton mills as then conducted"[2]—a reluctance for which he was not at all disposed to blame them.

There were thus special difficulties, over and above those common to most manufacturers at that time, in securing an adequate and efficient supply of labour at New Lanark. The people round about, including those of the neighbouring town of Old Lanark, hated the mills, and would not work, or send their children to work, under the factory system. Workers had to be drawn from far and wide. Of the adults, many were Highlanders, used to the very different conditions of the crofter's life, and hating the factory into which they had been driven as a last refuge from starvation. With them, Owen says, were mixed a number drawn from the

[1] For a graphic account of the evictions in the Highlands, see Marx, *Capital*, vol. i. p. 752 ff.   [2] *Life*, p. 79.

lowest stratum of the urban proletariat. There had been always a scarcity of workers, even of these unsuitable types, and those who were secured did not mix well, and formed a very poor basis for the building of a happy and ordered community.

In these circumstances it is not surprising that the condition of both village and factory was very bad at the time when Owen assumed control. We have only his own account, and he may have exaggerated the evils which he found, in order to accentuate the contrast between them and the results of his management. But there is no reason to doubt the essential truth of his version. Drunkenness and immorality, he tells us, were very prevalent; thieving was common in every department of the works; housing conditions were disgusting, and filth was everywhere, both in the houses and in the streets of the village. The people were, indeed, for the most part very religious; but they belonged, he says, to many rival and disputing sects, so that they quarrelled fiercely, and seemed to consider their religion a sufficient excuse for the living of evil lives. In short, New Lanark, when Owen first went there, was as far as possible from being a model village or a place likely to attract visitors interested in hygienic or factory reform.

In addition to the adults, the mill workers included between four and five hundred parish apprentices—the unfortunate pauper children whom the Poor Law authorities were then in the habit of despatching in droves to any factory owner who would be good enough to take them—no inconvenient questions usually being asked about what happened to them when once they were off the hands of the parish. Dispossessed Highland

crofters, who hated the factory life and found
solace in the bottle, and helpless pauper children
were the best industrial material the ordinary
employer could secure. David Dale had solaced his
conscience by lodging the children comparatively
well, and giving them the rudiments of religious
instruction; but he had followed the prevailing
custom in recruiting labour for his mills.

Apart from these parish apprentices, the population of New Lanark was about 1,300 at the time
when Owen assumed control, and, in addition,
there were a few workers living a mile or so off in
the old county town—"Old Lanark," as Owen
habitually called it. The people of New Lanark
were housed by the firm—for Dale had built the
village as well as the mills. The great majority of
families lived in one room, without any adequate
sanitary arrangements. The streets were filthy,
and the houses very ill kept. Almost Owen's first
enterprise was to build an additional storey to
every house, and so secure two rooms for nearly
every household. But this was as far as even he
could go.

The parish children were aged from five to ten,
although their ages were officially given as from
seven to twelve. Like the rest of the hands, they
worked a thirteen hours' day, with an hour and a
quarter allowed for meals. Such education as they
received in the rudiments of religion, in reading,
and, for some, in writing, took place after these
hours had been worked. "But this kind of instruction, when the strength of the children was
exhausted, only tormented them without doing any
real good—for I found that none of them understood anything they attempted to read, and many

of them fell asleep during the school hours."[1] For the other children of the village, there was apparently not even this mockery of education.

Bad as the position of these children was, it was evidently much better than that of parish apprentices in other factories of the time. "The benevolent proprietor [Dale] spared no expense to give comfort to the poor children." A large house was built for their accommodation. "The rooms provided for them were spacious, always clean, and well ventilated; the food was abundant, and of the best quality; the clothes were neat and useful; a surgeon was kept in constant pay to direct how to prevent or to cure disease; and the best instructors which the country afforded were appointed to teach such branches of education as were deemed likely to be useful to children in their situation. Kind and well disposed persons were appointed to superintend all their proceedings. Nothing, in short, at first sight seemed wanting to render it a most complete charity."[2] Elsewhere Owen wrote that the boarding-house for the pauper children "was under an admirable arrangement."[3]

But all this care could not alter the fact that the whole system was wrong. The parish authorities insisted in sending the children into employment when they were far too young—" from mistaken economy," as Owen charitably described their motive.[4] And the hours of labour were far too long for either kindness or good food or education to be of much use. "Many of them became dwarfs in body and mind, and some of them were deformed.

---

[1] *Life*, p. 83. [2] *New View of Society*, Essay II, p. 45.
[3] *Address to the Inhabitants of New Lanark*.
[4] *New View of Society*, Essay II, p. 45.

Their labour through the day, and their education at night, became so irksome that numbers of them continually ran away, and almost all looked forward with impatience and anxiety to the expiration of their apprenticeship of seven, eight, and nine years, which generally expired when they were from thirteen to fifteen years old. At this period of life, unaccustomed to provide for themselves, and unacquainted with the world, they usually went to Edinburgh or Glasgow, where boys and girls were soon assailed by the innumerable temptations which all large towns present, and to which many of them fell sacrifices."[1]

Owen came at once to the conclusion that the only thing to be done was to end altogether this bad system. He therefore engaged no more pauper apprentices, and dispensed with them as the existing indentures ran out. He could not dispense with the other methods of recruiting labour from a distance. The work had to go on, and workers had to be secured. But here, too, he determined on a thorough reform. He was, indeed, far more dissatisfied with the management of the factory and of the adult labour than with the boarding-house for the parish children. "The whole system, though most kindly intended by Mr. Dale, was wretchedly bad, and the establishment had been constructed and managed by ordinary minds, accustomed only to very primitive proceedings."[2] Not only were the conditions of the workers very miserable; the factory was also ill organised from the standpoint of productive efficiency.

At first Owen tried to work with the old managers, and to bring them round to his point of view.

[1] *New View*, Essay II, p. 46. [2] *Life*, p. 84.

But he soon found this would not do. The old managers went, and after a time, when Owen's firm had disposed of the Chorlton factory, Mr. Humphreys, who had been his assistant there, came north to be works manager at New Lanark. But before this Owen had begun to carry out the big changes he had in view.

He did not attempt any sudden revolution. "The changes were to be made gradually, and to be effected by the profits of the establishment."[1] His first tasks were twofold: the rearrangement and improvement of the machinery, and the enlargement and building of houses, and laying of proper streets in the village. He acted from the outset on the principle which was the foundation of his social creed. The environment, material as well as moral, must be made good, if good men were to be developed or good material or moral results secured. He acted, not only on this principle, but with it firmly in mind. "This experiment at New Lanark was the first commencement of practical measures with a view to change the fundamental principle on which society has heretofore been based from the beginning; and no experiment could be more successful in proving the truth of the principle that the character is formed *for* and not *by* the individual, and that society now possesses the most ample means and power to well form the character of everyone."[2] We shall hear plenty later of this "principle" of Owen's; here it is merely recorded as having inspired from the outset his proceedings at New Lanark.

Owen's connection with New Lanark lasted for twenty-eight years in all, and for twenty-five of

[1] *Life*, p. 84. [2] *Ibid.*, p. 85.

these he was in active control of the establishment. The changes which he introduced were spread over this quarter of a century, and it is often difficult to say at what stage a particular change was introduced, or how long it remained in operation in a particular form. But, broadly speaking, Owen's work at New Lanark falls into two periods. The first and longest, stretching from 1800 to 1813, when he formed his third partnership to work the mills, is a time of quiet hard work, during which New Lanark was gradually transformed into the most successful establishment of the day, in its human as well as its commercial results. During these years Owen's work, hampered by friction with his successive partners, was confined to measures for the gradual improvement of the conditions of work and living among his employees; and even what he could do in these respects was strictly limited by exigences of profit-making. It attracted, until the end of this time, comparatively little public attention, and Owen did not either court public notice or take any marked part in public affairs. So far, he was in the eyes of the world only a very successful and exceptionally humane man of business, of whose theories nothing was known outside the circle of his friends.

The second period stretches from 1813 to about 1825. It begins with the publication of his earliest important writings—the *Statement Concerning the New Lanark Establishment* (1812), and the *New View of Society*, or *Essays on the Formation of Character*, the first two of which were publicly issued in 1813. It begins, also, with the formation of his third partnership, under which, for the first time, the financial restrictions on his measures at New Lanark were removed, only to be replaced by other difficulties hardly less galling. From 1813 onwards Owen was a public character and New Lanark a very celebrated place, visited by travellers from all parts of the world and deputations in search of enlightenment. Owen and his factory were, also, from 1816 and 1817 onwards, the storm-centres of two violent controversies—the struggle about factory legislation and hours of labour, and the religious controversy precipitated by his famous declaration at the City of London Tavern in 1817. From 1813 Owen, though he kept a tight control over the establishment, was less regularly in residence there, and more often away lecturing or pushing his proposals in public. In 1825 he practically left New Lanark altogether, and, though he remained nominally a partner till 1828, he had very little further to do with its control.

It is important to realise that only in the second of these two periods did he attempt to put any of his major designs into operation. The "Institution for the Formation of Character," which symbolised his conception of what a factory should be, was not opened until 1816, and only then was the system of education at the establishment fully developed. Thus, the entry of Owen's plans into their mature phase coincided almost exactly with the beginning of his public troubles. New Lanark, at its fullest development, was always a storm-centre of controversy as well as a place of pilgrimage; and Owen was most busy installing his system there at a time when he was most distracted between his work at New Lanark and his wider social and economic plans.

In this chapter I am dealing, as far as possible,

only with the earlier of the two periods outlined above; and I am also leaving over for separate treatment the most distinctive feature of the New Lanark system—the schools and playgrounds for the children. Owen himself always regarded the first thirteen years or so of his work at New Lanark as purely a preparatory phase. At the opening of the "Institution" on New Year's Day, 1816, he expounded to the workers his philosophy of life and society, and described its relation to what he had so far done. He had in mind a fundamental reconstruction both of human character and, by its means, of existing social and economic relationships. But this he could not attempt in a single commercial concern. His object, therefore, was in the early stages only to improve the environment of the workers, or the necessary preparation for the coming of a new order. "My attention was ever directed to remove, as I could prepare means for their removal, such of the immediate causes as were perpetually creating misery amongst you; and which, if permitted to remain, would to this day have continued to create misery. I therefore withdrew the most prominent incitements to falsehood, theft, drunkenness, and other pernicious habits with which many of you were then familiar; and in their stead I introduced other causes, which were intended to produce better external habits; and better external habits have been produced. I say 'better *external* habits,' for to these alone have my proceedings hitherto been intended to apply. What has yet been done I consider as merely preparatory."[1]

Coming among the workers of New Lanark as an

[1] *Address to the Inhabitants of New Lanark*, p. 13.

interfering stranger from the foreign south, Owen was at first markedly and naturally unpopular. "The workpeople were systematically opposed to every change which I proposed, and did whatever they could to frustrate my object. For this, as it was natural for them to dislike new measures and all attempts to change their habits, I was prepared, and I made due allowance for these obstructions. My intention was to gain their confidence, and this, from their prejudices to a stranger from a foreign country, as at this time the working class of the Scotch considered England to be, was extremely difficult to attain."[1]

Indeed, Owen's measures were quite certain to be regarded as an unwarrantable interference with the freedom of those whom he employed. Dale had allowed no public-houses in the village; but there were, of course, plenty at Old Lanark, only a mile off, but outside the jurisdiction of the mill. Owen did not object to these. But in New Lanark there were a number of privately conducted retail shops, and all of these did a thriving trade in spirits. One of Owen's earliest measures was to close all these shops, and replace them by stores owned by the firm, at which all necessaries were supplied. "I bought everything with money in the first markets, and contracted for fuel, milk, etc., on a large scale, and had the whole of these articles of the best qualities supplied to the people at the cost price. The result of this change was to save them in their expenses full twenty-five per cent., besides giving them the best qualities of everything, instead of the most inferior articles, with which alone they had previously been supplied."[2] It should be noted

[1] *Life*, p. 86. [2] *Ibid.*, p. 87.

that Owen supplied whisky at his store, but good whisky, in place of raw spirits.

Another matter which he took promptly in hand was that of sanitation. The village, when he took it over, was, as we have seen, in a deplorable condition. Most families had only one room, and this, naturally, very ill kept. Owen enlarged the houses, and built new ones, so as to give each family two rooms. But he wanted also to get them to keep these rooms clean. He began by abolishing the practice, hitherto customary, of depositing and piling up all manner of refuse in the streets, outside the cottage doors. This was carted away; proper streets were laid down; arrangements were made for the collection of refuse; and a repetition of the nuisance was forbidden. But it was more difficult to ensure cleanliness, the only means to health, inside the houses of the workers. Here Owen acted, not by prohibitions enforced by punishment, but by instituting a sort of health visitors. He got the workers to appoint a visiting committee, whose members were to endeavour by precept to improve the standards of cleanliness and domestic economy. At first his visitors were driven from the doors; but gradually they made headway, and the whole standard rose, until New Lanark became easily the cleanest and most sanitary manufacturing village in the country. This, like most of Owen's measures, was accomplished, over a period of years, without the imposition of a single punishment.

Next came the question of the workers' conduct in the factory. Theft, which had been very prevalent, was overcome by a careful system of checks, which enabled any offence to be immediately discovered and traced to its author. But Owen was not content with this. He instituted his much-ridiculed system of "silent monitors," to which he himself attributed much of his success. It can best be described in his own words.

"That which I found to be the most efficient check upon inferior conduct was the contrivance of a silent monitor for each one employed in the establishment. This consisted of a four-sided piece of wood, about two inches long and one broad, each side coloured—one side black, another blue, the third yellow, and the fourth white, tapered at the top, and finished with wire eyes, to hang upon a hook with either side to the front. One of these was suspended in a conspicuous place near to each of the persons employed, and the colour at the front told the conduct of the individual during the preceding day to four degrees of comparison. Bad, denoted by black and No. 4; indifferent by blue and No. 3; good by yellow and No. 2; and excellent by white and No. 1. Then books of character were provided for each department, in which . . . I had the conduct of each registered . . . for every year they remained in my employment. The superintendent of each department had the placing daily of these silent monitors, and the master of the mill regulated those of the superintendents in each mill. If anyone thought that the superintendent did not do justice, he or she had a right to complain to me, or, in my absence, to the master of the mill. . . . At the commencement of this new method of recording character, the great majority were black, many blue, and a few yellow; gradually the black diminished and were succeeded by the blue, and the blue were succeeded by the yellow, and some, but at first very few, were white."[1]

This curious device, out of tune as it is with modern ideas, probably had a considerable effect, not in itself, but in relation to the rest of Owen's proceedings. It was, indeed, like treating the workers as children; but the saving grace was in the childlike simplicity of Owen's own character. It was nearly impossible to be angry with him for long; what, done by another, would have been a ridiculous impertinence, he was able to carry off and to make effective, as soon as he had made himself understood and loved by the workers at New Lanark.

For, in time, not only did the hostility to him disappear: he became immensely popular. His first moves in combating the opposition which he had aroused were wise ones. He sought out those who had influence among the workers, and gradually made them understand his objects and point of view. Through the few he began to influence the many; but the prejudice against him was long in dying. The real change did not come until 1806. By this time cotton from the United States was being largely used in the mills. For a long time there had been friction between the British and American Governments, especially over the American claim to trade freely with France and the British claim to an unrestricted right of search at sea. This quarrel led, in 1806, to an American embargo on the export of cotton to England, and to a cotton famine in this country. Cotton prices soared; but, as no one knew how long the embargo would last, buying

[1] *Life*, p. 111.

at the high prices was a highly speculative affair. Manufacturers had to choose between shutting down their mills or taking the risk of producing at a very high cost what might be worth much less by the time it was sold. Owen and his partners decided to shut down; but he succeeded in persuading them to follow the example set by Dale when the mill was burnt down twenty years before, by paying full wages to all the operatives thrown out of work by this decision. The stoppage lasted more than four months, and more than £7,000 was paid out in wages to those unemployed in consequence of it. This seems finally to have won the hearts of the workers.

Probably it only completed a conquest well begun before. At all events, all the evidence agrees that Owen became immensely popular at New Lanark. His sincerity in wishing to improve the establishment, not so much as a means to profit as because he really valued human health and happiness, could not in the long run be questioned. "Henceforward," he writes of the workers, "I had no obstructions from them in my progress of reform, which I continued in all my ways, as far as I thought my married partners would permit me to proceed, and, indeed, until their mistaken notions stopped my further progress."[1]

How Owen won the confidence of his employees may be illustrated by certain incidents of which record has survived. One day two boys from the village had trespassed on the grounds attached to Owen's house in order to cut hockey-sticks or *shinties*. "If Mr. Owen sees us, won't we catch it?" said one to the other. A minute later Owen's hand

[1] *Life*, p. 88.

descended on the speaker's shoulder. "Perhaps you
don't know," said Owen, "that what you are doing
is wrong. It is wrong, and if your parents never
told you so, they neglected their duty. Take the
shinties you have cut for this time; but if you should
want some another day, don't steal them; thieves
never come to any good. Come to me, and I will
give you permission; then you can take them without doing any wrong."[1]

The narrator, one of the two lads concerned,
later became a teacher in the New Lanark schools.
He was seventeen, and he engaged to remain for
eighteen months. But after six months he went off
without any notice to try his fortune at the University. When he came back, he tried to avoid
Owen; but Owen came up to him, asked him about
his college life in Glasgow, and offered him his
place back, if he wanted it, without a word of
complaint about the past. He resumed his place as
a teacher, and remained for a number of years in
the school at New Lanark.[2]

Owen did not believe in punishment. During
the first years of his management he was, indeed,
driven to impose fines for drunkenness, and to dismiss those who got persistently drunk. But this was
a quite exceptional case, and even this form of
punishment was dropped at a later stage. Discipline at New Lanark was maintained by a strong
system of moral suasion, backed by the will and
energy of Owen himself. In particular he took no
disciplinary measures against those who opposed
his plans. "I never knew," says the writer quoted

[1] *Robert Owen at New Lanark*, by one formerly a teacher,
p. 8. The incident is also quoted in R. D. Owen, *Threading
My Way*, p. 74.　　　[2] *Robert Owen at New Lanark*, p. 7.

above, "of a single instance in which Mr. Owen
dismissed a worker for having manfully and con-
scientiously objected to his measures."[1] The evidence is consistent that, although there were
practically no fines or lesser punishments, Owen
secured an extraordinarily high level of conduct
and efficiency with only the rarest recourse to the
penalty of dismissal.

But, as we have seen, the measures so far adopted
appeared to Owen almost nugatory in comparison
with what he meant to do. He was already doing
some educational work at the mills; but he considered that all his measures would be nearly useless
unless he added to them a systematic plan of education for the children of the village. He had realised
the truth that character is formed above all in the
years of childhood, and that no steps taken with
the adult could counteract earlier adverse influences.
He must have good schools for the children and
play-schools for the infants; he must raise the age
for admission to factory work and give every child, as
far as possible, a good education before it was allowed
to begin working for a living. In 1809 he considered that the time had come to begin putting
his ideas on this point into practice. Accordingly,
he made preparations to erect new buildings to
serve as schools, playgrounds and lecture halls,
where children and adults could get the best education he knew how to give them.

Owen's views on education are discussed in a
later chapter. Here we are concerned with the
effect of these plans on his partners. As soon as his
preparations were made known to them, they
expressed their strong objection to this unnecessary

[1] *Robert Owen at New Lanark*, p. 5.

expenditure of money which would otherwise have been available for distribution as profit. Early in 1809 two of his partners made a special visit to New Lanark to inquire into his measures and plans. He apparently talked them round; for on their return he was presented with a large silver salver, with a flattering inscription congratulating him on his work.

But within a few months the proposed expenditure on schools and other "fancies" of Owen's again alarmed his partners, who held eight-ninths of the capital and, therefore, of the ultimate control. A reinforced deputation came to New Lanark, and the case was argued out anew. This time Owen failed to move them; and, as he would not consent to manage the business without a free hand, he offered to buy them out. They asked him to name his figure, and he named £84,000, which was not only £24,000 more than they had paid Dale, but was also apparently to be paid in cash, instead of being spread over twenty years. Owen's partners accepted these terms, and he at once formed a new partnership to take over the mills. One of his old partners, John Atkinson, who had been closely associated with him in Manchester, stayed with him, and was admitted into the new partnership, in which the other principal participants were two relatives by marriage of Mrs. Owen, by name Campbell of Dennistoun. Owen himself had a considerably larger share in the new partnership than in the old, but was still liable to be outvoted by the other partners.

The accounts of the old partnership were made up, and it appeared that, during the ten years it had lasted, "after paying the capitalists five per centum per annum for their capital, the profits of the firm amounted to £60,000."[1] Presumably this includes the profit on the realisation of the business.

The new partnership of five members—Owen, Atkinson, Dennistoun and the two Campbells— was formed in 1809, under the title of "The New Lanark Company," and lasted until 1813. Before long Owen's troubles were renewed. Two of his partners—Dennistoun and Alexander Campbell— had married daughters of a relation of David Dale's, Mr. Campbell of Zura. This Campbell, who was a friend of Owen's, entrusted him with the large sum of £30,000 for investment, in preference to placing the sum at the disposal of his sons-in-law, who were in business as merchants in Glasgow. The affair was originally arranged without their knowledge; but, on finding it out, they had a violent quarrel with Owen. This made good business relations difficult; and before long Owen's partners were again strongly objecting to his measures for improving the position of the workers. He was at this time busy with the erection of the buildings for the proposed new schools. At first he took no notice of their objections. "I proceeded in my own way, until they gave me formal notice not to proceed with the schools."[1] This was probably in 1812.

Thus checked, Owen at once formally resigned his position as manager of the mills, and with it his salary of £1,000 a year, retaining his position as one of the partners and the holder of the largest block of capital. But this did not settle the matter; his partners now insisted on a dissolution of the partnership and the sale of the mills. Owen offered

[1] *Life*, p. 120.

to name a sum which he would either give or take for the property. They refused, and insisted on a public auction.

Then followed a very difficult period. Humphreys, who had been works manager, was installed in Owen's place. Owen's salary had ceased, and all his money was locked up in the mill. His partners would advance him nothing from the business, and he was obliged to borrow for his personal expenditure. In short, the quarrel was very bitter.

At this time Owen had written his first book, *The Essays on the Formation of Character*, published a little later as *A New View of Society*. Shortly after the quarrel, he went for a prolonged visit to London in order to arrange for the publication of his essays, and also to push there his plans for the development of education on a national scale. He employed this visit, and the contacts which he established in London, for the formation of a new partnership to take over the New Lanark mills. In a pamphlet issued for private circulation[1] he described what he had done at New Lanark and what he was planning for the future. His object now was to form a partnership composed not of pure business men, but of persons with money who would take a benevolent interest in his schemes. In 1812 and 1813 he succeeded in gathering together a group which seemed to meet his need. It included William Allen, the rich Quaker, chemical lecturer and editor of *The Philanthropist;* another rich Quaker, named John Walker, who became Owen's close friend; Joseph Foster of Bromley, yet another member of the Society of Friends; Joseph Fox, a dentist, a friend of Allen, and a Nonconformist of

[1] *A Statement Concerning the New Lanark Establishment,* 1812.

some standing; Alderman Michael Gibbs, after-wards Lord Mayor of London, a Tory and a pillar of the Church of England; and, last but not least, the great Utilitarian, Jeremy Bentham.

With this group Owen came to terms for the formation of a new partnership. But his old partners had no intention of letting the very profitable New Lanark mills pass out of their hands without a struggle. They had insisted on a public auction, and they meant not only to buy, but to buy cheap. They knew that Owen had not the capital to buy the mills himself, and they had no idea of his measures in London, where they supposed him harmlessly occupied in publishing his essays and helping Lancaster and others in their educational campaign. Accordingly, they had good hope of buying the mills without opposition, and at a knock-out price.

With this object, Owen's old partners industriously circulated in Glasgow reports that the mills were doing very ill, that Owen, with his wild schemes, was an impossible manager, and that the New Lanark establishment was not worth half the sum they had given for it when the partnership started. They had paid, they said, £84,000; but they would be glad to get £40,000 at the coming sale. They decided that the latter sum should be the reserve price at the auction and were in excellent hope of buying the property unopposed.

As the day of the sale drew near, Owen, accompanied by three of his new partners—Foster and Gibbs and another[1]—arrived in Glasgow. But

[1] Owen (*Life*, p. 124) says that Allen was one of those who went with him to Glasgow. This does not appear to tally with Allen's own diary, as quoted in his *Life and Correspondence*, p. 181.

their connection was not disclosed, and the three intending purchasers put up at an hotel without giving anyone a hint of their business. Before the sale opened, Owen met his old partners, and formally offered them £60,000 for the property. This they refused to take, and he insisted that the reserve price should be raised to this sum.

The sale began, with £60,000 as the starting price. Owen's lawyer offered £60,100. His old partners replied with £61,000. So, by hundreds on his side and thousands on theirs, the bids mounted to £84,000. At this point his opponents retired for a consultation. On their return they again began bidding at £500 a time, Owen's lawyer still countering each bid with an advance of £100. Soon they also began bidding in sums of £100. The offers mounted to £100,000. Again Owen's opponents retired, and again they resumed bidding. At £110,100 they retired yet again. At this point one of the Campbells, a brother of Owen's old partners, came to Owen to attempt a settlement. Owen refused to withdraw. "Mr. Kirkman Finlay, who was the leading commercial man at that time in Glasgow, and was a friend of both parties, had been present for some time, and he now left the room, saying sufficiently loud to be heard by all present, 'The little one' (meaning the 100 bid) 'will get it.' "[1] The bids rose to £114,000, and Owen's lawyer promptly added £100. For the last time Owen's opponents consulted; but they could not persuade one of their number to go higher. At £114,100 the property was knocked down to Owen, who had decided with his new partners before the sale began to go up to a maximum of

[1] *Life*, p. 126.

£120,000. "Confound that Owen!" said John Atkinson to Kirkman Finlay, who had come back into the room. "He has bought it, and £20,000 too cheap!" "These," Owen comments, "were the partners who for so many months had been crying down the value of the establishment and saying they would be glad to get £40,000 for it."[1]

Owen's late partners had made so sure of their purchase that they had issued invitations for a dinner after the sale to celebrate the event. The dinner had to be held, despite the failure of their plans. Among the guests was Colonel Hunter, the Glasgow newspaper proprietor, who was by way of being a humorist. He rose and proposed a toast: "Success to the parties who had that morning sold a property by public sale for £114,100, which a little time ago they valued only at £40,000. Fill a bumper to a success so wonderful and extraordinary!"[2] The toast was not well received by the victims.

Owen was kept some days in Glasgow completing, with his new partners, the formalities of the transfer. Meanwhile, he received a message from New Lanark asking when he might be expected home. He sent word, and as soon as the business was done, he and his partners posted to New Lanark. "When we arrived within a few miles of the Royal Burgh of the Old Town of Lanark, we heard a great shout at some distance, and we soon saw a great multitude come running towards us, which at first much alarmed my Quaker friends. I did not know what to think of the number of people and the noise they made on approaching us. They called out to the postillions

[1] *Life*, p. 127.   [2] *Ibid.*, p. 128.

to stop the horses, and before we were aware of
their intentions they had untraced the horses from
the carriage, had desired the postillions to take
them on to Lanark, and, heedless of our urgent
entreaties, they began to drag the carriage, and
now it was up hill almost the whole distance to the
Old Town through which we had to pass. But their
numbers were such, and they relieved each other
so continually, that they went forward quicker
than our horses could have dragged us up those
steep hills."[1]

In fact, the people of both Old and New Lanark
had turned out in a body to welcome Owen home.
Thus he rode back into his kingdom.

His second partnership had lasted four years.
After allowing 5 per cent. for interest on capital,
it had realised a profit of £160,000, presumably
including the £30,000 increase in the purchase
price. Owen had apparently succeeded in making
the best of both worlds. He had made huge
profits, and he had earned the gratitude of those
whom he employed. His new partners returned to
London delighted both by their reception at New
Lanark and by the bargain they had made.

[1] *Life*, p. 133.

CHAPTER VII

LIFE AT BRAXFIELD

In order to present a connected account of the
events relating to New Lanark up to the formation
of Owen's third partnership, I have postponed all
reference to his private doings after he settled in
Scotland at the beginning of 1800. He and his wife
lived but a few months in Manchester. By January
1, 1800, they were established in Scotland, residing
in the house already mentioned, which stood in its
own grounds in the middle of the village at New
Lanark. Here, for some years, Owen and his wife
passed the summer months and Owen stayed in the
winter when he had to remain at the mills. But
usually in the winter they lived with David Dale, in
the big house he had built for himself in Charlotte
Street, Glasgow. The warehouses and offices of the
New Lanark firm were in Glasgow, and Owen had
to divide his time between the two places, usually
riding to and fro on horseback.

David Dale and Owen speedily became very
friendly indeed. Owen says that, from the time of
his marriage, they never exchanged one unpleasant
word—"and this was the more remarkable because
our religious notions were very different."[1] So far
from avoiding this subject, they discussed it freely
and at length. Dale would conclude their conversations by saying, "Thou needest to be very right,
for thou art very positive."[2]

[1] *Life*, p. 98.   [2] *Ibid.*, p. 99.

116

Dale was at this time over sixty—he was born in 1739—and was desirous of contracting his business commitments, which included several other cotton mills besides New Lanark. Owen helped him in this, both with advice and in a practical way. In 1802 he accompanied Dale's partner, George Macintosh,[1] on a visit to the Highlands to inspect a mill which Dale and his partner had started in a remote part of Sutherland. In the course of the journey, Owen was admitted to the freedom of the Burgh of Inverness. He has left, in his *Autobiography*, a good account of the journey, and of the difficulties of travel in the Highlands in those days.[2] He and Macintosh spent some time on the trip, and made it one of pleasure as well as business.

In consequence of Owen's advice, David Dale sold both this Highland mill and others in which he had an interest. He remained a director of the Royal Bank in Glasgow; but he was less active in business, and was able to pay summer visits to Owen at New Lanark. The two men became more and more friendly, and when Dale's health gave way, Owen was constantly with him in his last illness. He advised him in the making of his will, and was with him when he died in 1806.

Dale left behind him, in addition to Mrs. Owen, four unmarried daughters. These four came to live with the Owens. They were still children, and Owen took charge of their schooling. Soon after Dale's death he took them on an extensive tour through England and Scotland, "and visited in both countries every place deserving the attention of young travellers"[3]—a journey which will recall

---

[1] Father of the inventor of "macintoshes."
[2] *Life*, p. 100.   [3] *Ibid.*, p. 137.

Maria Edgeworth's *Harry and Lucy* to the minds of many of my readers. Later, one of the four died, two married ministers of religion, and the fourth went to live with one of her married sisters. Owen always spoke very affectionately of his sisters-in-law; but after their marriages he saw little of them. The clergymen and he could not sink their differences as he and Dale had been able to sink them.

Before this addition to Owen's household, he had acquired a family of his own. His eldest son, Robert Dale Owen, was born in 1801, and a second son, William, in 1802. "Then followed two daughters—Anne Caroline and Jane Dale—about two years between each. Then David Dale and Richard, and my youngest daughter, Mary, close the number of my family."[1]

Until 1808 Owen continued to live in the village of New Lanark, still passing most of the winter at Dale's old house in Glasgow. But, with the addition to his family of Dale's daughters, the New Lanark house became too small, and he took a long lease of Braxfield House, a big country house, which was only about a quarter of a mile away from the mills. The house had been the seat of the notorious Lord Braxfield, the Lord Justice Clerk who is chiefly memorable for his infamous conduct of the Scottish treason trials of 1794, when Muir and other members of the Scottish Corresponding Societies were sentenced to transportation,[2] and as

[1] *Life*, p. 98. There was also a son, the first-born, who died in infancy.
[2] See Meikle, *Scotland and the French Revolution;* Brown, *The French Revolution in England*, and contemporary reports of the trials.

the original used by Robert Louis Stevenson for his portrait of "Weir of Hermiston." Braxfield had died in 1799; but his son and his son's wife had lived at Braxfield House, and become friends of the Owens. From them he now rented the property. "We kept," says Owen, "our own carriage and horses, and also a carriage and horses and servants for my sisters-in-law. Our establishment, therefore, became an expensive one."[1] It must have been so; for Owen kept on Dale's house in Glasgow as a winter residence for some years longer.

Braxfield House is the scene which forms the domestic background to Owen's life at this period. His son, Robert Dale Owen, has left, in his own autobiography, pleasant memories of his boyhood there. "The estate of Braxfield is beautifully situated on the banks of the Clyde. The house stands in a bit of undulating table-land, then set in blue-grass, containing some thirty or forty acres; and the slope thence to the river was covered with thick woods, through which gravel paths wound back and forth till they reached the Clyde, a quarter of a mile below the mills. What charming nutting we used to have there!"[2]

But before the age for nutting the young Owens had a taste of their father's theories in practice. Robert Dale Owen records that, in infancy, he had the habit of screaming long and loud whenever he was denied anything that he wanted. "When the child screams from temper, my dear Caroline," said his father, "set him in the middle of the nursery floor, and be sure you don't take him up till he stops crying." "But, my dear, he'll go on crying by the hour." "Then let him cry." "It may hurt his

[1] *Life*, p. 137.   [2] R. D. Owen, *Threading My Way*, p. 44.

little lungs, and perhaps throw him into spasms."
"I think not. At all events, it will hurt him more if
he grows up an ungovernable boy. Man is the creature of circumstances." The cure was tried, and,
after five or six repetitions, it was effective. "The
infant culprit," Robert Dale Owen comments,
"had learned a great lesson in life—submission to
the inevitable."[1]

Perhaps this suggests the stern parent; but it is
clear that Robert Owen was the very reverse. His
children were very fond of him, and he made them
his companions from early childhood, always ready
to discuss and to explain, and eager to give them a
taste for straightforward dealing and a love for
natural beauty. On one matter which came up in
these conversations, there were difficulties at an
early stage.

Mrs. Owen was a strong Calvinist and a follower
of her father's religious principles. Owen held all
religious sects to be fundamentally in the wrong;
but he did not attempt to interfere with the religious
teaching which his wife began to give to the children as soon as they could even begin to take it in.
But the young Owens often heard their father dis-
cussing matters with visitors in a very different
strain. Robert Dale Owen, after being told repeatedly that Protestantism was the sole way of
salvation, pushed his inquiries of his mother concerning his father's views. She was compelled to
admit that she doubted if he was a believer. Young
Owen, terribly shocked and with all the fervent
pertinacity of the family, made up his mind that
something must be done. He took counsel again
with his mother, who was unwise enough to advise

[1] *Threading My Way*, p. 35.

him to pray that his father might be converted and made pious like his grandfather. "Then, with tears in her eyes, she added, 'Oh, if he could only be converted, he would be everything my heart could desire; and when we die he would be in heaven with us all.' "[1]

Young Owen made up his mind to attempt the conversion. "I called to mind some texts my mother had read to us about the mouths of sucklings, and what they might do." He took the first opportunity of tackling his father.

"I sounded my father by first asking him what he thought about Jesus Christ. His reply was to the effect that I would do well to heed his teachings, especially those relating to charity and to our loving one another. This was well enough, as far as it went; but it did not at all satisfy me. So, with some trepidation, I put the question direct whether my father disbelieved that Christ was the Son of God. He looked a little surprised, and did not answer immediately. 'Why do you ask that question, my son?' he said at last. 'Because I am sure——' I began eagerly. 'That he *is* God's Son?' asked my father, smiling. 'Yes, I am.' 'Did you ever hear of the Mahometans?' said my father, while I had paused to collect my proofs. I replied that I had heard of such a people who lived somewhere far off. 'Do you know what their religion is?' 'No.' 'They believe that Christ is not the Son of God, but that another person, called Mahomet, was God's chosen prophet.' 'Do they not believe the Bible?' asked I, somewhat aghast. 'No. Mahomet wrote a book called the Koran; and Mahometans believe it to be the word of God. That book tells them that

[1] *Threading My Way*, p. 56.

121

God sent Mahomet to preach the gospel to them and to save their souls.'

"Wonders crowded fast upon me. A rival Bible and a rival Saviour! Could it be? I asked, 'Are you *quite* sure this is true, papa?' 'Yes, my dear, I am quite sure.' 'But I suppose there are very few Mahometans: not near—*near* so many of them as of Christians.' 'Do you call Catholics Christians, Robert?' 'Oh no, papa. The Pope is Antichrist.'

"My father smiled. 'Then by Christians you mean Protestants?' 'Yes.' 'Well, there are many more Mahometans than Protestants in the world: about a hundred and forty million Mahometans, and less than a hundred million Protestants.' 'I thought almost everybody believed in Christ, as mamma does.' 'There are probably twelve hundred million people in the world. So out of twelve persons only one is a Protestant. Are you *quite* sure that the one is right and the eleven wrong?'

"My creed, based on authority, was toppling. I had no answer ready. During the rest of the walk I remained almost silent, engrossed with new ideas, and replying chiefly in monosyllables when spoken to. And so ended this notable scheme of mine for my father's conversion. My mother had claimed too much."[1]

The religious question was, indeed, the one obstacle to complete family happiness at Braxfield. Owen and his wife were very fond of each other, and the children very fond of both. But it was hard even for married love to sustain the burden of a firm conviction in the wife's mind that her husband was damned.

Young Owen's memories, however, are not

[1] *Threading My Way*, p. 60.

mainly concerned with such episodes as these. They are largely of the open air, the Braxfield woods, country sports and dancing, and the ordinary pranks of childhood. In his system of education for the workers' children at New Lanark Owen laid the greatest stress on play and sports and open air, and he did not forget these things in the upbringing of his own.

So the years wore on at Braxfield. Meantime, both Owen and his work at New Lanark were steadily becoming known to a wider public. As early as 1803 we find him taking a prominent part among the Scottish cotton spinners, as a member of the Committee of Management of the Board of the Cotton Trade, for which he drew up a special report protesting against the import duties on raw cotton and demanding their removal. The cotton trade, he said, was already employing over 800,000 persons and paying £13,000,000 annually in wages.[1] The duties encouraged foreign competition, and this was made additionally serious by the policy of France in excluding British cotton goods from markets under French control.[2] We shall find Owen returning to this attack on the cotton duties at the end of the Napoleonic Wars, when the protests of the trade were more effective.

Owen was also during these years actively push-

[1] The low wage per head is, of course, due to the extensive employment of children. The figures are in any case only an estimate. Baines (*History of the Cotton Manufacture*) estimated the number employed in 1832 at about 800,000, and the total number dependent on the cotton industry at 1,500,000. McCulloch (*Encyclopædia Britannica*) also gives 800,000 as the number employed.

[2] *Observations on the Cotton Trade*, 1803, reprinted in *Life*, vol. i. Appendix E (edition of 1858).

ing his views on education. It was apparently at
his instance that Joseph Lancaster, the founder of
the British and Foreign Schools Society (first known
as the Lancasterian Association), came to visit
Glasgow and New Lanark in 1812. Owen took the
chair at a public dinner to Lancaster in Glasgow,
and in his speech gave a first sketch of his then im-
mature views on the educational question. He was
already fully conscious of its importance. Education, he urged, is, "so far as depends on our operations, the primary source of all the good and evil,
misery and happiness, which exist in the world."
"The characters of children, in almost every family,
are materially influenced through life by those with
whom they early associate, and particularly by servants." The poor, as well as the rich, need education. "They must learn the habits of obedience,
order, regularity, industry and constant attention,
which are to them of more importance than merely
learning to read, write, and account." There must
be evening and Sunday, as well as day, schools
making "a combined system of discipline and education for the poorer classes." We have the means
to achieve this. "Our friend here, Joseph Lancaster, has prepared them ready to our hands."[1]

There is nothing very distinctive in most of this.
It sounds like an employer addressing a body of
fellow-employers on the value of education as a
business asset. It suggests methods most unlike
those which Owen actually adopted at New Lanark, and an uncritical adherence to Lancasterian
methods which, if it was ever in his mind, certainly
did not survive his meeting with the apostle of the
"monitorial system." But one passage in the speech

[1] *Life*, vol. i. (edition of 1857), p. 249 ff.

was real Owenism, and as sweeping as anything he ever said. "General bodily and mental differences between inhabitants of various regions are wholly and solely the effects of education."[1] What Owen meant by this we shall see more fully in the next chapter, which will enable us to measure both his divergence from the Lancasterian plan and his complete difference of attitude from those who urged education merely as a means to industrial discipline and increased production. Robert Dale Owen writes of Owen's attitude to Lancaster's plan, "My father, enthusiastic at first in its favour, gradually changed it for something more thorough and effective."[2]

The meeting with Lancaster in Glasgow, and the discussions which followed, caused Owen both to develop his educational thinking and to write his views down for public consumption. As we have seen, his long visit to London in 1813 was for the double purpose of getting his essays published and forming his new partnership to acquire New Lanark under conditions which would give him scope for an ambitious practical experiment. Before describing the events which followed his appearance as an author and the entry of his plans at New Lanark on a fresh phase, we will pause and take a brief survey of his educational ideas.

[1] *Life*, vol. i. (edition of 1857), p. 249 ff.
[2] *Threading My Way*, p. 77.

CHAPTER VIII

IDEAS ON EDUCATION

The best governed State will be that which shall possess the best national system of education." Owen wrote these words in 1814, when he was at the height of his successful experiment at New Lanark. They are the keynote of his *Essays on a New View of Society*, in the fourth of which they are to be found.[1] "Yet (will future ages credit the fact?)," he continued, "to this day the British Government is without any national system of training and education, even for its millions of poor and uninstructed. The formation of the mind and habits of its subjects is permitted to go on at random, often in the hands of those who are the most incompetent in the empire; and the result is the gross ignorance and disunion which now everywhere abound!"

Owen's admirers, as well as his critics, are apt to miss the point which was at the centre of all his schemes and visions—of his Socialism and his Co-operative experiments no less than of his work at New Lanark. The basis of Owenism was his theory of education, as a means to the formation of character and the possession of happiness. First and foremost Owen believed in the power of education, rightly directed, to turn the world's affairs into a prosperous course. He claimed for it everything, and made it the basis of good living, good fellow-

[1] *New View*, p. 88.

ship, and good work. It had power, he believed, to reconcile all differences, to destroy the rivalries of class, creed and country, to make the world a single Co-operative Commonwealth united by the bonds of reason and affection. Without it error and disunity were bound to persist; by its means the vast productive powers known to science would be unloosed for the common good of all.

Naturally, Owen did not believe that any sort of education would achieve these immense results. His faith was not merely a generalised belief in education for its own sake. He knew what kind of education he wanted, and what he meant it to effect. There were points on which he was wrong; but his method was based on certain essentially sound psychological ideas which have waited long for practical recognition by responsible educationists.

It was, of course, largely Owen's work in the schools of New Lanark that first made him a great figure in the world. From the moment when he assumed control of the mills there, he began planning the means of putting his educational ideas into practice. For some time he could do little, for lack of funds for the purpose; and, though he did a great deal later, he was always careful to explain that the New Lanark schools, even at their fullest development, were by no means a complete embodiment of his ideas. He was not a great capitalist, though he had control of a great business; and he was never free to do at New Lanark exactly what he believed to be best. Under his latest partnership he was, indeed, associated with men who did not make high profits their main object; but the removal of the financial obstacles to his plans only opened the way for others. His earlier partners had grudged him money for education; their Quaker successors were ready enough to spend, but they desired to give the New Lanark schools a strong religious bias, to which he strongly objected, and they were also sternly critical of the "rational amusements and exercises," such as dancing, singing and drill, which Owen wished to make an integral part of his educational work. Moreover, he had always to go slow and to take careful account of the Sabbatarian scruples, sectarian bias, and national suspiciousness of the Scottish villagers.

As we have seen, David Dale, Owen's predecessor at New Lanark, had also believed in education, and had done something before Owen's coming to provide for the needs of the "parish apprentices" who formed the bulk of the child labour in the factory. But he, like Owen's Quaker partners, had conceived of education mainly in terms of religious instruction, and his school, though well managed, did not at all suit Owen's purpose. Owen, moreover, wanted not merely to do his duty by the parish apprentices, of whom he got rid altogether as soon as he could, but to provide for every child in the village of New Lanark the best education that the conditions would allow. Thus, when the system of apprenticeship ceased in his factory, this, so far from ending his educational responsibilities, only set him free to take in hand the upbringing of the children of those whom he employed.

He was astonishingly successful. The schools at New Lanark, especially after the opening of his "New Institution" in 1816, became a show place for educationists from all parts of Great Britain, and for distinguished visitors from all over the world. Hardly a visitor went away without receiving a deep impression. The many accounts which they have left bear abundant witness to the success of Owen's practical work.

It may be said that this was no more than any man who really treated education as a serious matter could have achieved, with Owen's opportunities to help him. But the records show that it was far more than this; and that Owen was far ahead of his contemporaries, not only in his educational faith, but also in the methods which he employed. He was, indeed, ready to help any serious educational effort, even if he could not regard its methods as adequate or well conceived. We have seen that he took the chair for Joseph Lancaster at his meeting in Glasgow, and made a speech full of warm praise. He gave £1,000 to Lancaster's British and Foreign Schools Society—a very large gift for a man who had no considerable capital of his own. Moreover, despite his strong dislike of sectarian education, he offered an equal amount to Dr. Bell, the head of the rival "National Society" formed to promote the education of poor children in the principles of the Established Church. This offer was made to the leaders of the National Society on condition of their opening their schools to all children, without the imposition of doctrinal tests; but, although his condition was refused, he gave Dr. Bell £500 for the work of the Society.

While Owen gave generous help to both the rival Societies then active in promoting popular education, he soon ceased to be under any illusions as to the adequacy of either Bell's or Lancaster's methods. They were, in his view, a great deal better than nothing; but he would not admit them into his own schools, and he saw clearly that the monitorial system, promising great results in return for a very small expenditure, necessarily involved the use of methods which were based on false psychological premises, and could not possibly produce a satisfactory effect. Teaching and learning by rote could not be means to the formation of character; and to form character was, in his view, the first business of education.

"It must be evident," he wrote, "to common observers, that children may be taught, by either Dr. Bell's or Mr. Lancaster's system, to read, write, account, and sew, and yet acquire the worst habits, and have their minds rendered irrational for life." "Mental injury" to the children, he affirmed, might well result from certain of the schemes most in favour among orthodox educational reformers. "In proof of this statement, enter any of the schools denominated National, request the master to show the acquirements of the children; these are called out, and he asks them theological questions to which men of the most profound erudition cannot make a rational reply: the children, however, readily answer as they had been previously instructed, for memory in this mockery of learning is all that is required. Thus the child whose natural faculty of comparing ideas, or whose rational powers, shall be the soonest destroyed, if at the same time he possess a memory to retain incongruities without connexion, will become what is termed the first scholar in the class; and three-fourths of the time which ought to be devoted to the acquirement of useful instruction will be really occupied in destroying the mental powers of the children."[1]

Owen criticised Bell and Lancaster because,

[1] *New View*, Essay IV.

while they had suggested improvements in the "methods" of education, they seemed to him to have no conception of its living purpose and fundamental idea. But he regarded them as important pioneers, whose improvements could be used as the basis for a better system.

At bottom, Owen's different outlook rested on his view of human nature and the influence of training and environment on character. This view of Owen's has, of course, been often stated and often strongly criticised. Its real meaning has also, I think, partly because Owen was by no means a master of literary expression, been sometimes misunderstood. He summed it up, at the beginning of his *First Essay on the Formation of Character*, in these words: "Any character, from the best to the worst, from the most ignorant to the most enlightened, may be given to any community, even to the world at large, by applying certain means, which are to a great extent at the command, and under the control, or easily made so, of those who possess the government of nations." In the *Second Essay* he explains the basis of this belief. "Children are, without exception, passive and wonderfully contrived compounds, which, by due preparation and accurate attention, founded on a correct knowledge of the subject, may be formed collectively into any human character."

In other words, Owen had an almost boundless belief in the effect of environment and training on the character of the child. He did not hold, as some of his critics seem to suppose, that it was only necessary to alter the environment of the adult, in order to form his character into any mould that society might require. He insisted on the importance of training as well as environment, and held that, in order to be effective, education in the right ways of life must begin from infancy. "The governing powers of all countries should establish rational plans for the educational and general formation of the character of their subjects. These plans will be devised to train children from their earliest infancy to *think* and *act* aright, for which purpose they must be prevented from acquiring habits of falsehood and deception."[1]

Again and again this point recurs. Owen constantly stresses the truth that character is largely formed in infancy, and that the first years are those in which an impression is most easily made on the mind. "Much of the temper or disposition is correctly or incorrectly formed before he [the child] attains his second year; and many durable impressions are made at the termination of the first twelve or even six months of his existence."[2] It is, therefore, of no use to expect a general reformation in the character of the people unless the foundations are laid in a system of moral education for the child.

Owen, however, did not want to begin formal education too early. He knew the evil of overstraining the developing faculties, or permitting memory to usurp the place of reason and observation. Moral training must begin from infancy; but it must not at first take the shape of formal schooling, and, at all stages, it must be made interesting by appealing to the child's faculties and senses and not merely to his retentive power. Education at New Lanark included, for children of all ages, a large element of recreation and amusement. For

[1] *New View*, Essay I.   [2] *Ibid.*, Essay III.

the younger children, it was wholly of this kind. The New Lanark children were not admitted to the school until they were at least five years old; but, "from the time they can walk alone until they enter the school," the playground, with its open and covered spaces, was there for them to use and enjoy. "Each child, on his entrance into the playground, is to be told, in language which he can understand, that he is never to injure his playfellows, but, on the contrary, he is to contribute all in his power to make them happy."[1] The young child is not to be taught directly; but he or she is to be surrounded by an atmosphere of mutual consideration which will provide a right basis for the teaching that comes later. Owen's system of instruction for the young is, on its moral side, chiefly one of precept and communal example.

Character, then, in Owen's view will not be changed by any mere alteration of social arrangements, unless this includes a definite and comprehensive change in children's education. The right training of the next generation is for him always more important than the immediate remedying of economics or social grievances. Character-building is the basis of his social doctrine.

But, though Owen was apt under stress of excitement to make wild statements, he did not, I think, really hold the view often attributed to him that man is solely a product of environment, or that the formation of individual character is, wholly and without reserve, under social control. He is not always clear on this point; but it should be noted that in both the passages cited above, where he is trying to state plainly the essence of his doctrine,

[1] *New View*, Essay III.

he insists on the collective application of this theory. He says that any character can be given, not to each individual, but "to any community"; and he says that "children may be formed *collectively* into any human character."[1] In other words, his essential point is not that each individual is in every respect the pure product of his training and environment, but that societies collectively are the product of the forms of training and of social environment in which their members are brought up to manhood. This is a doctrine which may stand good as a social generalisation, when it is admitted that individual character cannot be explained completely in these terms.

Moreover, Owen repeatedly insisted on the importance of "nature" as well as "nurture," and does not aim, as some have supposed, at exalting the one at the expense of the other. "Man is born," he wrote in 1817, "with combined propensities and qualities, differing in degree of power and in combination, sufficient to create through life individuality and distinctness of person and character. But, however much the power and combination of these propensities and qualities may differ in individuals at birth, they may be all so directed by subsequent circumstances as to be made to form general characters, and these characters to be of any, of the most opposite nature—even to be made entirely *irrational* or *rational*."[2]

His point, then, is not that all individuals can be moulded by training into a uniform pattern of mind, but that, just as certain sects or parties im-

[1] *New View*, Essay II.
[2] *A Sketch of Some of the Errors and Evils arising from the Past and Present State of Society*, p. 22.

press on their members a common set of beliefs, however different the individuals holding them may be in cast of mind, so society as a whole can by collective action inspire in most of its members a common basis of moral belief, which is capable of governing their action for the common good. Men can differ widely in point of view, interests, personal traits of mind, and yet hold in common a code of beliefs and observances. Owen's aim is, by inspiring men collectively with a good code of social conduct, not to suppress their differences, but to enable them to live together in mutual charity and fellowship. This process, which can only be effective if it begins with the child, he regards as the essential preliminary to Socialism or any new social order based on rational principles.

It is important to get these points right, because, by mistaking them, so many critics have gone astray in their interpretation of Owen's educational ideas. He does not want to remake men after one image: he does want to leave scope for personal, as well as social, qualities to grow. And he has a firm faith in the capacity of childhood to learn and think for itself. "The strength and capacity of the minds of children," he wrote, "are yet unknown."[1] If he called them "passive compounds," he did not mean that they merely received what was put into them, giving no reaction according to their own differences and capacities. The whole system which he installed at New Lanark was the negation of any such idea. He was always stressing the need for the teacher to study the mind of each child, to treat each as a reasoning creature, to help it to understand as well as merely to learn or repeat by

[1] *New View*, Essay III.

rote. The children's minds are "plastic"; but "these original compounds, like all other works of the Great Directing Power, possess endless varieties,"[1] and each has to be appealed to by the ways that give easiest access to its individual mind.

Especially does Owen stress the importance of appealing to more senses than one, and of making sight, as well as hearing, minister to the work of education. In summer, he would have much of the teaching done in the open air, by country walks, by direct study of nature, and by simple play. Indoors, he would have teaching done by maps, charts, coloured blocks and squares, and so enlist the visual powers on the side of rational education. Most unlike many of his contemporaries, he is always warning the teacher not to overstrain the child's mind by too continuous a demand for attention, and not to warp it by imposing lessons mechanically learned without being clearly understood. "The boys and girls are to be taught in the school to read well, and to understand what they read."[2] Singing and dancing are to play a large part in the teaching as well as instruction in the rudiments of reading, writing, and arithmetic.

Above all, it has to be remembered that Owen was claiming education on these lines, not for a favoured few, but as the common right of all children, however poor their parents might be. He practised his principles at New Lanark, where he opened his schools to all comers, and after overcoming the initial suspicion felt for one who was both an Englishman among Scotsmen and a capitalist developing the hated factory system, he became immensely popular and deeply respected by

[1] *New View*, Essay II. [2] *Ibid.*, Essay III.

the factory workers, despite the prejudice raised against him on religious grounds.

His national advocacy of his educational doctrines began, moreover, with a plea for the children of the poorest classes in the community—those who were living on parish relief. He did not believe that all men were alike or equal; but he did hold that every child was fully capable of being trained to good or bad citizenship and good or bad service in the community. "How much longer," he asked, "shall we allow generation after generation to be taught crime from their infancy, and, when so taught, hunt them like beasts of the forest, until they are entangled beyond escape in the toils and nets of the law?"[1] When the whole country was troubled by the unemployment crisis after 1815, Owen urged that the only true remedy would be found in combining schemes of national employment with national training of the children. When, in 1818, the Government voted money in aid of church-building, in order to promote moral education, Owen addressed to the Archbishop of Canterbury an open letter in which he pleaded that this money should be used to build, not merely churches, but buildings which would serve the double purpose of churches and of schools, open to all without distinction of sect. As he had supported Dr. Bell and the National Society despite his own theological views, he was prepared to support the national Church if it would take seriously in hand the education of the people. At this stage of his career, he aimed rather at reforming the Church and making it truly national than at opposing it. He was willing to compromise, if only he could get those who had

[1] *New View*, Essay II.

power and influence to take up the cause of education.

The same note was struck in Owen's appeals to his fellow-manufacturers. For his own part, he clearly never cared for money, and it was almost a matter of indifference to him whether he was rich or poor. He spent freely on the causes in which he believed the fortune which he made, almost against his own will, by his business enterprise. But he saw the need of explaining to other employers that they, as well as the community, had everything to gain by following his example. "Like you," he wrote in his *Address to the Superintendents of Manufactories*, "I am a manufacturer for pecuniary profit." He went on to say that every manufacturer realised the need for getting the best machinery and taking the greatest care of it. "If, then, due care as to the state of your inanimate machines can produce such beneficial results, what may not be expected if you devote equal care to your vital machines, which are far more wonderfully constructed?"[1] At New Lanark, he pointed out, he had done his best to care for the minds and bodies of the workers, and "the time and money so spent, even while such improvements are in progress only, and but half their beneficial results attained, are now producing a return exceeding 50 per cent., and will shortly create profits equal to cent. per cent. on the original capital expended in these mental improvements."[1]

Owen's contention, then, was that education was a paying proposition for the manufacturer as well as a national and international need. He was putting forward, at a time when it was a far more startlingly novel view than it is to-day, the theory of the

[1] *New View*, Essay III.

138

economy of high wages and good conditions of employment. And he claimed that the abounding prosperity of the mills at New Lanark was a plain demonstration of the soundness of his doctrine. Indeed, he went further, believing that what he had achieved, both for the children and for the adult workers, was but a little in comparison with what might be done under more favourable conditions. Manufacturing, he believed, could be made to pay, and, at the same time, to afford a thoroughly good standard of life to all connected with it, as well as an education for all their children much superior to that which he had actually been able to provide.

Thus, at a time when it had become customary to employ children regularly in the mills at six years of age or even earlier, and to work them, with only one pause, for fourteen hours a day or even longer, Owen would have no children in his factory under ten years old, and was personally in favour of forbidding all employment under twelve years of age. He even expressed the opinion that no serious labour should be undertaken until the age of fourteen, and was entirely scornful of the prevalent doctrine that the labour of children was the necessary foundation of Britain's manufacturing prosperity. He wanted to see a universal enforcement of the ten hours' day, for adults as well as juveniles, and flung himself into the agitation for a maximum working day of ten, and in his later years eight, hours. Favouring continued education for children working in the mills, he realised the impossibility of securing this by evening classes superimposed on an excessive working day. These things are the commonplaces nowadays of educational reformers; but Owen was the pioneer of them long before Shaftesbury or Sadler had seriously taken up the agitation for factory reform. We shall see that he was mainly responsible for the Factory Bill introduced by the elder Sir Robert Peel in 1815, and finally passed in 1819 in a mutilated form of which Owen strongly disapproved, and for which he largely blamed Peel's weakness and lack of understanding.

At New Lanark, we have shown, he could not go so far as he desired. He kept all children both out of the mill and at full time schooling until ten, and he cut down the hours of labour in order that the older children might get some benefit from the evening schools which he provided. But he could not reduce working hours below ten and three-quarters —a position which he deplored in his evidence before the House of Commons Committee on the Factory Bill of 1816. He could not be more than a few steps in advance of the practice of his better contemporaries. He had, therefore, to place his immediate hopes mainly in the educational work he was able to do for the children under ten, before their entry into the mills.

Though this was a grave handicap, it fitted in to some extent with the stress which he laid on the formative influence of the early years. In 1816 he supplemented his playground for the younger children by an infant school, in which "the children were not to be annoyed with books, but were to be taught the uses and nature or qualities of the common things around them by familiar conversation, when the children's curiosity was excited so as to induce them to ask questions respecting them."[1] Owen filled the school, not only with pictures and models,

[1] *Life*, p. 193.

but with flowers and natural objects from the countryside. As they grew older, they were introduced to maps and charts. "When the best means of instruction or forming character shall be known, I doubt," Owen wrote, "whether books will ever be used before children attain their tenth year."[1]

We may doubt the truth of this dictum, and still admit the enormous value of the alternative methods on which Owen laid his stress.

I have not thought it worth while to discuss how much of these ideas was "original" in Owen's mind, and how much he derived from books, or from the study of the experiments of other educational pioneers. My own view is that he owed very little to others, arriving at largely similar conclusions with other pioneers by a different road based on his own experience and peculiar philosophy of character. But what does it matter? He was a pioneer, and a highly successful one. He has nothing to lose by sharing credit with others.

From 1800 to 1813, as we have seen, Owen pursued his educational work without any attempt to institute a propagandist campaign, or any public avowal of the wider meaning which it bore in his own mind. In 1813 he formed his new partnership with Allen, Bentham, and the other progressives whom he induced to venture with him; and, in the greater security which his new position seemed to give him, he plunged at once into a public exposition of his principles. In retrospect, it is easy to see in the *Essays on the Formation of Character* or *A New View of Society*, published in 1813 and 1814, the outline of Owen's whole social philosophy, including his "Socialism" and his religious heterodoxy. But

[1] *Life*, p. 194.

these were not equally evident to the men of his own time, and he was listened to with respect and even with sympathy in Government and upper-class circles. In the succeeding chapters we shall see how he gradually lost this position as a respectable and respected advocate of reforms, and came to be regarded as a dangerous person, with whom no member of the governing class ought to have any dealings. We shall see, too, how, driven from one kind of appeal, he had recourse to another, and carried his message among the common people.

In Owen's later years it was always possible for any fool or obscurantist, or for any politician of the Government or the Opposition, to reply to any argument of his by dragging up his alleged "Atheism" against him. His influence among the working classes began to grow from the very moment when the governing classes threw him over; but his position in respectable circles was irretrievably lost. He could no longer pursue with any hope of success his plan for achieving moral reform through the instrumentality of the Government.

Owen's reputation as an educationist suffered eclipse together with his political influence. He became, indeed, the first really creative force for adult education among the workers; but respectable educationists turned their backs on him, though a few, including Lord Brougham, always acknowledged his immense services in this field of work. In especial, teachers and those responsible for the direction of teaching methods forgot him, and this side of his work at New Lanark dropped out of mind, to be rediscovered through the work of pioneers in other countries. In this, as in most other matters, Great Britain has been singularly forgetful of her national heroes. Owen's educational practice exercised all too little influence on British pedagogy.

Nor did his educational theories fare much better. Connected in men's minds with his and his disciples' later experiments in the formation of Co-operative Communities, they were misunderstood and distorted into absurd meanings. He was supposed to have held that man's character can be re-made suddenly by the magic of a changed environment, whereas he was always careful in his theoretical writings to stress the degree in which character is unalterably formed in the years of childhood. Thus, he wrote of the difficulty of persuading grown-up people "to unlearn and to change long-acquired habits—a proceeding directly opposed to the most tenacious feelings of human nature."[1]

It is a pity, however, if the world therefore writes Owen off as no better than a harmless crank or enthusiast. For in his educational writings before 1816 there is a wealth of sound sense, with only a slight, and readily isolable, element of millennial nonsense. His theory of the formation of character is far sounder than is usually allowed: his stress on the moral basis of education as a way of working with nature is healthy, and worth the notice of educationists to-day; and his insistence on the necessity of sound health and healthy recreation as the foundations of educational work is still sorely needed by an age largely content with school-barracks and asphalt playgrounds in grimy urban surroundings. We may not be willing to go all the way with Owen, and declare categorically that "man's character is made for, and not by him."

[1] *New View*, Essay III.

But we are ready to recognise that mental habits, largely dependent as they are on health and bodily habits acquired in youth, are profoundly influenced by nurture, and to endorse, more readily than our fathers, the view that nine-tenths of the opinions widely held in society are products, less of any process of individual reasoning, than of the social and cultural environment and associations of those who profess them. "In every known region of the earth, up to the present hour," wrote Owen in 1817, "man has been compelled from infancy to receive the peculiar notions of some sect, some class, some party, and of some country. In consequence, each individual has been surrounded by four dense atmospheres of error and of prejudice, through which he must look at every object around him."[1]

It is easy enough to suggest that Owen wanted only to substitute his own errors and prejudices for those of others, and to proceed by a system no better than theirs. But I do not think this charge can be made good by reference to the practical work done at New Lanark, or in the Owenite schools started in later years by many of his disciples. Robert Dale Owen's account of the schools at New Lanark gives an impression of freedom that is borne out by the reports of other visitors. Owen was intensely fond of children, and keenly sympathetic with the child's outlook and attitude of mind. This kept him, as an educationist, from some of the rigidities which went to spoil and dehumanise his Socialist doctrines. He made many blunders, and was often more than a little absurd. But as an educationist, in both theory and practice, I think he had in him the root of the matter.

[1] *Sketch of Errors and Evils*, p. 24.

Probably the only people who would have had a really good time in the model Communities which Owen sought later to establish would have been the children. But, when we consider the standards of his age in the treatment of child life, can we find for him a more convincing *apologia?* While the leading educationists were devising plans for mass education on the cheap through the "monitorial system," Owen was already recognising that this was at best a shoddy substitute for real education, which must interest as well as instruct, and enlist on its side in the child's mind imagination far more than memory. And in an age where "health and real knowledge" were neglected for the attainment of wealth, Owen had vision to put first things first. "For every penny ground by parents from the premature labour of their offspring, they sacrifice not only future pounds, but also the future health, comfort, and good conduct of their children."[1] And lastly, in an age which frowned sternly on the recreations of the poor, Owen fostered dancing and music and healthy exercise among both children and adults who came under his control or influence; for "it has been and ever will be found far more easy to lead mankind to virtue, or to rational conduct, by providing them with well-regulated, innocent amusements and recreations, than by forcing them to submit to useless restraints, which tend only to create disgust, and often to connect such feelings even with that which is excellent in itself, merely because it has been so injudiciously associated."[2] At New Lanark and elsewhere, Owen's

[1] *Observations on the Effects of the Manufacturing System*, p. 13.
[2] *New View*, Essay III.

object was to associate the good and the pleasant, and to "lead mankind to virtue" by making, in school and village, an atmosphere and environment favourable to good sentiments and ideas.

CHAPTER IX

THE FIRST FACTORY ACT

Owen's *New View of Society*, or *Essays on the Formation of Character*, attracted a great deal of public notice. He took great care with the writing of them, revised them more than once, and submitted them before publication to the criticism of several of his friends, including James Mill and Francis Place, who were both intimates of his new partner, Jeremy Bentham, and leading lights among the Utilitarians. The *New View* and the other writings of this earliest period of Owen's literary activity are much more readable, and much better written, than his later works, which he was never at the trouble to revise, being too eager to seize rapidly every occasion of spreading his gospel. The *New View* appeared at first in separate parts—the first two *Essays* in 1813, and the third and fourth in the following year. They appeared in 1814 as a book, and were reprinted again and again during the next thirty years, both by Owen himself and by others. They contain, indeed, by far the best summary of his fundamental doctrines.

We have seen that Owen was busy with the publication of these essays at the time when he was forming his new partnership in 1813. During his long visit to London in that year he got to know a great many of the leading men of the day, and became intimate with a good number. Among the friends he made at this time were William Godwin, Shelley's father-in-law and the author of *Political Justice*, whose views had a great deal in common with his own, and whose great book may well have been one of the influences that helped to form his mind. He got to know also Francis Place, Malthus and most of the leading economists of the orthodox school, Jeremy Bentham, who became one of his partners at New Lanark, Wilberforce and Sir James Mackintosh. The circumstances of his introduction to Bentham are very characteristic of the Utilitarian leader.

"It was most amusing to me to learn the difficulty, owing to his nervous temperament, that he had in making arrangements for our first interview. . . . After some preliminary communication with our mutual friends James Mill and Francis Place, his then two chief counsellors, and some correspondence between him and myself, it was at length arrived at that I was to come to his hermit-like retreat at a particular hour, and that I was, upon entering, to proceed upstairs, and we were to meet half-way, upon the stairs. I pursued these instructions, and he, in great trepidation, met me, and taking my hand, while his whole frame was agitated with the excitement, he hastily said: 'Well, well! it is all over. We are introduced. Come into my study!' And when I was fairly in, and he had requested me to be seated, he appeared to be relieved from an arduous and formidable undertaking."[1]

Owen got to know, not only the leading Radicals and intellectuals like Place and Bentham, but also

[1] *Life*, p. 132.

many of the statesmen and great Churchmen of the day. Indeed, he specially wanted to get into touch with men of this class. "My chief communications at first were with the leading members both in Church and State; for I wished them to see and know all I was doing and intended to do, being conscious that all parties from the highest to the lowest would be benefited by my views of society."[1] Owen's aim at this stage was to get his rapidly developing plans taken up by the governing classes, and carried out with their support.

In the light of Owen's later career, it is at first difficult to understand the most favourable reception he got from such men as Lord Sidmouth, Lord Liverpool, then Prime Minister, the Archbishop of Canterbury, and a host of other great politicians and divines. But it is not really so surprising as it seems. The practical proposals put forward in *A New View of Society* were almost purely educational, and there was nothing on the surface of them to suggest any intention to subvert existing class-relationships. Owen's religious views, though they were stated by implication, were not obtruded, and did not appear to be essentially related to his schemes. He was accepted as an educational and factory reformer, with a fine record of practical achievement already behind him, advancing views well worthy of consideration on their merits for the improvement of a situation generally admitted to be deplorable. For, though the orthodox economists might defend as inevitable the effects of the factory system on the workers, they could not deny the prevailing distress or the evils calling for remedy.

Moreover, though the governing classes were

[1] *Life*, p. 149.

swift to stamp out "disaffection" and to repress any working-class movement of revolt or attempt at Trade Union organisation, they looked with critical eyes on the great "cotton lords" whose new-made wealth was already challenging their supremacy. They were quite prepared to consider reforms which infringed the liberties of the cotton lords, provided that there was in them no taint of Radicalism or of yielding to popular clamour. They saw, too, in certain aspects of Owen's proposals, means of actually stabilising their own authority, by making the workers more contented and diverting their minds from demands for political reform. They were therefore ready to listen, especially to a cotton-spinner whom his fellow-employers regarded with a growingly malevolent eye. Tories have often supported industrial reforms in order to "dish the Liberals"; perhaps the Archbishops and Cabinet Ministers who gave heed to Owen had some such idea present, with others, in their minds.

It must be realised, in addition, that Owen was, by all accounts, a charming and charmingly-mannered enthusiast. He had not, at this stage, developed that reputation as a bore which was his in later years. "One of those intolerable bores who are the salt of the earth," Leslie Stephen called him in his well-known biographical study.[1] But at this stage Owen was not a bore at all. He had not yet developed his later habit of ceaseless reiteration of the same arguments, of dogmatic assertion treated as equivalent to proof, and of obvious pity for all who doubted his conclusions. He was even a little diffident in the great company into which he had fallen. And, unlike many of his fellow-manufac-

[1] *Dictionary of National Biography.*

turers, he combined with a faculty of downright statement the manners of a courtier and a simple-minded friendliness which attracted all who met him.

The evidence of this is overwhelming. Even twenty years later, when the habits of age were already growing upon him, and respectable people had long hounded him out of their society, Harriet Martineau, who met him then for the first time, was impressed "by the candour and cheerfulness, the benevolence and charming manners which would make him the most popular man in England if he could but distinguish between assertion and argument, and abstain from wearying his friends with his monotonous doctrine."[1] The criticism applies to a later date; the praise can be referred equally to the time with which we are now concerned.

Francis Place, surely the least enthusiastic of mankind, speaks in these terms of his first meeting with Owen in 1813: "He introduced himself to me, and I found him a man of kind manners and good intentions, of an imperturbable temper, and an enthusiastic desire to promote the happiness of mankind. A few interviews made us friends."[2]

There is, then, no cause for surprise when we find Owen, from 1813 onwards, in familiar intercourse with Lord Sidmouth and Lord and Lady Liverpool, or, by special request, reading his unpublished essays aloud to Dr. Sutton, the Archbishop of Canterbury. It is clear, moreover, that these dignitaries were not merely polite, but took his proposals into serious consideration. In 1814, just

---

[1] H. Martineau, *Autobiography*, vol. i. p. 231.
[2] Wallas, *Life of Place*, p. 63.

after Napoleon's exile to Elba, Sidmouth, at Owen's request, circulated interleaved copies of the *New View of Society* to all the leading Governments of Europe and America with a request that they might be returned endorsed with the comments of the recipients. Many of them came back, and Sidmouth and Owen went through the comments together, and apparently found them mainly favourable. Then, at Sidmouth's own suggestion, copies were sent to all the English bishops, and later, by request of the Archbishop of Armagh, to the prelates of Ireland. John Quincy Adams, the American Ambassador, next asked for copies for the Governors of all the States in the American Union. Napoleon, at Elba, also received a copy, and, what is more remarkable, read it and made inquiries about the author.[1]

From 1813 onwards Owen was passing a good deal of his time in London, making friends and pushing his ideas. He stayed usually with his friend and partner, John Walker, who had a house in Bedford Square and an estate, Arno's Grove, at Southgate. Walker was a very rich Quaker and a man of no business, and, according to Owen, "untainted with its deteriorating effects." He entered enthusiastically into Owen's plans, took a large part in forming the new partnership of 1813, and became a lifelong friend, placing his London house permanently at his disposal, and actively helping him in his public proceedings. But, like Bentham, he never visited New Lanark or took any part in the business beyond lending his money.

Making friends at this rate, Owen speedily became a well-known and a popular figure. But his

[1] *Life*, p. 150 ff.

object was not to enjoy himself, but to further his developing plans. These first took practical shape in an agitation, which he appears to have started practically single-handed, for factory reform. In 1815, as we have seen, he took the lead among the Glasgow cotton lords in pressing for the repeal of the tax on the importation of raw cotton. In this he had the enthusiastic support of his fellow-employers; but he tried to couple with this demand in the interest of the manufacturers a second demand in the interest of the workers. A great meeting was held in Glasgow, with the Lord Provost in the chair. "I stated to the meeting my objects in calling it, and first proposed that an application should be made to Government to remit the tax upon the raw material of the cotton manufacture. This was carried unanimously by acclamation. I then proposed a string of resolutions to give relief to the children and others employed in cotton, wool, flax, and silk mills . . . but, although all were enthusiastically in favour of asking for the remission of the tax, not one would second my motion for the relief of those whom they employed. I then declined to proceed with them in the business of the meeting, and it therefore came to nothing. But I told them I should take my own course in both measures, independently of them."[1]

Thus, failing to carry his fellow-employers with him, Owen returned to London to appeal to the Government and to Parliament. At that time, there was practically no factory legislation in existence. The elder Sir Robert Peel, himself a great employer, had indeed got carried in 1802 the Act regulating the Health and Morals of Apprentices in

[1] *Life*, p. 157.

cottons mills which is sometimes called the first Factory Act. But this measure dealt only with cotton mills, and only with parish apprentices, a form of labour which was already dying out with the development of other sources of supply. It had been, moreover, from the first largely inoperative, owing to the lack of any effective provisions for inspection, and, in any case, it had only limited hours to twelve, abolished night work, and regulated boarding arrangements for the pauper apprentices, leaving inspection in the hands of the justices of the peace.[1] As the great mass even of child workers were not parish apprentices, and therefore fell outside the scope of the Act, the measure of 1802 was of account only as establishing in principle the claim of the State to regulate factory conditions.

Owen wanted something at once far more comprehensive and far more drastic. His proposals, submitted to the Glasgow meeting and afterwards embodied in a draft Bill, were to apply to woollen, flax, and other textile factories as well as to cotton mills, wherever twenty or more persons under eighteen were employed. He desired to prohibit all employment under ten years of age, and to require baptismal certificates or other proofs of age to be produced. He wished to limit the hours of work to a maximum of ten and a half per day, excluding one and a half hours for meals and half an hour for instruction. This was to apply to all workers under eighteen. All employment for those under eighteen was to be between five o'clock in the morning and nine at night, night work for juniors being forbidden. The daily half-hour of instruction was to

[1] See Hutchins and Harrison, *History of Factory Legislation*, p. 16.

be given for four years after the child's entry to the
mill, in a place specially provided and suitable for
educational work. The justices of the peace were to
receive yearly returns from all factories under the
Act, and were to appoint duly qualified inspectors
with power of entry to the factories at all times.
These inspectors, or visitors, were to be empowered
to require the employer to call in a doctor in case of
infectious disease, and to carry out at the employer's
own cost any measures the doctor might recommend. The penalties for breach of the Act were to
be fines of from £5 to £10 for each offence, half the
amount going to the informer who brought about
the conviction and half to the poor fund. Copies of
the Act were to be posted in all mills.[1]

These were Owen's proposals, far less drastic
than some now in force, but far too advanced for
his fellow-manufacturers in 1815. In addition to
pushing his views in London, Owen now undertook a great tour through the manufacturing districts in order to collect evidence in support of his
case. Taking Robert Dale Owen, now a lad of
fourteen, with him, he visited mill after mill, in-
quiring into the conditions of labour. Robert Dale,
in later years, still kept a vivid memory of his impressions. "As a preliminary measure we visited all
the chief factories in Great Britain. The facts we
collected seemed to me terrible almost beyond belief. Not in exceptional cases, but as a rule, we
found children of ten years old worked regularly
fourteen hours a day, with but half an hour's interval for the midday meal, which was eaten in the
factory. In the fine yarn cotton mills they were
subjected to this labour in a temperature usually

[1] *Autobiography*, vol. I.A., Appendix G.

exceeding seventy-five degrees; and in all the cotton factories they breathed atmosphere more or less injurious to the lungs, because of the dust and minute cotton fibres that pervaded it. In some cases we found that greed of gain had impelled the mill-owners to still greater extremes of inhumanity, utterly disgraceful, indeed, to a civilised nation. Their mills were run fifteen, and, in exceptional cases, *sixteen* hours a day, with a single set of hands; and they did not scruple to employ children of both sexes from the age of eight. We actually found a considerable number under that age.[1] It need not be said that such a system could not be maintained without corporal punishment. Most of the overseers openly carried stout leather thongs, and we frequently saw even the youngest children severely beaten. We sought out the surgeons who were in the habit of attending these children, noting their names and the facts to which they testified. Their stories haunted my dreams. In some large factories, from one-fourth to one-fifth of the children were either cripples or otherwise deformed, or permanently injured by excessive toil, sometimes by brutal abuse. The younger children seldom held out more than three or four years without serious illness, often ending in death. When we expressed surprise that parents should voluntarily condemn their sons and daughters to slavery so intolerable, the explanation seemed to be that many of the fathers were out of work themselves, and so were, in a measure, driven to the sacrifice for lack of bread; while others, imbruted by intemperance,

---

[1] Robert Owen, in his evidence to the Committee on the Bill, said children were commonly employed at five or six, and he heard of some working at three and four years old.

saw with indifference an abuse of the infant faculties compared to which the infanticide of China may almost be termed humane."[1]

Equipped with his evidence concerning the abuses which were prevalent, and with the example of his own factory to show that manufacture could be successfully carried on without them, Owen returned to London to pursue his campaign. He laid siege first to the Government, obtaining from the Chancellor of the Exchequer, Vansittart, a favourable answer to his plea for the repeal of the tax on cotton,[2] and from him and other Ministers an assurance of Government favour if he could induce the House of Commons to support his Factory Bill. Thereupon, Owen began persistently lobbying the members of both Houses, gradually gathering together a group of influential supporters. The question soon arose how the Bill was to be introduced, and who was to take charge of it in the House of Commons. Owen's group of members proposed the elder Sir Robert Peel, who had been responsible for the Act of 1802. Peel had not taken any part in the discussions up to that point, but it was agreed to approach him, and he consented to assume charge of the Bill.

Owen always held that, if Peel had speedily pressed the Bill forward, it could have been carried at once with comparatively little opposition; for the manufacturers had not had time to mobilise their forces against it. But Peel insisted on consulting his fellow-manufacturers; and the process of whittling down the proposals was soon begun. The

[1] *Threading My Way*, p. 101.
[2] The tax was, in fact, halved by the remission of the special war tax imposed in 1803.

reference to wool and flax and other mills was struck out in face of the opposition of these groups, although of the four great textile manufacturers of the time—cotton, wool, flax and silk—the flax mills were the worst and most unhealthy.[1] Moreover, the manufacturing interest was given abundant time to organise; for Peel, in introducing the Bill, announced that there was no intention of carrying it into law during the current session.

Actually, Peel's Bill did not become law until 1819; and by that time it had been mutilated out of all recognition, and Owen had lost all interest in it. But at the outset he spared no pains, living in London and spending all his time and energy in lobbying and propaganda on its behalf. For two parliamentary sessions he was in daily attendance to deal with this matter alone. In 1816 the House of Commons got so far as to appoint a committee to consider the Bill; and before this committee Owen gave detailed evidence both about the conditions at New Lanark and about the materials he had collected on his journey of investigation.

Before the committee was set up, Owen had appealed to a wider public than he could reach personally by publishing his pamphlet, *Observations on the Effect of the Manufacturing System*, which is in effect a statement of the conclusions reached as a result of his tour. It is well and vigorously written, and deserves to rank among his most important works. He begins by stressing the nature and the rapidity of the change which has come over England during the past thirty or forty years. "Prior to that period, Britain was essentially agricultural; relatively few persons were employed in trade or

[1] *Life*, p. 161.

manufacture or commerce. Now (by the Census of 1811) the agricultural population is only a quarter of the whole. The change is chiefly due to the rise of the cotton trade. It has brought a huge increase in wealth and foreign trade; but it has brought huge evils therewith."

Then he goes on to stress the importance of regarding the factory system from the standpoint of its effect not only on wealth, but also on health and character. "Hitherto, legislators have appeared to regard manufactures only in one point of view, as a source of national wealth. . . . The general diffusion of manufactures throughout a country generates a new character in its inhabitants; and as this character is formed upon a principle quite unfavourable to individual or general happiness, it will produce the most lamentable and permanent evils, unless its tendency be counteracted by legislative interference and direction. . . . The manufacturing system has already so far extended its influence over the British Empire as to effect an essential change in the general character of the mass of the people. This alteration is still in rapid progress; and, ere long, the comparatively happy simplicity of the agricultural peasant will be wholly lost amongst us."[1]

Moreover, the growth of wealth has engendered a love of luxury and a desire for yet more wealth, "which has induced its possessors to sacrifice the best feelings of human nature to this love of accumulation." This leads to oppression of the poor, who "are at present in a situation infinitely more degraded and miserable than they were before the introduction of these manufactures, upon the suc-

[1] *Observations on the Effect of the Manufacturing System*, p. 5.

cess of which their bare subsistence now depends.
. . . The governing principle of trade manufactures is immediate pecuniary gain, to which on the
great scale every other is made to give way. All are
sedulously trained to buy cheap and sell dear; and
to succeed in this art, the parties must be trained
to acquire strong powers of deception; and thus a
spirit is generated through every class of traders,
destructive of that open, honest sincerity, without
which man cannot make others happy, nor enjoy
happiness himself."[1]

"The effects of this principle of gain, unre-
strained, are still more lamentable on the working
classes, those who are employed in the operative
parts of the manufactures; for most of these branches
are more or less unfavourable to the health and
morals of adults. Yet parents do not hesitate to
sacrifice the well-being of their children, by putting
them to occupations by which the constitution of
their minds and bodies is rendered greatly inferior
to what it might and ought to be under a system of
common forethought and humanity."[2]

Thirty years ago, Owen says with some exaggera-
tion, "the poorest peasants thought the age of fourteen sufficiently early for their children to commence regular labour; and they judged well."
Even for the most robust adults, the working day
then never exceeded twelve hours, and holidays
were far more frequent. "Under these circumstances the lower orders experienced not only a
considerable degree of comfort, but they had also
frequent opportunities for healthy, rational sports
and amusements. . . . Their services were willingly performed."[3]

[1] *Observations*, p. 6.   [2] *Ibid.*, p. 8.   [3] *Ibid.*, p. 9.

But, since the factory system grew up, the hours of labour have been drawn out, tiny children have been employed in more and more unhealthy surroundings, and "the employer regards the employed as mere instruments of gain." So bad have things grown that, unless the lot of the workers is improved, the effect will sooner or later be to "plunge the country into a formidable and perhaps inextricable state of danger."

Thereupon, Owen outlines his proposals, adding some points not included in his draft Bill. He is against all employment under ten years of age, and holds that no child under twelve should work more than six hours. Thereafter, he proposes a maximum of twelve hours, including an hour and a half for meals. He further urges that no child shall be admitted into a factory until he or she can write and count as well as read, and, if a girl, sew as well.

Finally, he turns to answering objections. He does not anticipate serious objection from manufacturers to the raising to ten of the age for admission. They may, he says, object to a shorter working day; but he is convinced that, if the shortening is general, any addition to the cost of production will fall upon the consumer. Moreover, under a twelve hours' day the factories will turn out goods "nearly, if not altogether, as cheap"; and, in any case, improved health will be nationally ample compensation. "Is it to be imagined that the British Government will ever put the chance of a trivial pecuniary gain of a few in competition with the solid welfare of so many millions of human beings?"[1]

One touch in this remarkable pamphlet makes

[1] *Observations*, p. 15.

curious reading in the light of later history. Owen is pointing out that the new factory population is dependent on the export trade. "It is highly probable, however," he adds, "that the export trade of this country has attained its utmost height, and that, by the competition of other states possessing equal or greater local advantages, it will now gradually diminish." The new Corn Law of 1815, by raising the protective tariff and so increasing the costs of production, will, he thinks, hasten the decline of exports and destroy trade. He therefore urges its repeal, and the institution of free trade in corn as well as cotton.[1]

Owen's pamphlet was hardly likely to reassure the manufacturing interest; for he did not at all conceal his view that human happiness must be preferred to profits or "commercial prosperity." While the committee was sitting to consider the Bill, the manufacturers were busy organising the opposition. When Owen was called to give evidence, a manufacturer on the committee [2] put him through an examination so offensive and irrelevant that, on Brougham's motion, it was expunged from the minutes. But enough is left in the official record to show that the manufacturers spared no effort to stir up prejudice against Owen's case. Not content with doing what they could to rebut his evidence of factory oppression, they did their utmost to queer his pitch by dragging up against him his unpopular religious opinions, in the hope of inducing the committee to believe that whatever was proposed by a notorious infidel could not be right.

One method by which the attempt was made to discredit Owen was by sending a party of manu-

[1] *Observations*, p. 6.   [2] Sir George Philips, of Salford.

facturers to New Lanark to gather evidence against him as he had gathered evidence against them. It was, of course, not in quest of factory misery that the deputation went, but to nose out infidel practices. The minister of Old Lanark, who disapproved of Owen, was quite ready to help. Mr. Menzies, said Owen, had often dined at his table, and had always been well treated by him; but he had apparently been shocked by Owen's speech at the opening of the New Institution at New Lanark in January, 1816,[1] and he now described this speech as "of a most treasonable character against Church and State." Mr. Menzies had not been present himself; but his wife had attended, and he vouched for this view of the speech on her authority. He further accused Owen of favouring Dissenting ministers at New Lanark, and of allowing Dissenting meeting houses to be opened there, to the detriment of the parish church.

This meagre haul of scandal apparently sufficed for the deputation, which paid Mr. Menzies' expenses to London in order that he might report to the Government. But the Home Secretary, Sidmouth, was at this time a friend of Owen's, who had some time before given him a copy of the offending speech. Mr. Menzies retired from Sidmouth's presence with a flea in his ear.[2]

Owen's evidence before the committee of 1816 is of considerable interest. He was asked what advantages he expected from his Bill. He replied, "A very considerable improvement in the health of the operatives, both young and old; a very considerable improvement in the instruction of the rising generation; and a very considerable diminution in the

[1] See p. 208.   [2] *Life*, p. 162.

163

poor rates of the country."[1] He was at once tackled on the question of the economic effects of shorter hours on the cotton trade. He cited his own experience that reduced hours had not caused anything like a proportionate fall in output, because the moral and physical well-being of the operatives had improved. He did not agree that increased leisure caused the workers to become idle and vicious. On the contrary, better conditions made the operatives work better. "Such conduct to work-people is the most likely to make them conscientious, and to obtain more from them than when they are forced to do their duty." He was asked to state the number of children under ten employed in cotton mills. He replied that he had no figures, but "I conceive the number would be in exact (*sc.* inverse) proportion to the knowledge which the proprietors have of their own interest, and the interest of the children."[2]

He was insistent on the point that the proposed legislation would not prejudicially affect the trade, though it might in some cases skim off part of the surplus profit. "I find by actual practice . . . that the difference to the proprietors, taking every circumstance in the most favourable way in which they can be taken, will not be more than $\frac{1}{4}d.$ per yard upon the goods manufactured from the yarn spun at the manufactory; and I have every reason to believe, from the progressive increase in the quantity which has taken place regularly every month since this change [the reduction of hours] took place, that before the end of the year the yarn will be manufactured as cheap, working ten and

---

[1] Quoted Podmore, *Owen*, vol. i. p. 198.
[2] Podmore, p. 193 ff.

three-quarter hours per day, as ever we manufactured it working eleven and three-quarter hours
per day. The present loss is not more than $\frac{1}{4}d.$ in
1s. 8d."[1]

For two years Owen stuck manfully to his task.
But the Bill seemed still no nearer passage, and it
was being gradually whittled away in deference to
the manufacturers' objections. Early in 1818 he returned to the charge with two manifestos, addressed
respectively to the Prime Minister and to the manufacturers. The former, written after the Bill had
been drastically amended in committee, was an appeal to the Government to strengthen its provisions, and to extend it to all types of textile factories. "I doubt," he wrote, "whether nine hours
of regular and active employment, established as
the measure of daily labour to be required from
the working classes, would not be still more economical and profitable for the country" than the
hours proposed in the Bill.[2]

"I am fully aware," Owen continues, "of the
clamour which these propositions will at first call
forth from the blind avarice of commerce; for commerce, my lord, trains her children to see only their
immediate or apparent interest; their ideas are too
contracted to carry them beyond the passing week,
month, or year, at the utmost. They have been
taught, my lord, to consider it to be the essence of
wisdom to expend millions of capital and years of
extraordinary scientific application, as well as to
sacrifice the health, morals, and comforts of the
great mass of the subjects of a mighty empire, that

[1] Quoted Hutchins and Harrison, p. 22.
[2] *Letter to Lord Liverpool on the Employment of Children in Manufactures.*

they may uselessly improve the manufacture of, and increase the demand for, pins, needles, and threads; that they may have the singular satisfaction, after immense care, labour, and anxiety on their own parts, to destroy the real wealth and strength of their own country by gradually undermining the morals and physical vigour of its inhabitants, for the sole end of relieving other nations of their due share of this enviable process of pin, needle, and thread making."[1]

Owen appealed, not only to the Government, but also to his fellow-manufacturers. "I can have no motive to deceive you," he wrote. "My whole pecuniary interest is embarked in the same cause with you."[2] He went on to point out the absurdity of the position. "We complain that all markets are overstocked with our manufactures, and yet we compel our little children, and millions of adults, to labour almost day and night, to urge forward perpetually increasing mechanical powers, that these markets may be still more overstocked."[2] In this connection Owen developed a very important part of his economic opinions, a significant anticipation of later economic theories. "No evil ought to be more dreaded by a master manufacturer than the low wages of labour. . . . These, in consequence of their numbers, are the greatest consumers of all articles; and it will always be found that when wages are high the country prospers; when they are low, all classes suffer from the highest to the lowest, but more particularly the manufacturing interest. . . . The real prosperity of any nation may be at all times accurately ascertained by the

[1] *Letter to Liverpool*, p. 28.
[2] *To British Master Manufacturers*, 1818.

amount of wages, or the extent of the comforts which the productive classes can obtain in return for their labour."[1] Premature employment of children, overwork, and low wages are the real evils. "By such short-sighted practices you cut up your prosperity by the root, and most effectually kill the goose from which you would otherwise daily receive the golden egg."[1] These evils are "ten times more powerful opponents to our success as manufacturers, than all the competition which it is possible for foreign nations to create against us." And, finally, if costs of production are increased at all, the consumer will pay, and should pay, and any possible increase will be insignificant in comparison with "the perpetual fluctuations which are made in the prices of all articles by a few wealthy speculators buying up at once immense quantities of the raw materials."[1]

Owen's fellow-manufacturers were not reassured by these arguments, even when Owen argued that his pecuniary interest was the same as theirs. For one thing, they knew that he hardly cared a rap whether he made money or not, and that the articles of his new partnership at New Lanark positively prevented the making of any profit above a fair rate of interest on the money invested. The manufacturing interest wanted full freedom for the rapid accumulation of capital out of surplus profits, and this freedom was menaced by legislative interference. Therefore they fought his Bill, both for what it proposed, and for the threat of further interference behind it. They were not strong enough to get the Bill thrown out altogether; but they could hinder its passage, and make it largely

[1] *To British Master Manufacturers*, 1818.

ineffective by amendment. Peel, always inclined to compromise, gave away point after point in response to their complaints. Owen became more and more annoyed. By the middle of 1818 he had given up hope.

"I was so disgusted at the delays created by these interested members, and at the concessions made to them by Sir Robert Peel during the progress of the Bill through the House of Commons, that after attending the committee every day of its sitting during two long sessions, I took less interest in a measure now so mutilated, and so unlike the Bill which had been prepared by me; and I seldom attended the committee, or took any active part in its further progress."[1] In the final stages his place was taken by Nathaniel Gould of Manchester and by Richard Oastler of Yorkshire, commonly known as "the Factory King." Under their guidance the Bill at last became law in 1819.

But it was now a very different measure. It applied only to cotton mills. The minimum age for factory employment was nine instead of ten. The hours of labour were twelve, exclusive of mealtimes, or thirteen hours and a half inclusive. There was no regulation for persons over sixteen, and no provision of any kind for inspection. The fines were actually doubled; but this was of little account, as there was no one to enforce them. Owen always disclaimed all responsibility for the Act in the form in which it was finally passed into law.

But the Act was important, if not in itself, as a precedent for later legislation. It established for the first time the State's right to regulate the conditions of labour engaged in the ordinary market—

[1] *Life*, p. 167.

a very different matter from the regulation of the conditions of parish apprentices, who alone were covered by Peel's Act of 1802. And for the establishment of this right, the basis of the whole factory code, Owen was almost solely responsible, though he threw up the task in despair after forcing it into the sphere of practical politics. Apart from his brief connection with the Hours movement of the early thirties, his activity in promoting factory legislation stopped short in 1818. He had found wider questions for agitation; but his work stands as the basis on which the whole structure of protective legislation was raised in subsequent generations.

CHAPTER X

"MR. OWEN'S PLAN"

The year 1815 is a critical time in the history of Great Britain. For more than twenty years, with only a brief interval that was no more than a pause for breath, the country had been engaged in a great war for supremacy. The battles, indeed, had been fought on foreign soil and in part with foreign troops. But the sustaining power of the successive European alliances against France had been Great Britain, and on Great Britain had fallen the burden of paying and equipping the armies in the field. The financial strain had been very severe, and the National Debt had mounted by leaps and bounds during the struggle. But freedom from war at home had allowed the vast new powers of production unloosed by machinery to be rapidly developed, and British trade had won an almost unquestioned supremacy in the markets of the world. The "nation of shopkeepers" did indeed fight Napoleon out of the swiftly mounting profits of the new industrialism.

With the revolution in industry came inevitably a revolution in social relationships. A great class of new rich arose, partly among the "cotton lords" and other big employers aggrandised by the new methods of production, and partly among financiers and contractors enriched by the manipulation of war loans and military supplies. Behind these was growing up a great new middle class of professional men, factory supervisors, salaried men of business and retail tradesmen, who multiplied fast as the volume of commodities grew and the population migrated from the villages to the towns. Greatest of all was the change in the lower class. A nation of agriculturists, largely combining work on the land with petty industry carried on under the domestic system, was being rapidly converted into a factory proletariat, driven by necessity from the villages into the industrial districts, and multiplying with extraordinary swiftness under the double impulsion of the falling infant death-rate and the swelling demand for child labour in the new factories.

As long as the war lasted, the consequences of this radical change in the structure of society were not clearly seen. All things were subordinated to the successful prosecution of the war, and it was difficult to get attention for any purely domestic problem. The agitation for Parliamentary Reform, which had been a lively agitation in the 1780's, made no great stir till after 1815, despite its vigorous advocacy by Cobbett, and the hard organising work of Major Cartwright and his friends. The manufacturing interests, though they showed symptoms of hostility to the war, especially when the Berlin Decrees and the Orders in Council caused an industrial crisis, did not push their opposition to the extent of attempting to lead a popular movement for Reform. The Luddite disturbances of 1811 and the following years showed, indeed, the existence of a large mass of explosive material among the new working class, and the beginnings of militant organisation. But, despite the efforts of the Radicals to divert the machine-breakers into a campaign for political reform, the Luddite movement seems to have remained almost wholly economic in its aims and methods. Not till the long war was over did all the forces of discontent with the prevailing conditions begin to gather themselves together for a forward movement.

The ending of the war seemed like the beginning of a new era. As long as the struggle with Napoleon continued, men could attribute their misfortunes to it, and draw the moral that they must wait stoically until it was over. Were they out of work or making no profit? The war had closed the Continental markets. Were they called upon to pay for the war, but given no representation in Parliament or voice in the expenditure of their money? It was well known that wars were best waged by autocracies. Even France had turned her Revolution into a military dictatorship; and that was why she had held out so long. Were prices high? They would come down with the return of peace. Were current grievances left unremedied? The attention of Ministers must not be distracted from their task of bringing the war speedily to a victorious end. There was a good time coming when it was over. Then all markets would be reopened, and the land would flow with milk and honey. Then all abuses would be put right.

Things fell out very differently when at last, after the final episode of the Hundred Days, Napoleon was packed off securely to St. Helena, and the statesmen of the nations sat down to divide the spoils and rebuild the broken fabric of European society. Prices fell; but men soon found that they preferred high prices with money in their pockets to low prices with none. Markets were reopened, and manufacturers made haste to offer unlimited quantities of their goods for sale. But to what purpose, since none could afford to buy them? All classes clamoured for lower taxes. They were told they had forgotten the War Debt, the burden of which grew heavier with every fall in the level of general prices.

It appeared, then, that peace, too, had its miseries, or war its redeeming virtues. For war was a great consumer; and a great consumer was what industry, with its vastly increased productive power, was irresistibly impelled to seek. "On the day on which peace was signed," wrote Owen, "this great customer of the producers died." [1] Everyone who had provided war equipment or stores, or sold goods to those who drew money from the State for war services of any sort, suddenly found that his market was gone. The State, intent on winning the war, had bought regardless of cost, and manufactured by inflation the money to buy with. The customers who remained, and the poverty-stricken peoples of Europe, could not afford to buy even the cheapest goods beyond the bare necessities of life. The lavish spending of wartime was followed by a proportionately severe reaction.

Owen was at this time still engrossed in his campaign for the reform of factory conditions. But the situation which arose in 1815 seemed to him to open up a wider and more productive field of social activity. It is abundantly clear from his own writings that, while his disgust at the delays and compromises which attended the progress of the Factory Bill was a contributory cause to his withdrawal

---

[1] *Life*, p. 172.

from support of Peel's Bill, it was not his principal motive. He had found other work to do, and beside it the small measure of factory reform that was at once attainable seemed of little account. In the latter part of 1816 Owen threw himself into a new campaign which decided the whole future course of his life.

He gives, in his *Autobiography*, a graphic description of the economic prostration which followed the peace of 1815. "What was called the revulsion from war to peace had created universal distress among the producers in the British Islands. Barns and farmyards were full, and warehouses were weighed down with all manner of productions, and prices fell much below the cost at which the articles could be produced. Farm servants were dismissed, and no employment could be found for them, the manufacturers being in the same situation as the farmers, and obliged to discharge their hands by hundreds, and in many cases to stop their works altogether. The distress among all workpeople became so great that the upper and wealthy classes became alarmed, foreseeing that the support of the hundreds of thousands unemployed, if this state of things continued, must ultimately fall upon them." [1]

By the middle of 1816 the alarm had become general. At first the country remained quiet, despite the distress, and the thoughts of the upper classes turned rather to the improvement of trade and the relief of distress than to the repression of the spirit of revolt among the workers. A great meeting of all the notables was called, with the Duke of York as chairman, and the Duke of Kent

[1] *Life*, p. 168.

active in organisation, to consider methods of relieving distress. Besides the Royal Dukes, it was attended by the leading Churchmen and politicians of both parties, and by the political economists and prominent business men. The Radical Reformers, headed by Lord Cochrane, also attended in force, and tried to turn the meeting into a demonstration for the Reform of Parliament and against excessive taxation.[1] These last were voted down, and the meeting set up a committee to raise a fund for the relief of distress, and to recommend remedies for the distress. Robert Owen, who attended the meeting, was elected to the committee, of which the Archbishop of Canterbury, then a friend of his, was appointed chairman.

At the first meeting of the committee, Owen was asked, as a practical manufacturer, to give his views on the causes of the distress. "I said the cause of this apparently unaccountable distress seemed to me to be the new extraordinary changes which had occurred during so long a war, when men and materials had been for a quarter of a century in such urgent demand, to support the waste of our armies and navies upon so extensive a scale for so long a period. All things had attained to war prices, and these had been so long maintained that they had appeared to the present generation the natural state of business and public affairs. The want of hands and materials, with this lavish expenditure, created a demand for and gave great encouragement to new mechanical inventions and chemical discoveries, to supersede manual labour in supplying the materials required for warlike purposes,

[1] For an account of this meeting, see my *Life of Cobbett*, p. 202.

and those, direct and indirect, were innumerable. The war was a great and most extravagant customer to farmers, manufacturers, and other producers of wealth, and many during this period became very wealthy." [1]

Then peace had come, and the "want of demand at remunerative prices compelled the master producers to consider what they could do to diminish the amount of their productions and the cost of producing, until the surplus stocks could be taken out of the market. To effect these results, every economy in producing was resorted to, and, men being more expensive machines for producing than mechanical and chemical inventions and discoveries, so extensively brought into action during the war, the men were discharged, and the machines were made to supersede them—while the numbers unemployed were increased by the discharge of men from the army and navy." Hence the distress . . . "for the new power created by them new inventions and discoveries was already enormous, and was superseding manual power." [2]

Owen thus traced the prevailing unemployment to two connected causes—the end of the war and the rise of machine production, which the war had artificially stimulated. He was at once asked to develop his view, which was on the face of it directly contrary to the orthodox idea that machinery increased employment, and to present to the committee a full report embodying both his diagnosis and the remedies which he proposed. On this task he at once set energetically to work, and it was soon completed.

[1] *Life*, p. 171. For Cobbett's account of the same phenomena, see my *Cobbett*, p. 195 ff.   [2] *Life*, p. 172.

This report really marks the turning-point in Owen's career. It contains the first expression of his wider positive proposals, and marks the transition from Owen the factory reformer and educational pioneer to Owen the ancestor of Socialism and Co-operation. The transition is gradual, and Owen's Socialism appears first as a moderate plan for philanthropic reform to be carried out by the governing classes. But for all that it contains in germ the essence of his Socialist doctrine.

He begins by stating again his view of the causes of the excessive unemployment which followed the peace. "The immediate cause of the present distress is the depreciation of human labour. This has been occasioned by the general introduction of mechanism into the manufactures of Europe and America, but principally into those of Britain, where the change was greatly accelerated by the inventions of Arkwright and Watt. . . . The introduction of mechanism into the manufacture of objects of desire reduced their price; the reduction of price increased the demand for them, and generally to so great an extent as to occasion more human labour to be employed *after* the introduction of machinery than had been employed *before*. The first effects of these new mechanical combinations were to increase individual wealth, and to give a new stimulus to further inventions. . . . There appeared to be no limit to the acquirement of riches and the description of power which wealth creates. The war itself . . . seemed but a new stimulus to draw forth our exhaustless resources. . . .

"But peace at length followed, and found Great Britain in possession of a new power in constant action, which, it may be safely stated, far exceeded the labour of one hundred millions of the most industrious human beings in the full strength of manhood. To give an instance of this power, there is machinery at work in one establishment in this country, aided by a population not exceeding 2,500 souls, which produces as much as the existing population of Scotland could manufacture after the mode in common practice fifty years ago! And Great Britain contains several such establishments! . . . Thus our country possessed, at the conclusion of the war, a productive power which operated to the same extent as if her population had been actually increased fifteen or twenty fold; and this had been chiefly created within the preceding twenty-five years." [1]

It is easy to see that Owen was inclined to estimate the total increase of productive power in terms of its increase in the cotton industry, which chiefly had fallen under his own observation. This, of course, showed the advance in technique at its greatest. The change was much less in the wool industry, and in a different plane altogether in the metal industries, while many occupations were still hardly touched by the process of change. In agriculture there had been a marked advance, but by no means to the same extent as in the textile industries. This vitiates some of Owen's arithmetical calculations; but it does not invalidate his point that the new inventions, especially in a falling market, had hugely depreciated the price of human labour power.

He goes on to describe the situation which followed the end of the war. "Now, however, new

[1] *Report to the Association for the Relief of the Manufacturing and Labouring Poor*, pp. 3 ff.

circumstances have arisen. The war demand for the productions of labour having ceased, markets could no longer be found for them; and the revenues of the world were inadequate to purchase that which a power so enormous in its effects did produce: a diminished demand, consequently, followed. When, therefore, it became necessary to contract the sources of supply, it soon proved that mechanical power was much cheaper than human labour. The former, in consequence, was continued at work, whilst the latter was superseded; and human labour may now be obtained at a price far less than is absolutely necessary for the subsistence of the individual in ordinary comfort." [1]

The supersession of human labour and the forcing down of wages, Owen adds, mean the diminution of the home market; and thus the circle of distress grows ever wider. "The working classes have now no adequate means of contending with mechanical power." One of these results must follow: either the use of machinery must be discontinued (but this is impossible in any one country in face of international competition); or millions of human beings must be starved, while machines take their place; or, thirdly, "advantageous occupation must be found for the poor and unemployed working classes, to whose labour mechanism must be rendered subservient, instead of being applied, as at present, to supersede it." [1]

This, then, is the basis of Owen's famous "Plan," the germ of his Socialism. He regards it as the duty of society to provide useful employment for its members, and sets out to devise a plan of social organisation which will achieve this end.

[1] *Report*, p. 6.

Owen was not alone in urging the necessity for measures to increase employment. The Government, perhaps acting under his influence, had issued a proclamation earlier in the year calling on all who could to provide employment; but, as no methods of doing this had been proposed, nothing had been done. Owen's aim was to put into a workable shape what was already admitted as a thing to be done if means could be found of doing it.

New Lanark, doubtless, furnished the substance of the idea on which Owen based his Plan. But there was an essential difference. New Lanark was essentially a factory; producing goods for the market, and therefore liable to the vicissitudes of commercial demand. At a time when manufacturers were restricting production because they could find no market for their wares, it would have been useless to propose that employment should be provided for the unemployed by starting fresh manufacturing establishments to produce goods for sale through ordinary commercial channels. This, of course, was the difficulty which seemed, as it seems nowadays, to render impracticable all plans for the finding of work. Owen saw that the dearth of employment was due to the lack, not of human, but of economic demand; and he set himself to provide work that would not be subject to the limitations of the commercial market. His Plan, in its original form, was essentially a way of providing work for the unemployed, and at the same time laying the foundations of a better social order.

In outline, it was this. He proposed that, instead of relieving the unemployed out of the poor rates, those in authority should set aside a capital sum, on which interest would accrue, and use this sum to found "Villages of Co-operation." These villages, modelled on New Lanark, were to be economic units, based throughout on a co-operative principle. For each village a considerable tract of land was to be bought or rented on a long lease. On a suitable site, preferably near the middle of the estate, the village was to be built, in the form of a great co-operative establishment. About 1,200 souls, including men, women and children, might, he suggested, be a suitable population for each village. The main occupation of the villagers would be work on the land; but they would also have workshops and factories of their own in varying degrees. For the most part, the village would produce the goods required for its own subsistence, buying as little as possible from outside, and selling only its surplus produce in the open market. But, as the number of villages increased, they would also growingly exchange their surplus products one with another. There would be, Owen held, no difficulty in so organising the scheme that each village would produce a surplus, at least adequate to pay interest on capital, after providing an excellent standard of living for all the inhabitants. For men could easily produce more than they consume, both in manufactures and in agriculture. The quantity of land needed by each village community would, of course, vary with the character of the soil and the proportions in which agriculture and manufacture were carried on. But, essentially, the proposed Villages of Co-operation would be communities "founded on the principle of united labour and expenditure, and having their basis in agriculture." [1] 500 would

[1] *Dialogue on the New View of Society*, 1817, p. 6.

be the smallest, and 1,500 the largest, population suitable for the experiment.

Convinced of the huge economies of "united labour," Owen believed that its application to agriculture would produce effects like those he had experienced in manufacture. He had acquired, from his early contact with Dalton and other scientific friends, a profound belief in the possibilities of applying chemical discoveries to agriculture. "The cultivation of the soil," he said many years later, "is capable of being made a beautiful chemical and mechanical process, conducted by men of great science and highly educated minds." [1] He wanted to found Villages of Co-operation which would be as efficient in tilling the soil as his New Lanark factory was in the production of yarn.

The economic basis of the proposed villages was thus to be mainly that of a scientific agriculture designed to produce what the villagers themselves needed for good living. And the principle of "co-operation" and "united labour" was to be applied to their methods of living as well as to their work. The village was to be a great group of buildings in which the inhabitants were to dwell as a united community. Each family was, indeed, to have its own apartment; but sitting, reading and recreation rooms were to be common, and meals were to be taken together and cooked in a common kitchen. A separate boarding-house was also to be provided for all the children over the age of three, only the infants sleeping with their parents in the family apartments. The buildings of the village were to be erected in a great hollow square, with certain

[1] *Six Lectures Delivered in Manchester*, 1837, p. 54.

public buildings, surrounded by playgrounds for the children, in the middle.

Naturally Owen laid great stress on the schools; for the whole village was designed as an educational, no less than an economic, unit. One building was set apart for an infant school, with a lecture-room and place of worship for the adults above. Another was to be a well-equipped school for the older children, and there was to be a good library and reading-room for the adult villagers. His object was, by education, to retrieve the harm done by the existing system to the characters of the adults, and to bring up the children in a better way.

Owen's "parallelogram" of buildings was to be surrounded on all sides by gardens, in which the elder children were to be employed for part of the day on the lighter tasks. Beyond the gardens were to be roads, and only on the other side of these roads, well away from the village and shut off by the garden belt, the factories or workshops and other industrial buildings of the community. Owen was jeered at for his "parallelograms of paupers"; but certainly this part of his scheme entitles him to rank as a pioneer of town-planning. The idea in his mind, further developed in his later work, was essentially that of the Garden City, properly planned and with a careful separation of the factory area from the residential quarter.

It has to be borne in mind that in this first sketch of his Villages of Co-operation Owen was putting forward, not his ideal, but a plan for the relief of the pauper unemployed. He was appealing to the ruling classes and to the Government to replace the degrading poor-law system by saner measures; and he had to bear his audience constantly in mind. It would have been useless to propose an ideal system, or one based on principles of equality. Owen's villages, in this first sketch of his proposals, have to be compared, not with an ideal of social organisation but with the existing systems of poor relief, the existing workhouses and institutions, or at any rate with the plans of other reformers for an improved poor-law system. If they are regarded in this light, much of the criticism levelled against them is seen as quite beside the point.

Owen's report, after outlining his scheme, went on to deal with the question of cost and the methods of putting it into operation. The capital cost, he reckoned, of starting one of his villages would be £96,000 if the land were purchased, or £60,000 if it were only rented. This included all buildings and roads, furnishing and equipment, and farming stock. Spread over 1,200 persons, this cost, including land, worked out at £80 a head, or £4 per annum at 5 per cent. Once started, the community would, he held, be self-supporting, and able both to pay interest and, over a period, repay the principal.

For the starting of the scheme, he favoured Government action. "In fact, many of the benefits to be derived to society at large will not be realised until the plan becomes national." [1] But, failing action by the Government, "there are several modes in which the plan may be effected. It may be accomplished by individuals, by parishes, by counties, by districts, etc., comprising more counties than one." [2] It may, he says, seem expensive; but it will be reproductive expenditure, and really

[1] *Report*, p. 20.   [2] *Ibid.*, p. 16.

the most economical. "In one generation it will supersede the necessity for poor rates," [1] which the combined operation of the Speenhamland system of relief and the distress following the peace had already made a crushing burden. "Under the existing laws," he points out, "the unemployed working classes are maintained by, and consume part of the property and produce of, the wealthy and industrious, while their powers of body and mind remain unproductive." [2] He would make these unproductive classes productive, and at the same time place them in surroundings which would increase their efficiency and happiness instead of degrading them. "The preventive principle," he says, "must be the basis of legislative proceedings."[3] Finally, he urges that the existing poor law is radically unsound, and must be reformed, but not by abandoning the poor to their fate. His plan must be adopted, or before long the whole social system will be violently subverted by men who, demoralised by misery, will be incapable of rebuilding it on sounder lines.[4]

Such was Owen's report, which he presented in due course to the committee over which the Archbishop of Canterbury presided. The committee had asked for a mouse; they received a mountain. "The Archbishop and the committee appeared to be taken by surprise, and appeared at a loss what to say or do." [5] But, while the report was in preparation, the Government had itself appointed a parliamentary committee, with Sturges Bourne as chairman, to consider the revision of the Poor

[1] *Report*, p. 23.   [2] *Ibid.*, p. 8.   [3] *Ibid.*, p. 19.
[4] *Dialogue on the New View of Society*, p. 13.
[5] *Life*, p. 182.

Laws. Finally, it was recommended that, as Owen's report dealt mainly with this question and contemplated important legislative action, it would be best for him to present it to the Sturges Bourne committee rather than to the Archbishop's committee, which was concerned mainly with raising a national fund for the relief of distress. Lord (then Mr.) Brougham, who was a member of both bodies, undertook to bring it to the notice of the parliamentary committee, and to suggest that Owen should appear there to be examined and to present his scheme.

The centre of interest accordingly shifts to the Sturges Bourne committee, before which, early in 1817, Owen was summoned to give evidence. At the time appointed, he went to the committee room and began to arrange his papers, which included drawings and plans of his proposed villages. There was a full muster of members. But after some whispered conversation the chairman asked Owen to withdraw, as the committee wished to deliberate in private before hearing him. For two whole days he was kept waiting while the members held acrimonious debate on the question whether they should receive his evidence. Finally, it was decided by a majority that he should not be heard, and Brougham, who had been strongly on his side, was sent to inform him. The reason for the decision was not disclosed.

Thus rebuffed by the parliamentary committee, Owen had to make up his mind how to proceed. He decided at once to appeal to the public with a full exposition of his plans. He began by publishing in the newspapers an imaginary examination of himself, as he thought it should have been con-

ducted by the committee.[1] This he followed up
with a further account of his proposals, under the
title, *A Sketch of Some of the Errors and Evils arising
from the Past and Present State of Society*.[2] These were
intended to prepare the way for a series of public
meetings, to be addressed by himself, and to be
held at the City of London Tavern, where the
original meeting to form the Association for the
Relief of the Poor had been held the previous year.
These meetings were called "to consider a plan to
relieve the country from its present distress, to re-
moralise the lower orders, reduce the poor rate,
and gradually abolish pauperism with all its degrading consequences."[3]

Sturges Bourne's committee, Owen held, was no
fair or impartial tribunal. It was "sitting with the
foregone determination to rob the poor of their just
and until then their legal rights—that is, the right
to efficient relief when unable to work or to find
employment, and that relief should be given in
accordance with the dictates of humanity for
suffering poverty, and not in the cruel manner in
which it is now [1857] doled out to them in the
present practice at many workhouses."[4] The majority of members "had made up their minds, influenced by the Malthusian irrational doctrines of
over-population, to depress the poor out of existence, instead of finding them employment at
decent living wages"[4]—unfortunately all too
true a description of the new poor-law policy
which was then in the ascendant. They were
not prepared to consider a plan which, like

---

[1] This is the *Dialogue* from which I have quoted above.
It appeared in the papers of July 30, 1817.
[2] August 9, 1817.   [3] *Life*, p. 184.   [4] *Ibid.*, p. 214.

Owen's, was based on a flat denial of Malthusian theories.

Owen disbelieved wholly in the so-called "law of population"; and in the papers which he now made public, he devoted a good deal of attention to combating the Malthusian view. "The fear of any evil to arise from an excess of population, until such time as the whole earth shall become a highly cultivated garden, will, on due and accurate investigation, prove a mere phantom of the imagination, calculated solely to keep the world in unnecessary ignorance, vice, and crime. . . . It is the artificial law of supply and demand, arising from the principle of individual gain in opposition to the well-being of society, which has hitherto compelled population to press upon subsistence." [1] The trouble is, not that we *cannot* produce enough, but that we do not, for lack of buyers able to pay.

Owen had no intention, now he had decided to appeal to the public, of allowing his views to fail for lack of publicity. He actually purchased thirty thousand copies of the newspapers each day they contained the articles expounding his views. He sent a copy, franked by a friendly Member of Parliament, to every parish minister, to every member of both Houses, to the chief magistrates and bankers in every town, and to every other notable he could think of. The coaches were actually delayed one day for twenty minutes by the despatch of this shower of journals.

Moreover, he republished the articles expounding his views in pamphlet form, and circulated forty thousand free copies, which were all gone in three days. He "was then constrained to stop so expen-

[1] *Dialogue*, p. 12.

sive a process "; for he had spent in two months £4,000 on publicity alone, newspapers, on account of the Stamp Tax, then costing 7*d.* or 8*d.* each.[1]

Meanwhile, on August 14, 1817, his first meeting had been held. The notables with whom he had been associated on the Archbishop's committee did not attend; but the leading economists were present, headed by Colonel Torrens and Ricardo, and there was a big muster of Radicals, including Henry Hunt, T. W. Wooller of *The Black Dwarf*, and Alderman Waithman of the City Corporation. The large hall was crowded, and very many were turned away.

Owen gave at this meeting no detailed exposition of his Plan. He was concerned rather to answer the criticisms levelled at it by the orthodox economists. "A country," he said at the outset, "can never be beneficially wealthy while it supports a large portion of its working classes in idle poverty or in useless occupation." And he went on to answer the charge that his scheme would create paupers, by asking whether "to train a child carefully and well, from earliest infancy, be a likely means to create, increase and perpetuate pauperism." "It is downright mockery," he said, "of common sense to talk about religion, and of improving the condition and morals of the poor and working classes," while they are surrounded by every incitement to vice and, in their misery, given no encouragement to virtue. "The learned, inexperienced men of the present times are wrong" in their adherence to Malthusian doctrines; they have no remedy to propose because they cannot see beyond the limitations of the commercial system. Individualism cannot furnish a

[1] *Life*, p. 215.

remedy. "You know not, my friends, how I shall rejoice when we shall sink the individual and unite him cordially with his fellows."

At the close of his speech Owen proposed a string of resolutions to the meeting. The first three declared the misery of the people and the disastrous burden of the Poor Laws. The fourth attributed the misery to the decline in the value of manual labour. The fifth declared that "it is not probable manual labour can regain its proper and necessary value . . . unless other arrangements shall be formed by society, purposely devised to give employment to all who are competent and willing to labour." The later resolutions proposed the setting up of a "Committee of General Investigation" to report upon Owen's Plan, and urged the opening of a subscription with the object of founding Villages of Co-operation. Owen further read a letter supporting the proposal from Mr. James Johnson of Chelsea, and reported an offer to provide land for an experimental village.

The discussion [1] opened with a speech from Colonel Torrens, putting the orthodox economic objections to the Plan. But the main opposition came from the Radicals, who were then in full cry against the prevailing high taxation. "Orator" Hunt moved an amendment to Owen's resolutions, attributing the distress to this cause, and Thomas Wooller seconded him. Alderman Waithman accused Owen of desiring to "shut the people up in barracks" and to destroy their manly independence. William Hone made a speech supporting the Malthusian view, and attributing the distress to over-population. He urged that Owen's Plan

[1] See report in Hone's *Reformists' Register*, August 23, 1817.

would encourage this, and that "its leading principle, all things in common, turns the whole country into a workhouse." At some point Owen's first three resolutions were carried; but finally, after Hunt's amendment had been narrowly beaten, the meeting was adjourned for a week in some disorder. "Let us alone, Mr. Owen," said Hone, in an editorial commenting on the discussion.

In a letter to the papers two days later, Owen gave his impressions of the meeting. He described his scheme as a "plan of amelioration and reformation without revolution," and attacked the demands of the political reformers. "A reform of any of our great national institutions, without preparing and putting into practice means to well train, instruct, and advantageously employ the great mass of the people, would inevitably create immediate revolution, and give new and extensive stimulus to every bad passion. He credited the Radicals with "genuine good intentions," but held their proposals to be premature. "Those who opposed the principles and plan that I advocated were some of the younger disciples of the much-dreaded notions respecting the evils of a too rapid growth of population; the advocates of reform, not founded on previous training, instruction, and productive employment of the people; and some of the opposers of all measures of Government." [1] The Ministers, he held, were still favourable to his plans.

Indeed, this seems to have been the case; for before the resumed meeting Owen went to see Lord Liverpool, the Prime Minister, and secured his assent to placing the names of the Ministers on his

[1] Newspapers, August 16, 1817.

proposed Committee of Investigation. He was given full liberty to do this, "short of implicating us as a Government." [1] Thus armed, he returned to face his audience again.

The second meeting at the City of London Tavern, on August 21, 1817, was always subsequently regarded by Owen as the vital turning-point of his career. For reasons which remain obscure, he had decided to take a course which he was sure would destroy his influence and popularity with the governing classes, to whom so far his appeal had been addressed. He had taken this decision quite deliberately, and had written out carefully some days in advance the passage of his speech in which he proposed to carry it into effect. He consulted no one—told no one what he proposed to do.

He began his speech with a renewed exposition of the causes of the distress. "Mechanism, which may be made the greatest of blessings to humanity, is, under the existing arrangements, its greatest curse." Something must be done to raise the value of labour, and find work for the unemployed. "That something must be employment on land." To give each labourer a cottage and land of his own would make things better; but it would be very expensive and wasteful. "Not by individualising man in his proceedings either in a cottage or in a palace" would a remedy be found.

Then Owen came to the passage in his speech which he had premeditated so carefully. "If the new arrangements proposed really possess all the advantages that have been stated," he asked, "why have they not been adopted in universal practice,

[1] *Life*, p. 220.

during all the ages which have passed? . . . **My** friends, I tell you, that hitherto you have been prevented from knowing what happiness really is, solely in consequence of the errors—gross errors—that have been combined with the fundamental notions of every religion that has hitherto been taught to men. . . . By the errors of these systems, he has been made a weak, imbecile animal; a furious bigot and fanatic; or a miserable hypocrite; and should these qualities be carried, not only into the projected villages, but into Paradise itself, a Paradise would be no longer found." "I am not," he added, "of your religion, nor of any religion yet taught in the world."

Having said this, amid mingled hisses and applause, in which the latter predominated, Owen went back to his more immediate subject. He claimed that in the proposed villages there must be absolute religious freedom, and "no particle of religious intolerance." There should be, for many years, no change in national institutions—no reform of Parliament, such as the Radicals desired. But the new villages should have full local self-government, and should serve as a means of preparation for national self-government. Then, in a significant passage, he disclaimed the idea that his Plan was meant only for the unemployed; "for they will be found to afford the most desirable arrangements for all the present surplus working population." He had put forward his Plan originally as an alternative to poor relief: he now broadened it into a general plan of social reorganisation. He then withdrew all his resolutions except the proposal for a Committee of Investigation, and put this to the meeting.

This time the Radicals had thoroughly packed the hall. They carried a resolution rejecting Owen's Plan, and citing heavy taxation as the cause of the distress.[1] He declared his resolution lost, and terminated the meeting. So ended the first episode in the public history of Owenism.

On the day following Owen met Brougham in the street. "How the devil, Owen," said he, "could you say what you did yesterday at your public meeting! If any of us (meaning the then so-called Liberal Party in the House of Commons) had said half as much, we should have been burned alive—and here are you quietly walking as if nothing had occurred!"[2]

It is extraordinarily difficult either to measure the effects of Owen's "denunciation of all religions," as it was generally called, or to understand what exactly was in his mind in making it. Some of his biographers, following his own account in his *Autobiography*, have written of it as bringing his influence with the "respectable" part of society suddenly and dramatically to an end. But this view, as we shall see, is untenable in the light of the events of the next few years. All "respectable" people by no means abandoned Owen at this stage. But it is true that his utterance cost him a good deal of support. *The Times*, for example, which had hitherto favoured his plans, at once became hostile, and the bishops no longer made a pet of him. He had, in fact, given a weapon to his opponents which could thereafter always be used against him with

[1] *Reformists' Register*, August 30, 1817. Owen's account (*Life*, pp. 221 ff.) is slightly different, but Hone's seems the more plausible.
[2] *Life*, p. 226.

deadly effect. From this time he was pursued steadily with the charge of Atheism, and this was always used to discredit his plans. But a large section of the upper class was not at all disposed to be shocked by Owen's religious views, though even less disposed to follow his example. There was no immediate stampede of his outraged supporters; but gradually the attacks upon him told, and his influential backers fell away. The full effect of his words of 1817 was only felt when they were dragged up against him in later years.

In a sense, therefore, he was right in regarding the episode as the critical point in his career; but his biographers are apt to go wrong by antedating its effects. Owenism, in its aspect of secularism, did not come to birth as an organised movement till many years later.

Owen's motives are more difficult to understand. Hitherto, he had pursued his crusade with marked circumspection, carefully avoiding such a statement of his views as would alienate official and influential support. He had appealed to the Government and the upper classes for favour, and had received a good measure of sympathy. The opposition had come, not from the Church, but from the political economists, who were by no means religiously minded, and the Radicals, who included a good sprinkling of "infidels." Why, then, did he go out of his way to make the denunciation of false religions the central theme of his second lecture?

I suppose the answer is simply that he said what he thought. He hated compromise, and probably he was getting very tired of being bandied from one committee to another with no practical result. If this was all he got by being reticent, why should he not say out all that was in him? This view of his was no newly acquired belief. He had held it firmly, as we have seen, from boyhood. He did believe that the fundamental obstacle to progress lay in men's readiness to blame one another, and that, as man was the creature of circumstance, all blame was beside the mark. He heard the poor denounced for their vices; and he held these vices to be the product of evil conditions. Men opposed his schemes, because they did not realise that the making of virtue and vice was in their hands. Religions made them take this false view. Therefore religions must be denounced one and all. It was not tactful; it seriously prejudiced, if it did not destroy, the chance of getting his plans taken up by those in power. But I think he had already lost hope and patience. He determined to say what he felt, and chance the result. "The victory is gained," he said at the meeting. "Truth openly stated is omnipotent."[1] And he believed it.

Yet this is not quite all that must be said about this episode. It marks also the first emergence in Owen of a propensity which, from this time, steadily grew upon him. For the first time at this meeting he spoke in an apocalyptic vein—as if he felt himself a prophet. Some have called this a streak of madness in him. In old age, it reached at least the point of an obsession, and, even in middle age, I think it wrecked a great deal of his work. Hitherto, Owen has been the great reforming man of business; from this point he begins to turn into the prophet and to appear as a visionary in the eyes of ordinary men. His visions were fine visions; they inspired many. But they had the defect of their

[1] *Life*, p. 224.

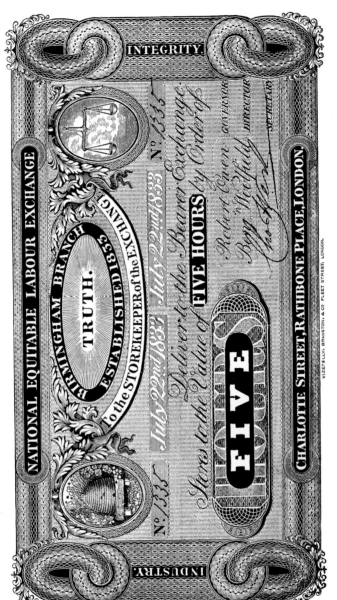

LABOUR NOTE

Issued by the London Equitable Labour Exchange

quality. From the moment when this apocalyptic vein seized on Owen he could never argue a case—he could only see visions and dream dreams. And he gradually lost, I think, that firm grasp of the world of fact which had made him the greatest practical social innovator of his day. He gained instead the power of prophecy, which made him the father of Socialism and of many movements; but, in a real sense, all prophets are mad. Owen went a little mad in 1817, and he went on getting madder to the end of his days.

CHAPTER XI

THE DAYS OF PETERLOO

Owen, as we have seen, believed in later years that his "denunciation of all religions" had been the turning-point of his career. But there were much more solid reasons for a change in the attitude of the governing classes towards his benevolent plans. In 1815 and 1816 the Government was chiefly seeking for remedies for the prevailing distress; in 1817 it was already far more concerned with the suppression of organised movements of discontent. As the distress and unemployment continued, it was inevitably accompanied by a growth of unrest. Riots occurred in the factory districts; there was a recrudescence of the Luddite disturbances of a few years before. Machinery seemed more than ever to be taking the bread out of the poor man's mouth. Moreover, the ending of the war had let loose the pent-up forces of political unrest. Everywhere the Radical leaders now got a ready hearing; the name of Cobbett became suddenly a household word.

We have seen how the Radical Reformers made an incursion into the meeting called to consider the distress, and put forward their claim that the trouble was due, not to a natural prostration of trade, but to misgovernment, the heaped-up debt, high taxation, paper-money, and the abuses of sinecurism and patronage. This message was carried through the country during 1816; and Cobbett, bringing down the price of his *Political Register* to a penny, became the accepted mouthpiece of the popular movement. His *Addresses to Journeymen and Labourers* were read everywhere, and secured a huge circulation. From sporadic rioting and unorganised strikes that achieved nothing, the factory workers seemed to be swiftly advancing towards an ordered campaign with the radical reform of Parliament and the ending of unproductive privilege as its declared and immediate objects.

Panic took hold of the governing classes. The Society of Spencean Philanthropists, followers of Thomas Spence, the pioneer of land reform, called a mass meeting in Spa Fields in London in December, 1816. The Spenceans were a small body; but the meeting was largely attended, and a section of the crowd, on leaving it, marched in procession through the City. A riot broke out, and some damage was done; but the affair was soon over, and nothing further came of it. Cobbett, Hunt and the other recognised Radical leaders were strongly against rioting; and their influence told.

Nevertheless the Spa Fields affair, insignificant in itself, was the spark that set reaction alight. It was regarded as a symptom, not merely of widespread unrest, but of an organised insurrectionary conspiracy. A Spencean "plot," which had probably no existence save in the imagination of the governing class, was made the excuse for drastic precautionary measures. Canning made an alarmist speech in the House of Commons, and Committees of Secrecy were set up by both Houses of Parliament to investigate the "plot." At the same time spies and informers, such as the infamous

"Oliver," [1] were spread abroad among the Radical and working-class organisations, where they not only fabricated false news freely to tickle Lord Sidmouth's ears, but also played the part of provocative agents, inciting the workers to rebel in order that they might betray more startling "plots" to the Government.

The reports of the two Committees of Secrecy leave no room for doubt as to the state of panic into which the governing classes had fallen by the beginning of 1817. The members of the House of Lords committee report that "they have found such evidence as leaves no doubt in their minds that a traitorous conspiracy has been formed in the metropolis for the purpose of overthrowing, by means of a general insurrection, the established Government, Laws, and Constitution of this kingdom, and of effecting a general plunder and division of property . . . and that designs of this nature have not been confined to the capital, but have been extended, and are still extending, widely in many other parts of Great Britain, particularly in some of the most populous and manufacturing districts." The House of Commons committee, in what it described as " a fair and not exaggerated statement," declared its belief in the existence of a nationally organised movement, under the leadership of the Spencean Societies, in which "nothing short of a Revolution is the object expected and avowed." "It has been proved, to the entire satisfaction of your committee, that some members of these Societies, acting by delegated or assumed authority as an executive committee of the whole, conceived

[1] See the Hammonds' *The Skilled Labourer* for an account of his career.

200

PENNY TOKENS

From the London and Birmingham Labour Exchanges
(The original tokens are in cardboard, printed on one side only)

the project, and endeavoured to prepare the means, of raising an insurrection, so formidable from numbers as by dint of physical strength to overpower all resistance."

Many details of the "plot" were included in the reports, which dwelt repeatedly on the supposed objects as the overthrow of the entire constitution and the confiscation of all land and other property. Barracks were to be surrounded and set on fire by armed men; the banks and Government buildings were to be seized; an infernal machine had been devised, and exhibited to the committee, for clearing the streets of cavalry. Finally, both committees expressed the view that the existing laws were quite inadequate for dealing with the situation, and that emergency repressive laws must be passed.

Hot upon the reports came the repressive legislation. On March 4, immediately after their presentation, the Habeas Corpus Act was suspended. Further special Acts were speedily rushed through both Houses. The right of public meeting was drastically restricted, and made subject to the approval of the magistrates. Reading-rooms were made subject to licence, which could be withheld or withdrawn if, in the opinion of the magistrates, they purveyed undesirable reading matter. Attempts to seduce soldiers or sailors from their allegiance were made punishable with death. But more important than any of the special Acts was the suspension of Habeas Corpus, which made any leader of radical opinion liable to summary arrest. Cobbett, realising that to stay in England would be merely to invite arrest, fled to the United States, whence until 1819 he despatched his writings regularly for publication in England.

These events, or rather the panic underlying them, fundamentally changed the attitude of the upper classes to projects of social reform. Repression, instead of the relief of distress, became in their minds the great necessity, and everyone who proposed schemes for bettering the lot of the workers became to some extent suspect of complicity in treasonable designs. Owen himself had obviously at this stage not the smallest intention of instigating or supporting working-class revolt, much less any revolutionary design. He was even against Parliamentary Reform, since he did not believe in political democracy save as a fruit of popular education, and considered political changes inappropriate as remedies for economic grievances. But he had a warm sympathy with the suffering poor, and he could appreciate their situation. So far from sharing in the general panic, he was only spurred by the gravity of the case to greater efforts to get his remedy adopted.

But though some of his upper-class supporters agreed with him that the remedy lay, not in repressing the symptoms of evil, but in curing the evil itself, this was not the mood of the majority. The proposals for poor-law reform turned, from measures of relief, into plans for stiffening up administration so as to reduce it and make it more deterrent. Schemes for Villages of Co-operation, which had been regarded as harmless philanthropy before, now took on a sinister appearance. Panic does not reason; it hits out blindly. So the governing class of England hit out blindly in 1817.

Owen, it is clear, was not fully conscious of this change of attitude, or of its causes. There is in his *Autobiography* no mention of the repressive measures which were actually in execution while he was making his speeches at the City of London Tavern. He was so busy pursuing his own plans, which seemed to him far more important than anything else, that the sensational events of the year made little impression on his mind. It must, of course, be taken into account that Owen's own story of these events was written down many years later, in his old age, and that time had doubtless blurred his immediate impressions. But he could hardly have written it as he did, if he had fully appreciated at the time the changed political atmosphere and its decisive effect on the policy of the governing classes.

Thus it comes about that, while the country is undergoing a three years' terror of repression, culminating in 1819 in the "Peterloo massacre" and the "Six Acts" strengthening the "Gagging Bills" of 1817, Owen goes on urging, almost without change of substance, his Plan for the relief of the poor. The Plan, indeed, changes its form, as it becomes clear that there is no chance of its national adoption by the Government. Owen is driven more and more to appeal to local bodies or groups of individual sympathisers to give his method a trial, and to trust to the example of small-scale experiment for its wider adoption. But he hardly changes at all the direction of his appeal. It is still to the rich and powerful, rather than to the poor themselves, that he addresses his plea. His Plan is still to be executed for the poor and not by them.

Indeed, a long time was to pass before Owen assumed in any sense the position of a working-class leader. The growth of an extensive movement of agitation among the workers, manifested in the big strikes of 1818 and 1819, moved him only as a symptom of a fundamental disease—something to be put right by his scheme of social reorganisation. His attitude was still that of the benevolent master of men, and not at all of the leader of a popular movement. The whole campaign of agitation, led by the political Radicals such as Hunt and Cobbett, seemed to him to be on quite wrong lines. They had no use for him and his "parallelograms of paupers"; and he had none for their desire to place political power in the hands of men who would lack knowledge and education to use it aright. Seeing far more clearly than they the real economic causes of the distress, he saw that their projected remedies were no remedies at all. They were still unconscious of the real meaning of the revolution wrought by machinery, and tended to regard the new capitalism and all its works merely as an unintelligible and inimical power. Owen believed in machinery and understood it; but, unlike the orthodox economists, he saw that it was a potent cause of the prevailing distress, and held that the cure lay in devising and applying means for its social control. His attitude at this time was, in a sense, what we should call nowadays a sort of benevolent State Socialism, to be achieved by authority working from above. But it differed materially from the State Socialism of later days in its insistence on the necessity for the greatest possible measure of local devolution and autonomy. In this difference lay the germ of its later development on what we should now call Guild Socialist lines.

It would, however, be a misnomer to call Owen, at this period of his life, a Socialist of any sort. He was that rarest of phenomena, an utterly disinterested critic of a system by which he had himself

risen to greatness. But he could not escape the consequences of his own experience. He had been used
to move, so far, in circles where autonomy passed
without challenge. At New Lanark he was the
benevolent despot, caring for the welfare of his children—the factory workers. In London he figured
as "the benevolent Mr. Owen," and mingled
chiefly with men of the governing class and imbued
with autocratic ideas. He knew Francis Place and
Bentham, indeed; and he had other friends among
the Radicals. But it was with the philosophic
Radicalism of the middle-class Utilitarians, and
not with the struggling Radicalism of the workers
and the militant reformers, that he had been
brought into close personal contact.

Owen was, moreover, still actively engaged during these years in developing his plans for the
government of New Lanark, and this helped to determine the cast of his mind. It is hard for a man
to be at once autocrat in his own factory and leader
of a democratic agitation outside it. Not till he had
virtually left New Lanark in other hands did Owen
pass over to his new rôle of popular leader; and, as
we shall see, the transition was never complete. He
remained half the benevolent employer to the end,
even when he was leading the great working-class
revolt of 1832–1834.

To the affairs of New Lanark we must now return, taking up the story again at the point which
was reached with the conclusion of the new partnership of 1813, which seemed at last to have associated with him a congenial group ready to aid him
to the full in his benevolent designs. We shall soon
see that a common benevolence is not a sufficient
guarantee of harmonious co-operation.

CHAPTER XII

LATER YEARS AT NEW LANARK

While Owen was largely in London during the years between 1813 and 1817, he was by no means allowing affairs at New Lanark to stand still. We broke off the story of the New Lanark mills at the point when he had just formed his new partnership with William Allen, Fox, Foster, John Walker, Gibbs and Jeremy Bentham. He had now for a time a much freer hand for the development of his schemes; for the new partnership was not formed primarily with a view to profit. The deed of partnership definitely laid down that "all profits made in the concern beyond five per cent. per annum on the capital invested shall be laid aside for the religious, educational and moral improvement of the workers, and of the community at large." [1] So far as money went, he had therefore now very full scope for action; for the concern had been making very large profits, and, though it was hit by the slump after 1815, it weathered this difficult time far better than most. Owen pressed on energetically with the building of his new schools, and with other plans for improving factory conditions. He reduced the hours of work to ten and a half, or twelve including meal-times, at the beginning of 1816, provided free medical attendance for all, started a Sick Club and a Savings Bank, threw open the woods as a

[1] Liddell, *Memoir of David Dale.*

206

public pleasure-ground, and in general pursued his course as by far the most enlightened employer of his time.

It is interesting to note that, although most of the workers at New Lanark were on piece-work, they were keenly in favour of the shorter working day, and were soon able to avoid loss of wages by increased output. In 1817 they presented an address of thanks to Owen on the anniversary of the introduction of shorter hours. They desired also to give him a piece of plate; but this he refused to accept, and the sum collected was applied to the relief of distress. Moreover, they petitioned Parliament in favour of Owen's Factory Bill.

Owen's greatest care, however, was the realisation of his educational schemes. On January 1, 1816, his new buildings were ready, and he delivered an *Address to the Inhabitants of New Lanark at the Opening of the Institution for the Formation of Character*, which was afterwards widely circulated in pamphlet form. We have already quoted his reference to all his work at New Lanark up to that time as merely preparatory, because directed merely to the removal of material abuses and the improvement of external habits.[1] He meant now to probe deeper. "The Institution, when all its parts shall be completed, is intended to produce permanently beneficial effects; and, instead of longer applying temporary expedients for correcting some of your most prominent external habits, to effect a complete and thorough improvement in the *internal* as well as *external* character of the whole village."[2] This was to be done by means of education of the children.

No child was to be employed till it was ten years

[1] See p. 101.   [2] *Address*, p. 13.

old. Up to that age they were to pass through an education planned in two preparatory stages followed by a "fuller course." In summer, much of the education, including nature study, was to be in the open air, and there was to be plenty of "dancing, singing, playing upon some instrument," and in the case of boys "military exercises"—"for it is intended to give them as much diversified innocent amusement as the local circumstances of the establishment will admit." For the children over ten there were to be evening schools, and for the adults "accommodation for reading, writing, accounting, sewing, playing, talking and walking, as well as regular lectures, dances and concerts in the hall of the Institution. No restraint was to be placed on private judgment or religious opinion.[1]

Once again, Owen went on to expound his view of the formation of character by physical and moral environment. Wickedness and misery have proceeded "solely from the ignorance of our forefathers." "What ideas individuals may attach to the term millennium I know not; but I know that society may be formed so as to exist without crime, without poverty, with health greatly improved, with little, if any, misery, and with intelligence and happiness increased an hundredfold; and no obstacle whatsoever intervenes at this moment except ignorance."[2] He attacked the false education of the "learned," as based on the very prejudices he wished to remove, and denounced religious dogma,[3] almost as vigorously as in London a year later, as the cause of ignorance and disunity. He said that his aim was to withdraw from society the "germ" of all party and sectarian quarrels; and "as little

[1] *Address*, pp. 14 ff.   [2] *Ibid.*, p. 27.   [3] See p. 192.

do I admit of the divisions and distinctions created on imaginary lines which separate nation from nation." [1]

Finally, he expressed his sense that he could put his principles but very imperfectly into practice at New Lanark, and warned his hearers against the danger of too rapid an overthrow even of the evil systems of the past. "You must go on under the old system till a new one is proved by practice to be essentially superior." . . . "This change will bear no resemblance to any of the revolutions which have hitherto occurred. These have been alone conducted to generate and call forth all the evil passions of hatred and revenge; but that system which is now contemplated will effectively eradicate every feeling of irritation and ill-will which exists among mankind." [2]

In establishing his new schools, Owen conceived himself as laying the only sure foundation for a revolutionary change for the better. At the least, within a few years he had made them the most famous educational establishment in the world, and a place of pilgrimage for enthusiasts from many countries. Between 1815 and 1825 nearly twenty thousand names were inscribed in the visitors' book at New Lanark; [3] and the visitors ranged from the future Czar Nicholas of Russia to deputations from parochial bodies and humble believers in the new educational ideas.

I have given, in an earlier chapter, an outline of Owen's educational theories. His practice followed them closely. His Infant School, the first in England and the model very inadequately followed by

[1] *Address*, p. 26.   [2] *Ibid.*, p. 35.
[3] R. D. Owen, *Threading My Way*, p. 115.

Brougham and Wilderspin some years later, was a place for play and not work, a kindergarten which Owen instituted almost contemporaneously with the better-known continental experiments of Pesta-lozzi and others. And, in the schools for the older children, as much use as possible was made of the appeal to eye and ear, music being prominent in the curriculum, and the walls of the schoolrooms hung round with maps, pictures of birds and beasts, illustrated historical time-charts, and similar de-vices. History and geography took a large place in the teaching, and both were taught from an inter-national point of view. Books were used, though Owen would have preferred to do without them for the younger children. But it was not easy to find suitable books. Maria Edgeworth's stories were read; but readers of *Rosamund and the Purple Jar* will not be surprised to hear that "even those contain too much of praise and blame to admit of their being regarded as unexceptionable." [1]

The new schools prospered greatly; but already there was a fresh cloud on the horizon. Owen's previous partners had interfered because they wanted higher profits. He had guarded against such interference by the new terms of partnership; but he was soon to find that there were other restric-tions on his freedom of action. The most active of his new partners was the Quaker, William Allen. "He was active, bustling, ambitious, most desirous of doing good in his own way, and had kind feelings and high aspirations"[2]; but Owen also describes

---

[1] I have no space to give a full account of the New Lanark Schools. Readers are referred to R. D. Owen's excellent *Outline of the System of Education at New Lanark* (1824), and to the long account in Podmore's *Owen*, vol. i., pp. 126 ff.

[2] *Life*, p. 131.

him as meddlesome and given to intriguing behind his back. The root of the trouble was that Allen was not merely religious, but exceedingly pious, and haunted, as his diary shows, by a permanent horror of infidelity in all its forms. Owen's religious views appeared to him dreadful and subversive, and he was in ceaseless panic lest New Lanark, under Owen's guidance, should become what he termed "a manufactory of infidels." He had insisted, when the deed of partnership was drawn up, on the insertion of a clause providing for religious education, based on the Scriptures, and he accused Owen of infringing this clause, and was constantly pressing for its full observance. Moreover, he objected strongly to the dancing, singing and military exercises [1] which Owen had introduced into the curriculum, and greatly preferred the Lancasterian system of education to that in force at New Lanark.

Allen is very plainly self-revealed in his diary—a queer but characteristic mixture of puritanism, piety, philanthropy, meddlesomeness and financial canniness. It is amusing to read the pious self-questionings and petitions for divine guidance under stress of which he joined the partnership, and to find, in the same paragraph, how the canny philanthropist, with no sense of incongruity, safeguarded himself absolutely from possible business loss.

"Much tried in mind, in considering whether it would be right for me to yield to the pressing solicitations . . . to join in the Lanark concern, for the sake of keeping up this most interesting establishment for preserving the morals, and promoting the

---

[1] These seem, in fact, to have been merely physical drill and evolutions, with no militaristic character.

comfort and happiness of the workpeople; and I
trust I felt what would warrant me to go so far as
I did. The parties came under an engagement to
secure me from loss for one year, and that they
would take my shares, if I felt uneasy and disposed
to relinquish them, on my giving notice in the ninth
month next. If this is not in right direction, I
humbly hope that I may be favoured with an in-
timation in my own mind to that effect, and be
graciously helped to act accordingly." [1]

After the new partnership had definitely started,
Allen seems to have been for a time reassured. He
began negotiations with the Government with a
view to getting a Royal Charter for New Lanark;
but it appears that nothing came of this. But his
troubles soon began anew. He visited New Lanark
in 1814, and, walking with Owen, "had much painful conversation on the subject of his peculiar
opinions." "Alas!" he wrote, "Owen, with all his
cleverness and benevolence, wants the *one thing*
without which parts and acquirements and benevolence are unavailing." [2] In the following year he
became still more troubled, and corresponded at
length with Owen, whom he accused of altering the
whole basis on which the factory was run. "I
fondly hoped that one establishment might be
found in which it should be proved that it was possible to provide for the comfort, for the morals, and
the happiness of a poor population, without injury
to the pecuniary interests of the employers " [3]; but
he had not bargained for having to sanction the
teaching of "infidel" doctrines. He again insisted
on the strict observance of the articles dealing with
religious education.

[1] *Life of W. Allen*, p. 181.   [2] *Ibid.*, p. 209.   [3] *Ibid.*, p. 245.

In 1818, after Owen's meetings in London, relations became still more strained, and three of the partners—Allen, Foster and Gibbs—paid a special visit of inspection to New Lanark, where they received an address of thanks to the proprietors from the workers, and where Allen addressed a public meeting in which he stated the religious views of the partners in opposition to Owen's. He also visited the local clergy, who had nothing to say against the conduct of the villagers, and reported that there was no drunkenness and no sign that Owen's religious views were making converts among the workers. He requested one minister to visit the schools regularly, and to write to them "if he saw any attempt made to introduce anything contrary to revealed religion." "I begin to hope," he wrote in his diary after this visit, "that even this undertaking may be blessed, and that, perhaps, we were permitted to enter into it to prevent New Lanark from becoming a seminary for infidels." [1]

Matters were patched up in 1818; but the trouble continued, and in the years from 1822 to 1824 it came to a head, Allen announcing that he would withdraw unless drastic changes were made. Again Allen, Foster and Gibbs came to New Lanark, and this time they were not to be put off. Owen was compelled to dismiss some of his teachers, and to install an orthodox Lancasterian, John Daniel, as head of the schools. Dancing was no longer to be taught at the company's expense, and the only music or singing was to be "instruction in psalmody." Public readings from the Scriptures and "religious exercises" were made part of the curriculum, and both the kilts, which many of the

[1] *Life of W. Allen*, p. 356.

children wore, and the classical tunics, which Owen had introduced as a costume for the dancing, were banned, as "we are of opinion that decency requires that all males as they arrive at the age of six years should wear trousers or drawers." [1]

From this time the New Lanark schools, and indeed the whole establishment, practically passed out of Owen's hands. He retained his financial interest until 1828, and remained nominally manager till 1825, but virtually the new conditions so hampered his freedom that the place was no longer his. He had made his great experiment, with enduring results; but he had not succeeded in finding a group of capitalists who would give him a free hand to put his plans into effect.

Long before the crisis came at New Lanark, Owen had found other things to occupy his energies. After the abortive meetings at the City of London Tavern in 1817, he returned for a time to New Lanark, and then, taking with him his sisters-in-law, went for an extensive continental tour, largely in company with Professor Pictet, of Geneva. He travelled to Paris with Pictet and Cuvier, the naturalist, on a French frigate, and, armed with introductions from the Duke of Kent and other notables, had a remarkable reception. He had interviews with the Duke of Orleans (Louis Philippe) and the Prime Minister, and became friendly with Humboldt and La Place. He was, indeed, lionised in Paris, where he remained some time before going on with Pictet to Geneva.

In Switzerland Owen paid a round of visits to the new schools organised by Father Oberlin, by Pesta-

[1] Quoted *New Existence*, part v., p. 8.

lozzi, and by Fellenberg. Oberlin's Catholic school seems to have impressed him more than Pestalozzi's, of whom he writes that "his theory was good, but his means and experience very limited." He was "much pleased with the honest, homely simplicity of the old man, but thought his school but "one step in advance of ordinary schools." [1] He was much more attracted by Fellenberg's college at Hofwyl, and after his return sent his two eldest sons there to be educated. [2]

In company now with his partner John Walker, Owen proceeded from Switzerland into Germany, and stayed for some time at Frankfort, where the German Diet was in session. He was again very well received, thanks to his introductions, by the German political leaders. But he did not remain very long, as he had made up his mind to attend the Conference of the Great Powers, then about to meet at Aix-la-Chapelle, and to present to it his *Two Memorials on Behalf of the Working Classes*. In these Memorials, which were actually laid before the Conference by Lord Castlereagh, he restated his essential doctrines, pleading for international action to restore the purchasing power of the workers and to institute schemes of education for the development of character. The new inventions, he urged, had destroyed the value of labour; before their coming "the manufacturing system had attained that point which gave the highest value to manual labour compared with prices." The great inventions had made production infinitely easier. "The grand question now to be solved is, not how

---

[1] *Life*, p. 244.
[2] For a good account of education at Hofwyl, see R. D. Owen, *Threading My Way*, chap. v.

a sufficiency of wealth can be produced, but how the excess of riches, which may be most easily created, may be generally distributed throughout society advantageously for all, and without prematurely disturbing the existing institutions or arrangements in any country." "Already, with a population under twenty millions and a manual power not exceeding six millions, undirected except by blind private interest, she [Great Britain] supplies her own demand, and overstocks with her manufactures all the markets of the world into which her commerce is admitted; she is now using every exertion to open new markets, even in the most distant regions, because she feels she could soon supply the wants of another world equally populous with the earth. Instead, however, of thus contending with other nations to supply their wants, and thereby, under the present arrangements of society, diminish the value of their manual labour, and depress their working classes, she might most advantageously for herself and them extend the knowledge which she has acquired of creating wealth, or new productive power, to the rest of Europe, to Asia, Africa and America." The system of fixing wages by the fluctuations in the supply and demand of labour "served the purpose in a tolerable degree while wealth was produced mainly by manual labour"; but the mechanical revolution has made it obsolete, and a source of general misery. International action to change the system is therefore necessary, and Owen asks the Conference to appoint a Commission to report on his work and schemes, and issue recommendations to the next Conference of the Powers. Nothing, of course, came of these suggestions, though it appears that Owen's Memorials were actually discussed at Aix-la-Chapelle.

From the final attempt to persuade the Governments of the world to take action Owen returned to look after his affairs at home. Francis Place, going through some old papers, had unearthed a booklet, originally published by one John Bellers in 1696 under the title *Proposals for Raising a Colledge of Industry of All Useful Trades and Husbandry*, in which proposals in some respects closely resembling Owen's were brought forward. This, with certain other papers, Owen now reprinted and issued. He also resumed his propaganda campaign at the point at which he had left it in the previous year. Early in 1819 he published an *Address to the Working Classes*, significant of the coming change in the direction of his appeal. But he had not yet quite given up hope of the upper classes; nor had they wholly thrust him out, though he had now to meet the charge of "infidelity" at every turn. Among those who still gave him steady support was Queen Victoria's father, the Duke of Kent, with whom he remained on terms of close intimacy till the Duke's death in 1820. We have seen how the Duke of Kent furnished him with introductions on his foreign tour, and he in return was able to give the Duke valuable help in straightening out his tangled financial affairs. When, in 1819, Owen again appealed for a Committee of Investigation to examine his plans with a view to action upon them, the Duke of Kent agreed to act as chairman both at the meeting called to discuss the proposal and of the committee itself. How far Owen was, even at this stage, from having lost all influential associates can be seen from the names of those who consented

to serve on the committee which he now established. Besides the Duke of Kent, the committee
included the Duke of Sussex, the elder Peel, David
Ricardo, Tooke, Torrens, Alderman Matthew
Wood, Sir William de Crespigny, and a number of
other notables. The bishops, indeed, had abandoned Owen; but he had still a respectful hearing among the economists and Liberals of the
day.

Moreover, the report presented by this committee was distinctly favourable to his plans. After
referring to the prevalent distress and the impera-
tive need for a remedy, it goes on to say that
"remedies will be most readily found in any plan
that may provide employment for the poor principally in agricultural labour; which, while it shall
tend to secure industrious habits, may be rendered
conducive to a system of training up the young in
improved moral conduct. . . . The committee consider that the plan proposed by Mr. Owen com-
bines many practical results connected with the
advantages above stated, and therefore are of
opinion that an establishment should be found by
way of experiment, and which, it is computed, may
in the first instance require an advance of capital
not exceeding £100,000." They recommend the
raising of this sum at 5 per cent. interest, and estimate that it will be possible to repay the whole out
of profits over a period of years. A definite appeal
is made for the amount needed.

Both the Duke of Kent as chairman and the committee in its report referred to the question of
Owen's religious views. "Mr. Owen," the committee reported, "is not known to have in any one
instance endeavoured to alter the religious opinions

of persons in his employment." They had not asked him for any declaration of his own religious views, being fully satisfied with this fact and the knowledge that "his character is distinguished by active benevolence, perfect sincerity, and undisturbed tranquillity of temper. They had examined the objections offered to the Plan; "but none of those stated has appeared as founded in reason or in fact."

At the same time, the committee made it quite clear that they were only prepared to recommend a very modified form of Owenism. "In the establishment which is now proposed there would be no community of goods nor any deviation from the established laws of property. Mr. Owen has expressed an opinion in favour of a state of society in which a community of goods should exist, but he has never considered it essential to the success of such an establishment as is now proposed, nor regarded it as a condition of his superintendence." Stress was laid on the fact that Owen had offered to act as superintendent of the proposed village, and had pledged himself that the interest on the capital should be paid.[1]

An attempt was now made, under the ægis of this influential committee, to raise at least the sum needed for the starting of a single village on the lines which Owen had laid down. Through the summer and autumn the committee's appeal for funds remained open; but in November William Tooke, who had acted as secretary, had to write to Owen announcing a failure to raise any considerable sum. A little later the committee was dis-

[1] This report is printed in Owen's *Autobiography*, vol. Iᴀ, Appendix Q.

banded, its work having come to nothing in a practical sense.

There is further evidence that in 1819, two years after his declaration of war on established religions is supposed to have put him out of court, Owen's Plan was still being seriously considered in quite respectable circles. During that year Owen gave a lecture in Leeds, and in August a deputation from the Leeds Guardians, headed by Edward Baines of the *Leeds Mercury*, the most famous journalist of the North of England, and the mouthpiece of middle-class Radical opinion in the West Riding, came to New Lanark on a visit of inspection, the Guardians having under consideration a proposal to adopt Owen's Plan as a substitute for the existing poor-law system. The whole report of this deputation is well worth reading.[1] "Mr. Owen's establishment at New Lanark," it states, "is essentially a manu-facturing establishment, conducted in a manner superior to any other the deputation ever wit-nessed, and dispensing more happiness than per-haps any other institution in the kingdom where so many poor persons are employed. . . . In the edu-cation of the children the thing that is most remark-able is the general spirit of tenderness and affection which is shown towards them, and the entire ab-sence of anything which is likely to give them bad habits—with the presence of whatever is calculated to inspire them with good ones. The consequence is that they appear like one well-regulated family, united together by the ties of the closest affection. In the adult inhabitants we saw much to commend. In general they appeared clean, healthy and sober. Intoxication is almost unknown."

[1] *Autobiography*, vol. IA, Appendix R.

The deputation expressed itself in favour of an experiment at Leeds based on Owen's Plan, and recommended that his system of education should be at once applied to the workhouse children. They could not at once recommend the setting up of a full colony on his Plan, as this would need legislation. But they left no doubt that they were in favour of the scheme.

While these events were in progress, Owen had tried another way of bringing his plans before the country. A vacancy occurred in the parliamentary representation of Lanark Burghs, and Owen offered himself as a candidate. This was in 1819, and, of course, in the days of the old, unreformed Parliament. There were few voters, and many of them expected to be bribed. Owen's opponent bribed, and he did not; but, by his own account, he was beaten only by four votes. At the General Election of the following year he stood again, but was once more beaten. Owen was not destined for Parliament, in which, indeed, he would have been very much a fish out of water. He could never have accommodated himself to the parliamentary atmosphere, or brought himself to take any interest in the greater part of the proceedings. His defeat was for him a fortunate event, and it looks as if he half knew this at the time; for he does not appear to have pressed his candidature with any serious degree of attention. Before the second contest was over, he was fully absorbed in other concerns, of which the chief was the preparing of his well-known *Report to the County of Lanark*, in which he embodied a new and maturer statement of his immediate proposals.

CHAPTER XIII

THE BEGINNINGS OF OWENISM

The *Report to the County of Lanark* is by far the best
and most comprehensive exposition of Owen's
social doctrines. In it, he is for the first time fully
speaking his mind, and expounding his Plan, not as
a mere expedient for the relief of unemployment,
but as the basis of an alternative social order. It is
in form a report to a committee appointed by the
Upper Ward of the County of Lanark, which doubtless had in mind merely a method of relieving distress. But Owen went far beyond his brief, enunci-
ating clearly his new social gospel. It was in the
doctrines first clearly stated in this report that the
Owenite movement grew up as a movement of
Socialism and Co-operation. There are phrases in
the report which mark its transitional character;
but essentially it marks the change from Owen the
reformer to Owen the Socialist pioneer.

It begins with an unequivocal statement:
"Manual labour, properly directed, is the source of
all wealth and of national prosperity." Such labour,
Owen says, can always produce a surplus over the
consumption necessary to maintain the labourer in
considerable comfort. This will remain true, "in
all parts of the world, under any supposable increase
of population, for many centuries to come." The
problem is not to produce enough, but to distribute
what can be readily produced. "It is the want of a

222

profitable market that alone checks the successful and otherwise beneficial industry of the working classes." "The markets of the world are created solely by the remuneration allowed for the industry of the working classes, and those markets are more or less extended and profitable in proportion as those classes are well or ill remunerated for their labour." "But the existing arrangements of society will not permit the labourer to be remunerated for his industry, and in consequence all markets fail."

Clearly, Owen urges, this deficiency of employment arises from some defect in the mode of distributing the "extraordinary addition of new capital" which the Industrial Revolution has produced. His report is an attempt to outline the necessary remedies.

He begins with the currency question, then a theme of violent controversy in connection with the younger Peel's Act of 1819, under which cash payments, suspended since a short while after the outbreak of the wars following the French Revolution, were to be gradually restored. Owen, like Cobbett, hated paper-money, but he also agreed with Cobbett in holding that Peel's Act, increasing by deflation the value of all accumulated fortunes and especially the burden of interest on the War Debt, would inevitably press down yet further the real wages of the workers.[1] Owen's remedy was the creation of a new standard of value and basis for credit—the foreshadowing of the system introduced later in his Equitable Labour Exchanges. "The natural standard of value," he wrote, "is in principle human labour, or the combined manual and mental powers of men called into action." He

[1] See my *Life of Cobbett*, p. 278 ff.

called for the practical application of this principle. "The average physical power of men has been calculated, and the average of human labour can be ascertained; and, as it forms the essence of all wealth, its value in every article of produce may also be ascertained, and its exchangeable value with all other values fixed accordingly; the whole to be permanent for a given period. Human labour would thus acquire its natural and intrinsic value, which would increase as science advanced. The demand for human labour would be no longer subject to caprice, nor would the support of human life be made, as at present, a perpetually varying article of commerce, and the working classes made the slaves of an artificial system of wages, more cruel in its effects than any slavery ever practised by society, either barbarous or civilised. This change in the standard of value would immediately open the most advantageous domestic markets until the wants of all were amply supplied."[1]

Owen pleads, then, for a new standard of value, based on productive power, as a means to the assuring of a good standard of living for all. "That which can create new wealth is, of course, worth the wealth which it creates. The producer should have a fair and fixed proportion of all the wealth he creates." All articles must be exchanged at "prime cost," in which Owen apparently includes interest on capital, through a "convenient medium for expressing labour value." The value of a day's labour, calculated on this basis, would certainly be not less than five shillings' worth of

[1] Students of Marx will not need to be reminded how much Marx owed to Owen, though he applied Owen's diagnosis to a different purpose.

goods. The new standard would "benefit the land-holder and capitalist as well as the labourer" by eliminating the risks due to commercial fluctuation and the evil system of "buying cheap and selling dear."

All this is by way of preamble to a new exposition of Owen's scheme for Villages of Co-operation. These, he now plainly insists, must be "founded on the principle of united labour, expenditure and property, and equal privileges." Agriculture, with manufacture as an appendage, will support more population than the manufacturing system and in higher comfort. But there must be the fullest application of science to both. Spade culture (*i.e.*, intensive cultivation), combined with science in agriculture, would produce more improvement than the steam engine in manufacturing. The plough, with extensive cultivation, is not so productive as the spade allied with science.

In the new villages Owen aims at destroying the evils of the division of labour. Skilled manual work is being largely superseded by mechanism, and with it goes the need for specialisation of labour. "Minute division of labour and division of interests are only other terms for poverty, ignorance, waste of every kind, universal opposition throughout society, crime, misery, and great bodily and mental imbecility." Therefore, each child must receive an all-round education, and each adult combine manufacturing with agricultural work. "Instead of the unhealthy pointer of a pin, header of a nail, piecer of a thread, or clodhopper, senselessly gazing at the soil or around him, without understanding or rational reflection, there would spring up a working class full of activity and useful knowledge, with habits, information, manners and dis-positions, that would place the lowest in the scale many degrees above the best of any class which has yet been formed by the circumstances of past or present society."

Education is, of course, to be the basis of this new order. "The children in these new schools should be trained systematically to acquire useful knowledge through the means of sensible signs, by which their powers of reflection and judgment may be habituated to draw accurate conclusions from the facts presented to them. This mode of construction is founded in nature, and will super-sede the present defective and tiresome system of book learning, which is ill calculated to give either pleasure or instruction to the minds of children. . . . It is only by education, rightly understood, that communities of men can ever be well governed."

Again, in this report, Owen outlines the formal organisation of his proposed communities; but on this point he adds little that is new, save in deal-ing with their methods of government. The super-intendents, he says, must have practical knowledge of both agriculture and manufactures, and must comprehend the new principles and take pleasure in putting them into execution. The modes of government will depend on the parties who form the various associations. Those formed by land-owners or capitalists will be under such persons as they appoint; but those formed by co-operative action of the middle or working classes should be fully self-governing. Again, however, Owen affirms his objections to representative government and elections, urging that, in order to avoid these and their results in faction and friction, the government should be entrusted to all the members between certain fixed ages, who would apportion among themselves the various functions.

Finally he urges that, once his villages are started, they will speedily supersede other ways of living or producing. "There will be no desire or motive for individual accumulation of wealth"; for all will have amply enough. War will cease; courts of law, prisons and punishments will soon be no longer required. The world will settle down to a new way of full and co-operative living.

This report seems to have taken the Committee of the County of Lanark by surprise. In their own report, they pay handsome tribute to New Lanark, and express themselves strongly in favour of "the more practical parts" of Owen's proposals. "Careful study," they say, would be needed before they could pronounce on the report as a whole. But up to a point they were clearly favourable, and at the County meeting called to receive both reports a resolution was moved for the institution of a model village, "instead of a Bridewell," on land offered by Mr. Hamilton of Dalzell at a rent to be fixed by an impartial person. Criminals, among others, were to be sent to this proposed village for reformation, and Owen was to be asked to act as superintendent. He objected to this curious distortion of his Plan, and apparently the whole project dropped for the time, though it was in a measure revived, under different conditions, in the Orbiston community of 1826.[1] By that time, however, Owen was far away, busied with a much larger experiment of his own.

[1] See p. 239.

During the next four years Owen was largely occupied by his recurring disputes with his New Lanark partners; but he also engaged in energetic propaganda in support of his schemes. In 1822 he made his last attempt to get his Plan put into practice under the auspices of the benevolent rich, founding in London the British and Foreign Philanthropic Society, which launched an appeal for £100,000 to start a model Village of Co-operation, and actually secured promises of £50,000, including £10,000 from Owen himself. The Earl of Blessington, Brougham, Joseph Hume, Sir William de Crespigny, Hamilton of Dalzell, Lord Torrington and other notables were connected with this Society, and John Galt, the novelist, was its secretary.[1] Nothing, however, was done, and it appears that in the midst of the scheme Owen's interest was diverted elsewhere.

For, towards the end of 1822, he was invited to Ireland, then in a condition of acute misery, to expound his system. He lectured all over the country, and had a really remarkable reception. A great series of meetings was held in Dublin, with the Lord Mayor in the chair. The Catholic clergy appear to have been fairly friendly, but the Protestant clergy opposed Owen strongly. Finally, in May, 1823, he helped to found the Hibernian Philanthropic Society, with the support of Lord Cloncurry and a number of other notables. Again a subscription was opened, but the Society expired after Owen's return to England. His brief visit, however, bore fruit later in the Ralahine community of 1831.[2]

[1] Account in *Robert Owen's Journal*, various issues, 1851–2.
[2] See p. 239.

I have called the *Report to the County of Lanark* the real beginning of Owenism as a social, or Socialist, system. Indeed, although it was addressed to an assembly of landowners and gentlemen, it was really the foundation of Owen's appeal to the workers. We have seen how the Radicals opposed him at his London meetings in 1817. Hunt and Hone had attended the meetings. Hone, in his *Reformists' Register*, had headed a leading article "Let Us Alone, Mr. Owen," and had written in this strain: "Robert Owen, Esq., a benevolent cotton-spinner, and one of His Majesty's Justices of the Peace for the county of Lanark, having seen the world, and afterwards cast his eye over his very well regulated manufactory in the said county, imagines he has taken a *New View of Society*, and conceives that all human beings are so many plants, which have been out of the earth for a few thousand years, and require to be reset. He accordingly determines to dibble them in squares after a new fashion; and to make due provision for removing the offsets. . . . I do not know a gentleman in England better satisfied with himself than Mr. Robert Owen. Everybody, I believe, is convinced of Mr. Owen's benevolence, and that he purposes to do us much good. I ask him to *let us alone*, lest he do us much mischief. . . ." And then, of Owen's Plan, he adds that "its leading principle, ALL THINGS IN COMMON, turns the whole country into a workhouse."[1]

William Cobbett, then in exile in America, wrote more brusquely still. "A Mr. Owen, of Lanark, has, it seems, been before the committee with his schemes, which are nothing short of a species of

[1] *Reformists' Register*, August 23, 1817.

monkery. This gentleman is for establishing innumerable *communities* of paupers! Each is to be resident in an *inclosure*, somewhat resembling a barrack establishment, only more extensive. I do not clearly understand whether the sisterhoods and brotherhoods are to form distinct communities, like the nuns and friars, or whether they are to mix together promiscuously; but I perceive that they are all to be under a very *regular discipline;* and that wonderful peace, happiness, and national benefit are to be the result! How the little matters of black eyes, bloody noses, and pulling of caps, are to be *settled*, I do not exactly see; nor is it explicitly stated whether the novices, when once they become confirmed, are to regard their character of pauper as indelible, though this is a point of great importance. Mr. Owen's scheme has, at any rate, the recommendation of perfect novelty; for of such a thing as a *community of paupers*, I believe no human being ever before heard. . . . Adieu, Mr. Owen of Lanark."[1] And elsewhere Cobbett referred contemptuously to "Mr. Owen's parallelograms of paupers."

Owen was fully conscious at this time of his lack of contact with the workers. "At this period," he wrote, "I had had no public intercourse with the operatives and working classes. . . . They were at this time strangers to me and to all my views and intentions. I was at all periods of my progress, from my earliest knowledge and employment of them, their true friend, while their democratic and much mistaken leaders taught them that I was their enemy, a friend to all in authority, and that I

[1] Cobbett's *Political Register*, August 2, 1817.

desired to make slaves of them in these villages of unity and mutual co-operation."[1]

The tone of this reflection, so clearly marking off the workers as a "they" distinct from Owen's "I," throws a light on his relations to the working-class movement, even at the time of his fullest absorption in it. He always thought of the workers as "they," and of himself as a being destined to serve them indeed, but of a different world. He would gladly sacrifice friends, fortune and reputation in their cause; but it was beyond his power to think of himself save as a benevolent being coming among *them* from another world.

Nevertheless, at least from 1820 onwards, Owen was rapidly gathering a large body of working-class disciples. He had first directly appealed to the workers in his *Address to the Working Classes* in 1819;[2] but the object of this had been rather to dissuade them from class-hostility to the rich than to stimulate action on their part. He adjured them, instead of cherishing feelings of anger towards the rich, to reassure them that no spoliation of their wealth was intended. "You will say to those who are now in possession of riches, honours, power and privileges, which they have been taught to value: 'Retain these in perfect security as long as you can hold them in estimation. Our whole conduct and proceedings shall be a pledge to you that we will never attempt to dispossess you of any part of them. . . . The cause of contest between us will henceforth cease. We have discovered its irrationality and utter uselessness. . . . The rich and the poor, the governors and the governed, have really but

---

[1] *Life*, p. 221.   [2] *Autobiography*, vol. IA, Appendix P.

one interest. . . . The notions and arrangements which at present prevail through society are necessarily destructive of the happiness of all ranks.' " Owen at this stage thought the rich, appealed to in these terms, would withdraw their opposition to the uplifting of the poor.

It is hardly surprising that the Radicals regarded Owen as merely another and a madder poor-law reformer like many they had known. The *Report to the County of Lanark,* and Owen's lectures during the next few years, put his proposals in a different light. These did not convert Hone or Hunt or Cobbett, or the older generation of Radicals, who were horrified at his notions of community of goods and united labour devoted to mass production—ideas which they, as lovers of the old peasant England of the past, regarded as monstrous subversions of liberty and mere variations on the evil theme of the new factory system. But among the younger workmen, who had perforce come to regard the new productive system as a fact to be accepted, Owenite ideas began to make rapid headway. In 1820 a small group of workmen met in London to discuss the new Co-operative principles. Their leader was George Mudie, a printer recently come from Scotland, and another was Henry Hetherington, afterwards famous as the oft-imprisoned publisher of the *Poor Man's Guardian,* and an active worker in the Chartist and other working-class movements. In the following year this group started the Co-operative and Economical Society, and Mudie started the *Economist,* the first definitely Owenite and Co-operative newspaper. It announced itself as "explanatory of the New System of Society projected by Robert Owen, Esq." It lasted for fifteen months, and ran into two volumes.

I have no intention, in this book, of attempting to tell the story of the rapid spread of this movement or of the allied working-class movements during the ensuing ten years. "From 1820 to 1830," writes G. J. Holyoake, "Co-operation and communities were regarded by the thinking classes as a religion of industry. Communities, the form which the religion of industry was to take, were from 1825 to 1830 as common and almost as frequently announced as joint stock companies now."[1] In fact, Societies based on Owenite principles sprang up in many parts of the country, and London had many experiments in Co-operative organisation.

This decade was indeed the seeding-time of all the great working-class movements. Hodgskin, driven by Birkbeck and Place from the control of the newly formed Mechanics' Institution in London—to which we find Owen lecturing in 1825— was delivering his lectures on "Popular Political Economy" and writing his *Labour Defended*. The Radical agitation in politics was gathering its forces for the struggle of 1830–1832, and preparing the ground for the Chartist movement. William Thompson, the economist, who was a disciple of Owen, published in 1822 his *Principles of the Distribution of Wealth* and in 1827 *Labour Rewarded*, in which he put forward practical plans for the formation of Co-operative communities on the Owenite principle. And younger men, such as William Lovett, the future secretary of the Chartist London Working Men's Association, eagerly drank in the

[1] Holyoake, *History of Co-operation*, p. 71.

Owenite gospel and set out to preach it as the basis of working-class action. In 1826 came the London Co-operative Society, of which Lovett became storekeeper, and in the following year the London Co-operative Community Fund Association, an attempt to raise capital for a Village of Co-operation in the neighbourhood of London, the Union Exchange Society, forerunner of Owen's own Labour Exchange of 1832, and the Brighton Co-operative Association. In 1828 William King and his associates in the Brighton Society started the *Co-operator*, best and most informative of the early Owenite papers. In 1830, according to the Brighton *Co-operator*, there were already three hundred Co-operative Societies scattered up and down the country. Of these we shall have something to say later. Here we need only record the extraordinarily rapid development of Owenism and Co-operation as a creed of the younger generation among the workers. For, although many of these bodies had some middle-class help, they were nearly all predominantly working-class.

During the years of most rapid advance after 1824, Owen was himself largely absent from England and almost completely out of touch with the practical movements instituted by his disciples. For in 1824, after his last agreement with his partners had practically taken the control of New Lanark out of his hands, he had gone to America, hoping to conquer the New World when the Old seemed to be failing him. In the United States there were already a number of "Communities," which, though they were based on religious principles, were in some respects like his proposed Villages of Co-operation. He had published in

1818 a pamphlet, by a Quaker named W. S. Warder, describing one of these, "The Religious Society of the People called Shakers." Another religious community, the Rappites, led by George Rapp, an emigrant from Würtemberg, had settled in Indiana, on the Wabash, and had called its settlement "Harmony." The Rappites in 1824 desired to move to a new site, and Owen heard that their village and lands were for sale as they stood. He left at once for America to inspect them, and speedily made up his mind to buy the entire estate, which he renamed "New Harmony," and proposed to make the seat of the first real attempt to put his theories into execution.

The community of New Harmony is dealt with in the next chapter. Here what concerns us is only that it absorbed nearly the whole of Owen's attention during the period from 1824 to 1829. He came back to England for brief visits in 1825 and 1827; but for the rest of the time he was in America, either lecturing or attending to the affairs of the new community. In 1825 he severed his managerial connection with New Lanark. His sons settled in New Harmony and became American citizens. Mrs. Owen went on living at Braxfield until 1828, when Owen finally sold his shares in New Lanark, and financial stringency caused her and his daughters to seek a smaller house. His daughter Anne died in October, 1830, and in the following spring Mrs. Owen died.[1]

It is extraordinarily difficult, though some of their letters have survived, to grasp the relations

---

[1] Mary, Owen's youngest daughter, died in 1832, and his only surviving daughter, Jane, then joined her brothers at New Harmony.

between Owen and his wife during the later years of their married life. While her husband pursued his public plans, first in London and on his tours throughout the country, and then in America, Mrs. Owen remained at home in New Lanark, not even accompanying her sisters on their continental journey in 1818. From 1813 onwards Owen was from home a great deal of the time, and from 1824 to 1829 he paid only flying visits to Scotland. Even after his return to Great Britain in 1829, he was almost wholly in London or in various parts of England lecturing, and his wife and daughters saw practically nothing of him. He and his wife corresponded regularly, and it is quite clear from their letters that there was no quarrel, and even no coldness between them; but the fact remains that Owen had apparently no need of his wife's companionship. He writes to her reporting his public doings and commenting on men and affairs—affectionately in a way, but seeming to take her and their affection pretty much as a matter of course. Her letters, reporting such small concerns as her life offered, and dwelling especially on the poor health of their daughter Anne, can only be described as plaintive. Again and again she speaks of her need for him, and urges him to come to her. "Oh, my dear husband, how much I feel the want of you to advise with in a time of so much anxiety.[1] . . . . I hope you will remember next Thursday, the day when we became *one*—thirty-one years ago, and I think from what I feel myself that we love one another as sincerely and understand one another much better than we did thirty-one years ago. My

[1] In connection with Anne's illness.

sincere wish is that nothing may ever happen to diminish this affection."[1]

Caroline Owen loved her husband; but she had the sense of his neglecting her. She had, of course, never entered into his views, and his religious opinions had deeply shocked her. It must have grieved her, too, when her sons, and at least one of the daughters, Jane, followed Owen's creed rather than hers. Perhaps the divergence of views helped to account for the growing distance between husband and wife. But I think the true explanation is rather different. From the time when Owen threw himself into the public advocacy of his plans, he had no room in his mind for anything else. Hazlitt called him "a man of one idea," and he accepted the phrase and justified what it implied.[2] But there was more in it than this. Like a character in one of the stories of Henry James, I believe that Owen, from the time when he became a public man, ceased to have any "private life." He lived in and for his idea; apart from it he virtually ceased to exist at all. He became a humanitarian, and lost his humanity. The "man of one idea" went far to spoil the idea by straining it too far and placing too much weight upon it. And, by the same strain, he went even further towards spoiling the man. He became an embodied principle, and forgot his wife. One affection only the universal benevolence for humanity could not drive out. He remained a great lover of children—actual human children, and not merely childhood in the abstract. This stayed with

[1] Letter 233 in Co-operative Union Collection, dated April 23, 1830.
[2] *Life*, p. 105.

him till the end; but for the rest I feel he became in his later years less a man than a walking principle, and that this goes far to account for his failures. He made his world cold with universal benevolence; and the Spiritualism of his old age was a belated grasping after the warm human contacts he had sacrificed to his conception of "the cause." He would have been a better prophet, and more a man, if he had known how to do things by halves. But that the "man of one idea" could never do.

CHAPTER XIV

NEW HARMONY

Of the many Communities or Villages of Co-operation established during his lifetime, Owen was directly connected with only two—New Harmony and Queenwood. Orbiston in Scotland was started by a body of his disciples while he was absent in America; Ralahine in Cork was opened in 1831, when Owen was busy preparing the ground in England for the great working-class movements of the following years. With these, and with many less important experiments in community-making, he had nothing to do personally, though of course his influence counted for a great deal with the promoters. And, of the two Communities in whose organisation he played a personal part, his connection was much the closer with New Harmony, of which he was the sole founder and for a considerable period chief controller.

As we have seen, Owen bought New Harmony in 1825 from the Rappites—a religious community of German peasants who had lived there a frugal, but apparently contented and modestly prosperous existence. He paid £30,000 for the property, just as it stood—lands, village, and such equipment as the Rappites did not take with them to their new home. Harmony, as it was then called, was an estate of some 30,000 acres in Posey County, Indiana, on the banks of the River Wabash, which flows into the Ohio. The soil was good, and there was excellent pasture and orchard land. The village was substantially built, and included, besides community buildings and cottages, various industrial undertakings—a silk mill and a woollen mill among them. It had served for some time as a local market centre for the sparse population of the surrounding district.

Why did Owen choose the United States as the field for his first experiment? To some extent, no doubt, the choice was a matter of chance. The Rappite colony was in the market, and there were obvious advantages in starting on a site already laid out and cleared and actually developed for the purposes of an enterprise in some degree resembling that which he proposed. But there were other reasons. The New World had a glamour of its own. It was less, Owen thought, under the domination of commercialism and class hostility, nearer to a natural order of society, less involved in its own prejudices and dissensions. Vested interests were there far fewer and weaker; there would be less distractions and less obstructions to contend with. In the vast spaces of the New World men breathed a freer air. Convention was less importunate; it was easier to set about doing a new thing in a novel way. In those days, men went to America in order to escape from commercialism.

Moreover, America had been already the scene of many experiments in community-making. The Rappite colony was not the only self-governing settlement conducted largely on a communist basis. There were several other religious communities working along similar lines, including the Shakers, of whose settlement Owen had already published a detailed account by a Quaker visitor. And, apart from these largely communistic peasant villages, there was nothing new to Englishmen in the idea of group colonisation in the United States. Morris Birkbeck and others had led bodies of emigrants who had settled down together in new communities, farming the land, indeed, on an individualistic system, but closely united for mutual help and social relationships. Cobbett, a few years earlier, had written from his farm in Long Island, whither he had removed out of the reach of Sidmouth's "Gagging Bills," to advise emigrants from Great Britain to come singly and settle down among the Americans instead of attempting to make national communities of their own;[1] but his attack on the practice serves to show that it was a familiar plan.

Nor was Owen even the first to dream the dream of an ideal community built up as an object lesson to the world in the free democratic atmosphere of the American States. On the morrow of the French Revolution, Coleridge, Southey and Wordsworth had planned to found Pantisocracy on the banks of the Susquehannah, their minds turning naturally from superstition-ridden England to the undeveloped new lands in which all things were possible. Owen felt a kindred impulse. Let London reject him, or merely talk round and round his plan without any real attempt to put it into practice. London, even the whole country of Great Britain, was too deeply sunk in commercialism for the new ways of living to be easily learnt in such uncongenial surroundings. Environment was the master of man; and in the new world Owen could make the environment to suit his plan.

[1] Cobbett, *A Year's Residence in America.*

Impulses such as these must have moved him when he bought Harmony from the Rappites. Indeed, certain of his own utterances make this fairly plain. He began his work in America with a round of lectures, and in his very first lectures, delivered in the Hall of Representatives at Washington, in the presence of the President of the United States and many of the leading politicians and public men, he gave an explicit statement of his reasons for choosing America as a field for propaganda and experiment. He was already well known in the United States, and a Society for Promoting Communities based on his principles had been started in New York in 1821 or 1822. He had, too, the benefit of being known by many who had visited, or heard reports of, New Lanark as one of the greatest of British manufacturers and philanthropists. His good repute had preceded him to America; his subsequent break with the Church and its supporters had neither penetrated there to any great extent, nor would it in any case have counted against him as it counted in Great Britain.

In the *Discourses on a New System of Society*, with which his American campaign opened, Owen began with a retrospective account of his own career. He told the story of his success as a manufacturer, of his social work at New Lanark, and of his mission as the apostle of the "new social system." In the matter of theory there was nothing new in these *Discourses*. They embodied a brief exposition on familiar lines of his own philosophy and proposals, followed by an outline of his plans and his motives in choosing America for the scene of his first great experiment. "By a hard struggle," he said, "you have attained political liberty, but you have yet to

242

acquire real mental liberty, and, if you cannot possess yourselves of it, your political liberty will be precarious and of much less value."[1] He denounced "the whole trading system" as "one of deception," and announced that he proposed to inaugurate the new system of community at New Harmony "on my own private responsibility, or with partners having the same principles and feelings with myself; or by the joint stock companies, under an act of incorporation from the state governments of Indiana and Illinois." He thus invited co-operation, expressing his usual confidence in the immediate and overwhelming success of his plan, and adding naïvely that he was "desirous that the knowledge of this change being about to commence should be speedily known over the Union, that as little capital as possible should be lost by its application to objects which might be rendered of no value by the new measures which may be soon carried into extensive execution in all the states."[2] Finally, Owen invited "the industrious and well-disposed of all nations" to come to New Harmony, and play their part in inaugurating the new order of society.

Owen followed up these lectures with others in other cities, and, as soon as New Harmony was opened, under the initial charge of his son William, settlers began to flock in. Eight hundred arrived in the first few weeks, long before proper arrangements could be made for their reception, or for setting them systematically to work. There was practically no selection of recruits: anyone who felt like coming came, and expected to find all ready for his reception. William Owen wrote to his father

[1] *First Discourse*, p. 11. [2] *Ibid.*, p. 14.

entreating him to stop this indiscriminate flow of settlers, and concentrate on securing the various types of skilled craftsmen who were urgently needed.[1] There was an acute shortage of housing room already, and great difficulty in getting building materials, as well as a dearth of skilled labour. This letter was written to Owen in England, where he had gone on a visit in the late summer of 1825 after setting the preliminary arrangements in train.

Socially and educationally, better progress was made. The schools were already in good order when all else was in confusion, and concerts, recreations and sports were speedily set going on the model of New Lanark. But the economic problem was far harder to tackle away in the wilds of Indiana, where nearly everything had to be made on the spot, as supplies could only be procured with great difficulty from outside. The surprising thing is that the Community did not break down under the strain of these early months. Instead, order was gradually introduced, and when Owen returned at the beginning of 1826, matters were going smoothly and with apparent success.

Owen had intended that, for the first three years, New Harmony should remain under his personal control, without any democratic government by the settlers, or any complete application of the principles of community. But, apparently pleased by what he found on his return, or urged on by enthusiasts among the settlers, he changed his mind, and, immediately on his arrival, a committee was appointed to draw up a constitution. This took shape in a plan of pure community,

[1] The greater part of the letter is quoted by Podmore, p. 295.

based on the full equality of all the settlers. The village was divided into six departments: agriculture; manufactures; literature, science, and education; domestic economy; general economy; and commerce. Each department chose an intendant, who in turn chose four superintendents—these officers together forming the governing council of New Harmony. Amid great enthusiasm the constitution was adopted, and for a time Owen's energy and practical capacity as a manager made the whole village, at least on the surface, into a contented and well-regulated Community.[1]

But already the seeds of dissension were being sown. Owen had brought back with him from Europe a number of influential disciples, including William Maclure of Ayr, who put a substantial capital sum into the venture. Most of these European friends concerned themselves mainly with the schools; but theoretical differences soon appeared. One, a Captain Macdonald, refused to accept the constitution on the ground that it involved elections and representative government, which were fatal to the free spirit of community and equality. Before long the objection to the elective system, and perhaps some practical difficulties in its working, led to a positive though amicable split, and two groups of settlers formed, on outlying parts of the estate, distinct subordinate communities of their own, governed not by elected leaders, but by a council of all the members

[1] The evidence for this is partly in the *New Harmony Gazette*, the magazine of the Community, and partly in private letters from the settlers—*e.g.* the letter of W. Pelham, quoted by Podmore, p. 302. See also R. D. Owen, *Threading My Way*.

between certain ages. One of these, Macluria, led by William Maclure, was governed by its five oldest members under sixty-five. This method was, indeed, based on that which Owen himself had advocated in his writings.[1] Religious differences also ministered to the division of the Community into smaller bodies, and further subordinate communities were soon founded. Macluria, however, subsequently reunited itself with the parent body.

From this point the history of New Harmony consists of a steady succession of constitutional changes, fresh experiments in division and reunion, and gradual relapse from the communal to an individualist system. In 1827 the village was reorganised into a number of separate societies based on occupation—a sort of Guild organisation apparently. But every attempt at reconstruction failed, principally because the settlers could not get on well enough together. There were wide social and racial differences which even faith in the new system could not overcome, and many of the settlers had not that faith. The curious can trace the detailed record of New Harmony in Podmore's *Life of Owen*, or in one of the books describing the various community experiments in the United States.[2] The failure was from the first inevitable; for a small Community of idealists, each with his own set of theories and each compelled to put theory into instant practice over the whole field of life and in circumstances of exceptional difficulty, offers the very maximum of opportunity for quarrels and divisions. The surprising fact is not that New

[1] *E.g.* in the *Report to the County of Lanark*.
[2] Or, if they prefer original sources, in the *New Harmony Gazette*, the magazine published by the Community.

Harmony collapsed, but that it lasted so long, and that visitors and residents bear testimony to the fine spirit which prevailed there even amid the dissensions and confusions which brought it to an end.

In 1827, after the reorganisation of the Community on occupation lines, Owen again went off on a visit to England. He returned in 1828, and a survey of the prevailing conditions made him admit his failure. "I tried here a new course for which I was induced to hope that fifty years of political liberty had prepared the American population. . . . I supplied land, houses, and the use of much capital. . . . But experience proved that the attempt was premature to unite a number of strangers not previously educated for the purpose, who should carry on extensive operations for their common interest, and live together as a common family. I afterwards tried, before my last departure hence, what could be done by those who associated through their own choice and in small numbers; to these I gave leases of large tracts of good land for ten thousand years upon a nominal rent, and for moral conditions only. . . . Now upon my return I find that the habits of the individual system were so powerful that these leases have been, with a few exceptions, applied for individual purposes and individual gain, and in consequence they must return into my hands." Owen's conclusion was that men could not be fitted to live in community save by precedent moral training. He therefore decided "to form such arrangements on the estate of Harmony as will enable those who desire to promote the practice of the Social System to live in separate families on the individual system, and yet to unite their general labour, or to exchange labour for labour on the most beneficial terms for all, or to do both or neither as their feelings and apparent interests may influence them."[1] In other words, he wound up the Community, leasing land still to such as wished to go on along more or less communal lines, or selling outright to such as wished to purchase. A good deal of land was thus sold. A large tract, however, remained in Owen's ownership, and was later transferred by him to his four sons, who all remained at New Harmony after the collapse, and became American citizens. When the whole affair was wound up, and a dispute about money with Maclure, who had joined with him in financing the enterprise, had been settled by arbitration in Owen's favour, he had lost about £40,000, four-fifths of his whole fortune, in the New Harmony experiment.

The terms in which Owen commented on the failure of New Harmony indicated that he had not lost faith in his plan for solving the social problem. Indeed, immediately on his return to England, he plunged into a new adventure, far more extraordinary than the purchase of New Harmony. He had made up his mind that his plans stood the best chance of realisation in the New World, less deeply rooted than the Old in the errors which he sought to destroy. He had failed in the United States; but he might succeed on the territory of the Mexican Republic, where large tracts of undeveloped land were being made over by the Government to promising concessionaires or bodies

---

[1] *New Harmony Gazette*, vol. iii. p. 204 (quoted Podmore, p. 322).

of settlers. He approached the Mexican Minister in London, whom he knew, and was most politely discouraged. But it was useless to discourage Owen, and he got his letters to the Mexican Government recommending his plan, and set out for Mexico. On the way, he stopped at Jamaica, and contrasted the comparatively prosperous and happy condition of the slaves with the condition of the factory workers in England. "The West Indian 'slave,' as he is called, is greatly more comfortable and happy than the British or Irish operative manufacturer or day-labourer."[1] He urged the abolitionists not to disturb these comparatively happy conditions. Most masters treated their slaves well; for they knew it was to their interest to do so.[2]

Owen found Mexico in a state of revolution. But this did not deter him. He tried to convert Santa Anna, the military leader, to his views, and believed in later years that he had done so. He even obtained from the Mexican Government a conditional promise of a large tract in Texas, then Mexican territory, for his experiment. The condition was the passing by the Mexican Congress of an Act establishing freedom of religious worship. But the Bill was thrown out, and the proposed concession came to nothing. After addressing Santa Anna and his generals at length on the new views, Owen left Mexico for the United States, where he was due to hold a debate on his religious views with a Universalist minister, the Rev. Alexander Campbell, at Cincinnati. Admiral Fleming, British naval

[1] *British Co-operator*, 1830, p. 93.
[2] Cobbett took much the same line against the abolitionists. See my *Life of Cobbett*, p. 257. Captain Marryat, in *Newton Forster*, presents a similar picture.

commander in the West Indies, and a personal friend of Owen, conveyed him from Mexico to New Orleans on a British warship.

From April 13 to April 21, 1829, Owen and Campbell held debate. Or rather, each in turn discoursed on the matters he believed to be at issue between them. Owen expounded his new system and its "twelve fundamental laws," and laid bare the errors inherent in all religious systems; Campbell spoke of the evidences for the truth of the Christian religion, and seasoned his discourse with a little abuse of Owenism. Neither answered the other's arguments, or made more than an occasional excursion on to common ground. Yet a thousand people listened to this unending flow of words, which makes a closely printed report of nearly five hundred and fifty pages.[1]

Among the audience at this astonishing tourney was Mrs. Trollope, mother of Anthony Trollope the novelist. She was astonished at the good reception given to Owen, when he ventured to question the fundamental doctrines of Christianity; but she saw that Owen's personality was the cause. "Never did anyone practise the *suaviter in modo* with more powerful effect than Mr. Owen. The gentle tone of his voice, his mild, sometimes playful, but never ironical, manner, the absence of every vehement or harsh expression, the affectionate interest expressed for 'the whole human family,' the air of candour with which he expressed the wish to be convinced he was wrong, if he indeed were so, his kind smile, the mild expression of his eyes—in short, his whole manner disarmed zeal, and produced a degree of

[1] *Debate on the Evidences of Christianity between Robert Owen and Alexander Campbell.*

tolerance that those who did not hear him would hardly believe possible."[1] Nevertheless, Owen's proposition, put by Mr. Campbell to the audience in the misleading form of a purely negative disbelief in the Christian religion, appears to have attracted only three votes. Owen, who put no proposition to the meeting, expressed himself as "much pleased with Mr. Campbell's little manœuvre, because I discover it pleases him and his friends. Truth requires no such support."[2]

From Cincinnati Owen proceeded to Washington, where he again visited the President of the United States, Andrew Jackson, and offered his services as mediator in the disputes with Great Britain. Bearing letters for the American Minister in London, he then returned to England, and interviewed the Foreign Secretary, Lord Aberdeen, with the result, by his own account, that the troubles between Great Britain and the United States were amicably settled.[3]

[1] Mrs. Trollope, *Domestic Manners of the Americans.*
[2] *Debate*, p. 446.
[3] *London Investigator*, vol. iii. p. 247.

CHAPTER XV

THE LABOUR EXCHANGE AND THE BUILDERS' GUILD

The years of Owen's absence in America were, as we have seen, a period of intense activity for the British working class. The growth of Owenism and Co-operation during this period, however, was confined to comparatively narrow circles, and hardly touched the great factory districts of the north of England. The great mass of the working class was engrossed in the struggle for political reform, and this struggle, while it played a great part in stimulating the capacity for organisation and in setting men to thought about social and economic problems, did not call into being any widespread movement under purely working-class auspices. The manufacturers and the middle classes as well as the workers wanted Parliamentary Reform; and, apart from a few outstanding figures such as Cobbett, the leaders of the Reform movement tended to be men drawn from these classes. While the workers and the middle classes were fighting in alliance for what seemed a common object, it was inevitable that the better educated and more freely circumstanced groups should take the lead.

Nevertheless, the Reform agitation furnished a stimulus by the aid of which independent working-class organisation rapidly developed. Organised by the reformers for political purposes, the workers in the factory districts turned their awakening to use in the forming also of more stable Trade Unions and other working-class societies. The repeal of the Combination Acts in 1824 enabled them to organise openly for industrial purposes; and, though the Trade Union Act of that year was passed under peculiar conditions and was repealed the following year in favour of a far less liberal measure, the prohibition of combination itself was not reimposed, and Trade Unions were enabled to organise on a more permanent and stable basis than before. The great outburst of strikes which followed the Act of 1824 showed how large a volume of unrest existed among the workers, and prepared the way for the great awakening of the following decade.

Moreover, even those movements which were partly under the control of the middle-class Radicals made a great contribution to the development of consciousness among the workers. The formation of Mechanics' Institutes, which began at Glasgow under purely working-class auspices, was actively taken up by the political Radicals who, wresting the control of the projected London Mechanics' Institute from its original promoters, formed it in 1823 as a purely scientific institution under the patronage of the middle-class educational reformers. Dr. Birkbeck and Brougham took the lead in this development, and within a few years Mechanics' Institutes were set up in nearly every considerable town. Although these were non-political bodies, and any intrusion of advanced doctrines was strongly resisted by their promoters in many districts, they contributed a good deal to the awakening of working-class activity. Men could not come together for technical education, and consider the progress of machinery and the application of science to industry, without having their minds turned to working-class ˙ industrial and political problems.

The student of radical movements during the years of the Reform agitation will find no difficulty in tracing the steady and rapid development of a distinctive working-class point of view, and the growth of a tendency to shake off the tutelage of the Benthamites and Broughamites and other middle-class groups. He will discover it significantly illustrated in the controversy over the control of the Mechanics' Institutes, in which Brougham and Birkbeck, aided by Francis Place, were victorious over J. C. Robertson and Thomas Hodgskin, despite the backing given to the latter by Cobbett in the *Political Register*. He will find it in the growth of distinct working-class political bodies, such as the Society for Radical Reform, which was formed in 1829, and the much larger and more influential National Union of the Working Classes, which arose out of it two years later, and was the direct progenitor of the Chartist movement. He will find it in the writings of men like Thomas Hodgskin, who proclaim labour, as the source of all wealth, entitled to the full product of its activity. And he will find it, last but not least, in the growth of the Co-operative and other Societies stimulated by the teachings of Robert Owen.

For, though Owenism as a theory aimed rather at the union of all the "industrious classes" than at any class action by the workers alone, the Owenism which gained ground rapidly during the twenties was of a different stamp. The men who founded Co-operative Societies for trade or propaganda after 1820, or started Owenite periodicals, were not all manual workers; but most of them were, and the driving force of the movement came from the working class. The Owenite doctrine of community had originally been put forward for adoption by the State and the benevolent rich. Its rejection in these high quarters set the intended beneficiaries thinking. "Why," they asked, "should we not do this thing for ourselves, making up by our numbers and solidarity for the lack of wealth and power?" The gospel of socialisation from above became in their minds a gospel of socialisation from below, to be achieved, from small beginnings, by the voluntary co-operation of the poor.

The beginnings were small indeed—far too small to attract any notice in the world of great affairs. The newspapers were far too full of the Reform agitation and the growth of Trade Unions to notice the small, quiet growth of Co-operative organisation. The mass of the workers had certainly never heard of Owenism or Co-operation until 1830, and the idea was thoroughly novel to many of the Trade Unions even in 1832. But the growth was none the less significant; for it ran parallel with the growth of a distinctive working-class consciousness, and the growing cleavage between the middle-class and the working-class reformers was steadily preparing the way for its more widespread acceptance. The Whig advocates of Parliamentary Reform had no intention of enfranchising the manual workers; and the middle-class Radicals, even if they were theoretical advocates of Manhood or Household Suffrage, had no intention of standing out for it against a compromise which would place power in the hands of the middle class. It was becoming, as Reform drew nearer, more and more evident that its certain effect would be only the dethronement of the landed oligarchy and the transference of power to the rising lords of industrial capitalism. The working-class leaders, even when they saw this, mostly supported the Reform Bill as a necessary step towards fuller emancipation. But it became clear that Reform would be only the beginning of a long further struggle, and that the workers needed separate organisation for the expression of their own needs and policy.

It is often suggested that the great agitation which followed the Reform Act, and passed during the next twenty years through its successive phases of Owenism and Chartism, was the result of the workers' disillusionment with the results of the Reform that had been carried through largely by their efforts. This is only half true. The forces that went to the making of the Grand National Consolidated Trades Union and the Chartist movement were rapidly gaining power and direction while the Reform struggle was still at its height. Until Reform was over and done with, they could not find expression in a mass movement of independent action; but all the ingredients were ready some years before the explosion actually occurred.

Owen came back to England, after the collapse of his experiment at New Harmony, just at the most critical period in this evolution of working-class consciousness. The two culminating years of the Reform agitation were also the years when the new forces began to take hold on the great masses of the factory workers and artisans. Circumstances, rather than his own volition, placed him at the head of the growing movement. He became its leader because his ideas were the one coherent expression of a widespread sentiment. The reaction against political compromise, and in favour of working-class self-help and direct economic action, found in him the man who seemed to express its aspirations in a new and appealing social system.

The years following Owen's return to England in 1829 were thus the busiest and most immediately influential of his life. He had finally left New Lanark in 1828, and his family was now living in a small house in Hamilton. The greater part of his property had been sunk in New Harmony, and much of it irretrievably lost. He had ceased to have much contact with Cabinet Ministers, bishops and members of the governing class, or with the em-ployers, who now regarded him as a dangerous lunatic. Putting no trust in purely political mea-sures or in parliamentary forms of government, he felt no desire to take part in the Reform agitation, then moving swiftly towards its climax, and occu-pying the first place in the thoughts of the active majority in all classes. Through all his incessant activities from 1829 to 1832, hardly a reference can be traced to the Reform movement, or even to such outstanding events as the Bristol Riots or the sack of Nottingham Castle. This, however, does not at all mean that he was playing only a minor part.

When Owen returned from America, Owenism, conceived now as a working-class gospel of Social-ism and Co-operation, had already made great headway. The pioneer Co-operative Societies and journals described in an earlier chapter, and the writings of Owenite Socialists such as William

Thompson, had exerted a steadily growing influence on the younger Trade Unionists and working-class leaders. Especially from 1828 onwards, largely under the influence of William King and the Brighton *Co-operator*, Co-operative Societies of every sort and kind multiplied with extraordinary rapidity, and many of them were based upon, and some almost indistinguishable from, Trade Unions.

Nowadays, when we speak of a Co-operative Society, we think primarily of a shop or store founded on mutual principles for the retailing of groceries and other household commodities. We may know, indeed, that there are other sorts of "Co-ops.," including a number of Societies of Producers associated for the making of boots or clothing or other commodities under conditions of democratic self-government. But these play but a small part in the movement as a whole, and the typical "Co-op." is the Society of Consumers associated for retail trade.[1] Behind these actual trading operations looms, indeed, a wider social purpose—a more or less clearly formulated faith in a new social order based on production for use instead of profit; and this social basis of Co-operation is an essential factor in its trading success and working-class appeal. But retail mutual trade is its principal business, and gives to the movement its characteristic structure and outlook.

In the days of which we are speaking, Co-operation had not settled down into its modern shape, or acquired a traditional structure. The object of the

[1] The great Co-operative Wholesale Societies with their productive departments are, of course, also Societies of Consumers, based primarily on the federation of the local retail stores.

founders of the early Co-operative Societies was primarily to give practical effect to the principles of Owenism. Most of them laid down definitely in their rules that their purpose was to found, or take part in founding, a Community or Village of Co-operation on the Owenite model. If they engaged in retail trade, as, except the Societies based directly on Trade Unions, most of them did, they sold goods to their members only as a means of diverting the profit of the middleman into a common fund which would thus be made available for the starting of a Community. Their activities were quite as much educational and propagandist as commercial; their aim was the creation of the New Society by their associated effort.

The Societies based directly on Trade Unions were in some degree different. When a body of fellow-craftsmen joined to form a Co-operative Society, their aim was necessarily to sell their goods, not to one another, but to the outside public. The initial purpose of these Societies of Producers was the same as that of the other Owenite bodies—the establishment of the new system on a basis of community; but their different origin and membership caused them to develop in a different way. They were brought more directly into connection with the day-to-day struggle of the workers for better wages and conditions and for the right of Trade Union combination; and they naturally related their action as Co-operators to their action as Trade Unionists, and tried to make Owenism serve them as a weapon in the struggle. The Consumers' Societies could only look forward to founding a Community when they had accumulated a substantial fund by mutual trade; the Trade Unionist

259

Co-operators did not see why they should not begin at once, within the limits of their own craft, to put the new principles into practice. Especially there was a strong inducement, when a dispute with their employers led to a strike or lock-out, to try to dispense with the need for any employer by founding a Co-operative Society to produce the goods.

Up to the time of Owen's return from America, the Societies which were formed were almost all of the mixed type. They were little groups of devotees, laying up store by mutual trade for the founding of Communities, and meanwhile pushing on their propagandist and educational work. Only about 1830 did the Trade Unions begin seriously to take up the new ideas, and found Societies of the "producer" type. And only when the movement spread to the Trade Unions did it acquire a real momentum, and come to be more than the peculiar creed of a small body of enthusiasts.

Owen's attention was speedily drawn to the rapid growth of his ideas, in the new shapes which they had acquired during his years of absence. "When Mr. Owen first came over from America," William Lovett wrote in his *Autobiography*, "he looked somewhat coolly on these 'Trading Associations,' and very candidly declared that their mere buying and selling formed no part of his grand co-operative scheme; but when he found that great numbers among them were disposed to entertain many of his views, he took them more into favour, and ultimately took an active part among them."[1] This change of attitude seems, in fact, to have developed side by side with the change in the nature

[1] Lovett, *Autobiography*, p. 43.

of the Co-operative Societies themselves. The Producers' Societies offered to Owen's optimism a prospect, which he could not find in the mere "Trading Associations," of rapidly altering the basis of society from capitalism to Co-operation. He began to see the vision which, a few years later, took shape in the Grand National Guild of Builders and the Grand National Consolidated Trades Union.

Producers' Societies were obviously far harder to set going than mutual Trading Associations. The latter had merely to buy wholesale a certain quantity of provisions and retail these to their own members; the Producers' Societies had to find a market outside. Very early in their development, the idea arose of a central exchange or bazaar, to which the products of each Society could be sent, and from which the members of each Society could buy what they required in exchange for the goods deposited. As early as the spring of 1830 the British Association for Promoting Co-operative Knowledge, founded as the central body for the Co-operative movement in 1829, opened an Exchange Bazaar in London.

But, while the newer recruits to Co-operation were developing action along these lines, the older plans of the movement were still being pushed forward. In May, 1831, the first Co-operative Congress[1] was held in Manchester, and it was resolved to take steps towards the founding of a Community of Mutual Co-operation. The idea was that two hundred Co-operative Societies should each subscribe £30, and send one of their members to be a citizen of the first Community. Owen dis-

---

[1] The Congresses were held half-yearly.

approved of the scheme, on the ground that the resources behind it were inadequate. At the second Congress, held in Birmingham in October, 1831, his name was added to the committee; but he withdrew. The third Congress, held in London in May, 1832, had to record the failure of the project. Only one Society had subscribed £6 on account, and one other promised to subscribe. The nascent Co-ops. of those years needed all the resources they could gather for their own internal development and for local propaganda.

Inevitably, the idea of founding a Community began to drop into the background, and more and more stress was laid on that side of the movement which was making the greatest practical advances. Early in 1832 a certain William King, apparently no connection of the Dr. King who had been the leader of the Brighton Co-operators and one of the chief inspirers of the movement's rapid growth, founded a second Labour Exchange at Gothic Hall in the New Road. But far more ambitious than either of these was Owen's own venture. In September, 1832, the National Equitable Labour Exchange began business in large premises in the Gray's Inn Road.

We have seen, in dealing with Owen's *Report to the County of Lanark*,[1] that as early as 1820 he had not only put forward the theory that labour is the true measure of the value of commodities, but also urged the practical application of the principle to commercial dealings. If the average physical power of a man or a horse could be calculated, so, he urged, could average human labour-power; and the correct way of valuing commodities, which

[1] See p. 222.

would render "all individual bargaining unnecessary," was by calculating the amount of average human labour-power incorporated in each commodity offered for sale. This principle he now sought to express in practice through the Labour Exchange. The new currency of "Labour Notes," which he issued from the Exchange, was the expression of the new measure of value.

Owen's "Labour Notes" have been often misunderstood. He did not propose to value, and he did not actually value, all goods solely in accordance with the number of hours spent in producing them. Apart from the value of the material, which was calculated in money at current market prices, he recognised different kinds of labour as differing in value, accepting as the basis of differentiation the actual money rates of wages payable to various types of workers. The price of an article was calculated by adding together the money value of the material, the current time-wages for the hours spent on the work, and a penny in the shilling for the expenses of the Exchange. The total in pence was then divided by 6, 6*d.* being taken as the average price of an hour's labour. The result of this sum was the number of hours of "labour-time" incorporated in the article. Thus materials 6*s.*, six hours' skilled labour at 1*s.* per hour = 6*s.*, commission 1*d.* per 1*s.* = 1*s.*; total 13*s.*, which, at 6*d.* per hour = 26 hours of labour-time.

Nothing would have been either lost or gained by this translation or re-translation of pounds, shillings and pence into labour-time, if the goods had really been worth the sums asked for them. But some were worth more and some less, and there appears to have been no adequate arrangement for valuation on the basis of what Marx subsequently called "socially necessary labour-time." One man might take twelve hours to make what another would make in six; and, while for some articles it was fairly easy to fix a standard time allowance, for others there was nothing for it but to accept the estimate of the maker. Thus some articles were priced too high and some too low; and when the Exchange opened, naturally people bought what was cheap, and left what was dear on the hands of the promoters. And, as the Exchange did not stand to make a profit in any case, it could not afford to make a loss.

It took time, however, for these defects to appear. For a time the Exchange seemed a triumphant success. Goods were both deposited in large quantities, some by individual Owenites and Trade Unionists, and some by the various Societies of Co-operative producers—tailors, bootmakers, carpenters, hatters, and the like. Sales too went on briskly; for those who deposited goods also bought goods made by workers in other trades, and there was also good custom from the general public. In December, 1832, a branch was opened for South London at the Rotunda in the Blackfriars Road, then a favourite meeting-place for all sections of the working-class movement. A similar establishment in Liverpool followed soon after, and other branches and independent exchanges sprang up elsewhere. But before this the parent body had been evicted from its premises in the Gray's Inn Road, as the result of a dispute with the landlord, who, after demanding a heavy rent, turned the Exchange out, and started a rival venture of his own. Owen's Exchange found new premises in Charlotte Street, Fitzroy Square, long to be the centre of Owenite activities in London.

Owen's "Labour Notes" have often been held up to ridicule. But, in the circumstances of the time, they were by no means so fantastic as they appear to-day. Private banks had everywhere their own issues of notes, which passed current only within a limited area; and in some cases the shortage of cash, especially during the Napoleonic Wars, had led private employers to issue special currencies of their own for the payment of wages. Owen's notes were distinctive in that they professed to be based on a new standard of value; but there was nothing very startling for those days in the mere fact that a private issue of notes was made. Indeed, there is clear evidence that the "Labour Notes" for a time were fairly widely accepted in London, not only by supporters of the new system, but even by ordinary tradesmen.

At Charlotte Street, in July, 1833, the Labour Exchange passed under new management. It was taken over from Owen by the United Trades Association, a federation of a considerable number of Trade Unions in London. Each of the Unions concerned, which included carpenters, painters, glaziers, sawyers, tailors, shoemakers, hatters, brass-workers and others, had instituted a fund, by means of a weekly levy, for providing productive work for its unemployed members. Thus the Trade Union was the Co-operative Society, and included production as one of its regular activities.

For a time, as we have seen, the Labour Exchange prospered. In 1833 a branch, which was in reality a quite separate enterprise, was set up in Birmingham, and for a time this too was successful.

But by the middle of 1834 business at both centres had considerably fallen off. The Birmingham branch wound itself up, paying all its debts in full, and sending a small surplus to the local hospital. The London body was not so happy in its ending, and Owen lost the whole of the considerable sum he had spent in its development. It seems clear that the London Exchange was in difficulties even before the great Trade Union crisis of 1834, with which we are about to deal; but it is most probable that what brought the Labour Exchange movement prematurely to an end was this crisis, in which, not only the great new Trade Union organisations, but also the greater number of the Owenite Co-operative experiments, were brought crashing to the ground.

In 1832, after a time of unparalleled political excitement, the Reform Act became law, and the first elections were held for the Reformed Parliament. The workers found themselves voteless, under a Government standing for the ideas and policy of the rising middle and employing class. The working-class groups which had opposed the alliance with the middle-class Radicals and desired to stand out for Annual Parliaments and Universal Suffrage gained immensely in power and influence; the rising excitement which had chiefly availed to push the King and the Lords into accepting Reform now expressed itself in the rapid development of the purely working-class Societies which stood for a more radical programme. The National Union of the Working Classes reached the greatest height of its activity and influence.

But, to a still greater extent, the workers, disappointed of their immediate hopes of political enfranchisement, turned their thoughts to industrial organisation. The Reformed Parliament, it was clear, would do nothing against the capitalists; for it represented largely their point of view. In the economic sphere, it appeared, the workers must act and agitate for themselves, and the Trade Union must be their principal instrument. There set in a feverish fit of Trade Union organisation.

In order that this movement may be clearly understood, it is necessary to recall a few earlier facts. In 1824 the repeal of the Combination Acts had for the first time set the workers free to organise openly on Trade Union lines. There were, of course, many Trade Unions before this; but they were nearly all small and local, and confined to a single trade. The idea of a "General Union" embracing workers of every trade and grade had, indeed, been preached here and there even in the days of the Combination Acts, and in 1818 John Gast, the leader of the London shipwrights and one of the chief figures in London Radical working-class circles, had actually formed "The Philanthropic Hercules, for the mutual support of the labouring mechanics"—the first recorded attempt at a general "Trades Union." Again in 1826 a similar attempt had been made in Manchester, and in 1829 John Doherty of Manchester had organised the cotton-spinners in Scotland as well as the north of England into a "Grand General Union of the United Kingdom," and had followed up this important step by helping to form, in 1830, the National Association for the Protection of Labour—the first widespread federation of Unions representing workers in many different trades and industries. The Association spread rapidly in Lancashire and Yorkshire, and conducted a highly successful newspaper of its own, under the title first of the *United Trades Co-operative Journal* and then of the *Voice of the People*. But before long it began to break up. The Lancashire section seems to have disappeared, leaving the great Spinners' Union as the outstanding society in the county. The Yorkshire section held together, and, as the "Leeds, Huddersfield and Bradford District Union," played its part in the troubles of the next few years.

Meanwhile, other big Unions were springing up. The Potters' Union, set up by Doherty in 1830, had branches in Newcastle-on-Tyne, Bristol, Derby and Manchester as well as Stoke-on-Trent. The great Builders' Union, formed probably in 1831 or 1832, united into a single body the separate national societies already created by some of the separate crafts, and swept into its net a host of small local trade clubs and societies. The agitation for an effective Factory Act set the textile workers busy organising Short-Time Committees throughout the Northern and Midland Counties. In 1830 "Tommy" Hepburn swept the miners of Northumberland and Durham into a single inclusive Union, which had a brilliant and troubled life of two years, before it was remorselessly crushed by the opposition of the coal-owners. Even the agricultural labourers in 1830–1831 flamed up into that "last revolt" which was remorselessly crushed by the Whig Government and the judges with the weapons of execution and transportation.

Most of the movements here described were primarily movements of direct economic revolt. The agricultural labourers wanted bread, the textile operatives higher wages and relief from long hours and evil factory conditions, the miners higher wages, shorter hours and some relief from the ghastly servitude of the pits. The builders and the potters, who were on the whole better off, saw their established trades threatened by new methods of work and the rise of large-scale employers or contractors. Each movement had its source in a positive economic grievance. But the men and women who flocked into the new Unions were in a highly impressionable condition, and their leaders had largely drunk of the new gospel of Owenite Co-operation. They felt the power of Union as a great new power, not to be confined within the limits of mere wage-bargaining or mere petitions to the middle-class Parliament for legal protection. The Union was the instrument through which they could act directly, and for themselves; and how could they employ it better than by following Owen's precept? Why should they not become their own masters, dispense with employers altogether, appropriate the whole produce of their collective labour, and exchange their products on fair terms one with another? Why wait for the slow coming of Owen's model communities? Why try to raise capital from the rich for starting Villages of Co-operation? Why not use the Union as a Co-operative Society or Guild, and so start at once the Millennium which their master, Owen, had so often proclaimed?

Owen and his disciples seized their chance. The little Owenite groups and societies became the missionaries of "Union" as well as Co-operation. Owen himself went ceaselessly up and down the country, lecturing and talking to the Union leaders. His correspondence, preserved at Manchester, is full of letters from his followers up and down the country reporting progress in converting the Unions to Socialism and asking his advice and help. From Manchester, Glasgow, Birmingham, Worcester, Nottingham, Derby, Stoke-on-Trent and a dozen other places; from builders, potters, glaziers, framework knitters and half a dozen other trades came proposals for Co-operative Societies, reports of such societies already formed, accounts of the conversion of the Trade Unions to Owenism, entreaties to Owen to come and lecture. Letters poured in from enthusiastic disciples, Union leaders, and active workers in every branch of the movement. Owen's prestige was tremendous; everywhere he had large and enthusiastic audiences and made converts to the new system. The factory operatives in the north, with some middle-class help, were agitating for Sadler's Ten Hour Bill. Owen in 1833 swung them off their feet and helped Doherty and others to organise the National Regeneration Society, which stood for nothing less than the eight hours' day, and meant to get it, if need were, by a universal strike. John Fielden, Cobbett's colleague as M.P. for Oldham, was almost the only manufacturing employer who backed Owen in this scheme. Oastler and the leaders of the Ten Hour movement looked askance at it. They had sowed the wind; they were like to reap the whirlwind.

By the middle of 1833, Owen had become established as the recognised leader of the Trade Union movement. The great stirring of the workers seized hold of his lively imagination, always ready to embrace millennial possibilities. The new era was dawning; within six months or a year the old system, with all its evils, would have passed away, and the new age of Co-operation would have begun. "You may accomplish this change for the whole population of the British Empire in less than five years, and essentially ameliorate the condition of the producing class throughout Great Britain and Ireland in less than five months." [1]

Among the many bodies which were at this time eagerly receptive of Owenite ideas was the great Operative Builders' Union, to which these words were addressed. The headquarters of the Builders' Union were at Birmingham, which was already a great centre of Owenite propaganda, and the home of a flourishing branch of the Labour Exchange. The Birmingham builders were at this time greatly under the influence of two young architects, Joseph Hansom and Edward Welsh, who were enthusiastic Co-operators. At their suggestion, strongly supported by James Morrison, editor of the *Pioneer*, the unofficial organ of the Union, Owen was invited to Birmingham to address the builders' delegates, representatives attending from Manchester as well as from the Midlands. Steps were taken in Birmingham to set going a Co-operative Society or Guild, and Owen set out on a round of lectures to the lodges of the Union throughout the country. In September the Grand Lodge, or "Builders' " Parliament, representative of the Union as a whole, met in Manchester. Owen's plan for a "Grand National Guild of Builders" had been previously circulated to the lodges, printed in full in the *Pioneer*, and expounded by Owen at a number of meetings. The Builders' Parliament, under Owen's guidance, spent a week in reorganising the Union

[1] *Address to the Operative Builders*, August 26, 1833, quoted from the *True Sun*, in Postgate's *Revolution*, p. 90.

on lines of "universal government," by which the various crafts were bound more firmly together into a single united body. It then adopted the plan for the National Guild,[1] and issued a "Friendly Declaration" announcing its new policy to the world. Sir Robert Peel, the declaration said, had given them the sound advice "to take our own affairs into our own hands."

"We have decided to follow this advice, and with this view we have formed ourselves into a National Building Guild of Brothers, to enable us to erect buildings of every description upon the most extensive scale in England, Scotland and Ireland." Then followed an outline, in the unmistakable Owenite style, of the advantages which would follow this course of action. The Guild would build better and cheaper than any master builder; it would support all its members and their families in infancy, sickness and old age; it would prevent unemployment by providing work for its unemployed numbers in erecting "superior dwellings and other buildings for themselves," and so raise the standard of life and ensure that the builders, their wives and their children "may live continuously surrounded by those virtuous external circumstances which alone can form an intelligent, prosperous, good and happy population"; it would enable just remuneration to be fixed "for the services of the Brethren according to their skill and conduct when employed by the public"; it would decide on the amount of work to be done; it would provide for the "re-education" of all the Brethren and the acquisition of new and better habits, and for placing all their children under instruction which would

[1] This is given in full in Appendix A, p. 325.

"enable them to become better Architects and Builders of the human character, intellectually and morally, than the world has yet known or even deemed to be practicable"; it would help on similar arrangements by "all other classes of producers"; it would "exhibit to the world, in a plain and simple manner, by quiet example, how easily the most valuable wealth may be produced in superfluity beyond the wants of the population of all countries," so that all classes would "perceive their interest in becoming superior producers," and "the present artificial, inaccurate and therefore injurious circulating medium for the exchange of our riches" would be "superseded by an equitable, accurate and therefore rational, representation of real wealth"; it would remove the causes of individual and national competition, jealousies and wars, and so "establish peace, goodwill and harmony, not only among the Brethren of the Building Guild, but also by their example among the human race for ever." Finally, it would "secure to the present Masters of all the Building Branches who will understand their business a far more advantageous and secure position in society than they have or can have under the system of individual competition between Master and Master and Man and Man." It would thus end in a real and cordial union of interests within the Guild, and exhibit the means of realising "the great Association for the Emancipation of the Productive Classes."[1]

The master builders, however, were less ready than the delegates of the Union to accept this glorious offering of universal harmony. Nor were

[1] Circular of the Builders' Union, 1833, quoted in Postgate, *The Builders' History*, p. 463.

T 273

their tempers improved when wage demands began to be combined with intimations that the reign of the employer was ending, and offers to admit master builders to the Guild as managers on proof of capacity and subject to re-election,[1] or when the Guild began to apply for contracts in competition with them. The men were in an aggressive temper, and put forward big demands: the employers met them with the lock-out, and with the weapon of the "document," a pledge renouncing membership of the Union, which was handed out to the workers in certain districts for signature. In Liverpool and Birmingham big strikes or lock-outs were already in progress. Soon Manchester and the rest of Lancashire became involved; then Derby and other centres in the Midlands; and finally London.

Meanwhile in Birmingham, the headquarters of the Union, the Guild had got to work. The influence of Hansom and Welsh secured a few contracts, and during the strike the Builders set out, with money advanced through these two sympathisers, to erect a great Guildhall of their own. Slowly, amid great difficulties and stoppages caused by shortage of funds, the work went on. But outside contracts were hard to get, and the great Union was unequal to the strain of financing both the Guild and the big industrial disputes into which it had been plunged. Hansom wrote to Owen begging him to find money to carry on the Guildhall; but as we shall see, Owen already had his hands full elsewhere. At length Welsh, Hansom's partner, defected from the cause, and after a time work on the Guildhall had to be stopped. The unfinished building eventually passed into Han-

[1] Birmingham letter, quoted Postgate, p. 90.

som's hands and was sold to clear off debts. It became a warehouse, and is still standing, or was until a few years ago.

But before the crash came, the affairs of the Builders' Union and the Guild, which was the Union under another name, had become involved in the far wider developments of Trade Union action under Owen's leadership which were manifested in the dramatic rise and fall of the Grand National Consolidated Trades Union. For Owen and his friends, the whole affair of the Builders' Union was only a side-show, or at any rate only a small part of a wider movement of general regeneration. The apocalyptic language of the declaration quoted above is to be read as applying not to the Building Guild alone, but to this wider movement. Owen had set out, not to reorganise an industry, but to put the whole management of society on a new footing—to usher in by industrial action a New Moral World.

CHAPTER XVI

THE "TRADES UNION"

From 1832 to 1834 the chief organ of the Owenite movement was the *Crisis*, a weekly penny paper edited first by Owen himself and his son Robert Dale, who had come back for a time from America, and later by J. E. Smith. Especially under Smith, one of the ablest of the early Socialist writers and a most forceful personality, it became a very powerful organ of Owenite opinion, dividing with James Morrison's *Pioneer* the rôle of expressing the Socialist aspirations of the great Trade Union uprising of the years following the Reform Act. Its very name was a sign of the times. For the Owenites, these eventful years were a crisis, not merely in the Trade Union movement, but for the whole human race. The end of the old order was at hand; the reign of reason was due to begin. Not only the Builders, but all the "Industrious Classes," had to be won over to play their part in the great change.

J. E. Smith, whose quarrel with Owen in the middle of 1834 was undoubtedly an important factor in the collapse of the Consolidated Union, was a most extraordinary person. Born in Glasgow, he was sent by his father, who was a strict Irvingite and a small employer, to Glasgow University, where he was trained for the ministry. Instead, however, of entering the regular ministry, he fell under the influence of one John Wroe, pro-

276

claimed as the Messiah by a small sect of devotees, known later as the Christian Israelites. Quarrelling with Wroe, against whom serious charges were made, he tried his hand at painting, and then came to London as an unattached preacher and lecturer. Here he fell under Owen's influence, and became one of the chief lecturers at Owen's Institution in Charlotte Street. Owen, recognising his powers, made him editor of the *Crisis*. After the breach he returned to preaching, evolved a mystical religion of his own, which he called "Universalism," and ended his days as the enormously successful editor of the *Family Herald*, having apparently quite forgotten his brief and influential spell of Socialist propaganda. Yet the work of the years when he was connected with Owen and "the Trades Union" certainly ranks him among the ablest and most vigorous of early Socialist writers. His *Letters on Associated Labour*, which appeared in the *Pioneer*, are masterpieces of vigorous propagandist writing.[1]

From October 7 to 14, 1833, a delegate Congress was in session in London at the National Equitable Labour Exchange. Owen presided, and addressed the Congress, which recommended the formation of a "Grand National Moral Union of the Productive and Useful Classes." All "Trade Unions, Co-operative Societies, Commercial Orders, Benefit Societies, and all other associations intended for the improvement of the working classes" were urged "to form themselves into lodges, to make their own laws and regulations—for the purpose of emanci-

[1] See his life, *Shepherd Smith the Universalist*, by W. A. Smith; also an article in the *D.N.B.*, which gives no account of his Socialist days, and a brief study in R. W. Postgate's *Out of the Past*.

pating the industrious and useful classes from the difficulties which overwhelm them." [1] This was the formal beginning of the Grand National Consolidated Trades Union. The *Pioneer*, in its first number on September 7, 1833, had already spoken of "the Union" as if it were established even then on a general basis.

Further meetings followed, up and down the country, and in February, 1834, a Congress of delegates meeting in London formally gave a constitution to the Grand National Consolidated Trades Union, known more commonly in its day as "the Trades Union," to distinguish it from Trade Unions and Trade Clubs less ambitious and inclusive. The growth of the new body was astonishingly rapid and comprehensive. It is stated, on apparently good authority, that within a few weeks more than half a million members were enrolled, and a writer in the *Pioneer*, its official organ, estimated the total number of Trade Unionists, in this and other Unions, as at the very least a full million. This was in the spring of 1834. Workers of every sort flocked into the new organisation. It enrolled not only skilled craftsmen and factory operatives in the major trades, but workers in every conceivable occupation. Agricultural labourers were enrolled in many districts, and formed into a distinct "Friendly Society of Agricultural Labourers"

[1] Reference taken from the minutes of a meeting held at Huddersfield on November 1, 1833, to support the project. Owen was in the chair, and "the delegates of the Unions meeting at Leeds" were urged to give their support in order to "unite all the industrious and useful classes." The document is preserved in the files of Owen's correspondence at the Co-operative Union, Manchester. For the plan adopted at the October Conference, see p. 327.

within the larger body. Lodges of "Industrious Females" were formed in many centres, and "Miscellaneous Lodges" enlisted not only manual workers in the scattered trades, but also many sympathisers from the professional classes. The aim of the Union, in Owen's mind, was nothing less than the inclusion in one great body of the whole of the "productive classes." He led the way by becoming a member, and his disciples in the Owenite Societies throughout the country followed his example.

It must not be supposed that all this growth came suddenly out of nothing. For a long time past, the Trade Union movement had been rapidly developing. The Parliamentary Committees of 1824 and 1825, which studied the whole question in connection with the repeal of the Combination Acts, admitted that these Acts had been quite ineffective in preventing the existence of Trade Unions. They had enabled the magistrates to suppress a particular Union which made itself obnoxious, and they had caused many Trade Unions to disguise themselves under the name of Friendly or Benefit Societies; but they had not prevented combinations from existing, or even from negotiating collective agreements with bodies of employers. Their repeal had only given an additional stimulus to a movement of organisation that was already of considerable account. The excitements of the Reform agitation had applied a further stimulus; and, as we have seen, by 1830 Trade Unionism was widespread and active in a large number of trades.

While, therefore, the formation of the Consolidated Union undoubtedly led to a great increase of membership, it is probable that the majority of those who joined it were already members of some local Trade Union or Benefit Society, and that a great deal of its growth was due to the merging of such societies in the new great organisation. Even so, the rapidity with which it spread is remarkable enough; if it had sprung suddenly out of nothing, the situation would be merely incredible.

We have seen that among the Unions which took definite shape between 1829 and 1832 were several powerful bodies aiming at the national organisation of particular industries. The Spinners, the Potters, and the Clothiers, as well as the Builders, formed national Unions which enrolled a large membership and pursued an aggressive industrial policy. Moreover, though John Doherty's attempt to form a "General Union" of all trades broke down, and the National Association for the Protection of Labour had broken up into its constituent sections in 1832, after a troubled existence of two years, its Yorkshire membership had held together in the strong Leeds, Huddersfield and Bradford District Union, which entered actively into the movements of 1834.

What was the relation of these five big Unions to Owen's Consolidated Union? To a great extent the position remains doubtful, and was probably ambiguous at the time. When the first plan of the new body was presented to the Conference of October, 1833, the Builders, and probably the others also, were represented, and it seemed clear that they were all regarded at the outset as sections of the Consolidated Union. What does not appear is to what extent they themselves accepted this position. The Builders, at least, did not attend the second Conference in February, 1834, at which a proper constitution for the Consolidated Union was first adopted; and it seems fairly clear that they did not regard themselves as bound by the decisions of the Consolidated Executive, and that, in February, 1834, they definitely decided to maintain their separate existence outside the "General Union."[1] But, from the standpoint of its leaders, the Consolidated Union was at least as much an idea as an organisation, and they were disposed to regard all Trade Unions as, by their very nature, coming within its scope. The position was never clearly defined. New Societies were founded in 1833 and 1834 as branches of the Consolidated Union, and old Societies declared themselves by resolution to be attached to it; but the precise definition of membership, and the assigning to the various bodies of their proper places within the comprehensive Society, was bound to be a matter of time.

As a step towards this process, it was necessary first of all to equip the new leviathan with a constitution.[2] This was done at the Conference held in February, 1834, to which apparently a broadcast invitation was sent out under Owen's auspices. There is some mystery about this Conference. The Conference of October, 1833, had decided that the next meeting should be held at Barnsley on March 31, 1834, and had appointed J. R. Turner, Secretary of the London United Trades Association, as Secretary. What then happened is not clear. The Conference summoned by Owen met in London in the middle of February, drew up a

[1] *Pioneer*, February 13 and 18, 1834.
[2] Printed in full in Appendix C, p. 328.

regular constitution and appointed a national executive for the Consolidated Union. "Last week and this," wrote the Owenite *Crisis*.[1] "the delegates of the Trade Unions have met in London. There are two Parliaments in London at present sitting; and we have no hesitation in saying that the Trades Parliament is by far the most important, and will, in the course of a year of two, be the most influential. It is much more national than the other; the constituency is much larger. The Union is composed of nearly a million of members, and universal suffrage prevails amongst them."

Yet, in the following month, in the advertisement columns of this same *Crisis*,[2] appears a summons to the Conference of the Grand National Moral Union of the Working Classes, to be held at Barnsley at the end of the month, in accordance with the decision of the Conference held the previous October. The notice makes no mention of the London Conference held in February, though this had been partly reported in the *Crisis*, and though it had formally elected an executive committee for the Consolidated Union. Whether this Barnsley Conference was ever held I do not know: I have been unable to trace any further reference to it. But it looks as if Owen, with characteristic impatience and autocracy, had ignored the decision of the previous October, and called the London Conference on his own initiative—perhaps with the consent of Turner and the London United Trades Association. If so, this may help to explain the non-attendance of the Builders, and the fact that none of the five big sectional Unions was re-

[1] *Crisis*, February 22, 1834.
[2] *Ibid.*, March 15 and 22, 1834.

presented on the executive of the Consolidated Union. Morrison, who had presumably represented the Builders on the provisional body, resigned his seat on the executive in February or March, 1834,[1] and may have left for this reason. But the whole episode is exceedingly obscure.

In any case, the constitution adopted in February became the accepted basis of the Consolidated Union. It was plainly designed to provide for the admission of the big sectional Unions, whether they took part in drafting it or not. Its governing principles were these. As far as possible, each trade or industry was to form a separate section within the Union, with its own rules and regulations, its own district lodges and officers, and its own governing council. But in each district also the lodges of the various trades were to be joined together in a central committee, and the Grand Council of the Union as a whole was to be composed of delegates from these central committees. The Grand Council, at its half-yearly meetings, was to elect the executive of four members. Thus, while the members were grouped nationally according to trades, the final power belonged to the districts, in which the various trades were brought together. This may account for the reluctance of such big Unions as the Builders to throw in their organisation fully with the Consolidated Union; for their own central governing bodies would have lost much of their power. Probably it was the realisation of this, as well as the division which may have resulted from the incidents mentioned above, that led the Consolidated Executive in April, 1834, to

[1] *Crisis*, April 12, 1834, where it is said that Morrison resigned "some weeks ago."

invite the five big Unions each to send a delegate to sit with it in determining policy.[1]

From the first, the Consolidated Union was definitely an Owenite body. It accepted and preached the full Owenite gospel, and looked forward to a complete change of system to be established by Co-operation among the productive classes. It urged all its sections both to open Co-operative Stores for mutual trading among their members, and, even more strongly, to engage in co-operative production and in particular to spare no effort in setting to work in their own workshops all members unemployed, on strike, or locked out. It adopted Owen's familiar views concerning the formation of character, the influence of environment, and the need for perfect goodwill as the basis of the new social order. It laid great stress on educational work among its members and their children, and adopted a strongly feminist attitude. Indeed, only one feature of Owenism, his hostility to all organised religions, was either left out or kept in the background, and this was probably due in the main to the influence of Morrison and J. E. Smith, who, enthusiastic Owenites on other points, did not share all their leader's views on the religious question.

The Consolidated Union was scarcely formed when troubles began to gather round it. According to the rules, no offensive strike could take place without the sanction of the executive; but defensive strikes could be called by the district committees. The object of Owen and of the executive was to conserve their resources as far as possible until they were ready to proclaim a

[1] *Pioneer*, April 19, 1834.

general strike of the whole working class, with at least the universal eight hours' day as its first objective, and perhaps even an immediate peaceful revolution. But this was out of the question in reality. As fast as the workers organised, they put forward demands to their employers. In many trades and districts, too, the employers took the offensive, and either sought to reduce wages, or declared war on the Union and presented the "document" to their employees for signature. The great "Derby turn-out," over this issue, began in November, 1833, before the Consolidated Union was even equipped with a constitution. All through the subsequent months, the Derby struggle drained away the Union's scanty funds, and, as dispute followed dispute, the strain became soon too heavy to be borne. A slump in trade made matters worse.

In March, 1834, came another smashing blow, delivered this time by the law. The famous "Tolpuddle Martyrs" were convicted. The offence of these six unfortunate Dorchester labourers was nothing worse than the administering of unlawful oaths in the course of forming a lodge of the Friendly Society of Agricultural Labourers under the Consolidated Union; but for this they were sentenced to seven years' transportation. At once Owen and the other Union leaders had to devote their attention to getting up a campaign for the quashing of this monstrous sentence. A London Dorchester Committee was speedily organised, with Lovett as Secretary, and meetings of protest were held throughout the country. In London, the agitation culminated in a monster procession, led by Owen, to present a petition to Lord Melbourne, the Whig Home Secretary. Owen visited Melbourne before the day, and he agreed to receive a petition, provided the deputation presenting it came alone and not at the head of a huge demonstration. The leaders, however, decided to proceed with the demonstration. A mass meeting was held in Copenhagen Fields, and at least 30,000 persons walked behind Owen and the deputation to Whitehall. The Government, in great alarm, had called out many regiments of soldiers; but there was absolutely no disorder. Melbourne, however, refused to receive the deputation, and the petition had in the end to be presented quietly on another day.

Monstrous as the Dorchester sentence was, no petitions or meetings and no protests of the Radicals in Parliament, where Cobbett, Fielden and Feargus O'Connor were prominent in the attack, availed to get it altered. The rise of the Consolidated Union had set the governing classes and the manufacturers in a panic, and the Whigs were all for strong measures. The Unionists, made angry, grew readier to strike; the employers, encouraged by the Government's attitude, locked their men out the more freely. A big strike of the London tailors in April was met by the presentation of the "document" by the masters. Already the Derby turn-outs were breaking down exhausted. The Consolidated Executive had to impose levy after levy in a desperate struggle to meet its obligations.

At this stage failure was inevitable, even if it had not been so from the first. But now the position was worsened by internal disputes. Next to Owen, by far the ablest men in the movement were Morrison and J. E. Smith. Morrison, originally associated with the Builders' Union, was editor of the *Pioneer*, recognised as the official organ of the Consolidated Union. J. E. Smith, whose contributions to the *Pioneer* under the name of "Senex" were among its best features, was editor of the *Crisis*, the official organ of the Owenite Co-operative movement. Owen now fell out with both these, his best, lieutenants. Different versions have been given of the cause of the quarrel. Morrison, in his account of it in the *Pioneer*, dwells chiefly on the religious differences between him and Owen, and Smith himself puts the point of difference even more strongly, writing that "the Union must divide—at present they are composed of two great parties, believers and infidels—and I conceive that Owen and I must separate to provide fuel for each."[1] But, if the fundamental difference was about religion, it found expression in other ways as well. Smith and Morrison objected to Owen bringing his religious views into the Union: Owen objected to their writing in the *Pioneer* and the *Crisis* articles calculated, in his view, to stir up class-hatred. He was willing to organise a general strike; but he insisted that it must be done in a spirit of universal charity and philanthropy. "All the individuals now living are the suffering victims of this accursed system, and all are objects of pity; you will, therefore, effect this great and glorious revolution without, if possible, inflicting individual evil . . . without bloodshed, violence, or evil of any kind, merely by an overwhelming moral influence, which influence individuals and nations will speedily perceive the uselessness and

[1] Letter of Smith (May 30, 1834), quoted in *Shepherd Smith the Universalist*, p. 103.

folly of attempting to resist."[1] Many of J. E. Smith's articles and lectures certainly did not live up to this ideal of charity. The atheist was the apostle of goodwill; the Universalist Christian the apostle of class war.

This was one fruitful cause of dispute. Another arose when Smith, in the *Crisis*, began to criticise severely the actions of the Consolidated Executive. The disputants agreed in desiring to prevent sectional strikes, and prepare the way for "a strong strike and a strike all together"; but Smith and Morrison held that the executive was not preparing the way, and the former at least argued that Owen's influence was bad. "He thinks," wrote Smith, "he can lead the people—he is not aware of the odium which attaches itself to his name. He is too full of himself to see it, and we have always been suppressing his name and his articles as much as possible. He cannot brook this any longer, and seeing that he cannot get everything his own way, he is going to start a new paper under the name of the *Union Gazette*, which he expects will swallow up all others. He means to work behind the curtain, and yet to be dictator. Now our move is to prevent this dictatorship, for we know it cannot be tolerated."[2]

Early in the year Morrison, who had been on the executive of the Consolidated Union, resigned his seat, and a little later Owen displaced the *Pioneer* from its status of official organ of the Union, in favour of his own *Gazette*. Early in July the *Pioneer* expired. Smith, in the *Crisis*, continued his attacks

[1] "The Legacy of Robert Owen," in the *Pioneer*, March 29, 1834.
[2] Letter of Smith, as above.

with increased vehemence, particularly when a member of the executive absconded to New South Wales with part of the Union's funds. Owen, who had previously tried to establish a strict censorship by the executive over all matter appearing in either paper, then shut down the *Crisis* also. Its last number appeared on August 23, and Smith thereafter dropped out of the movement.

When Smith left the Consolidated Union, it was already staggering beneath the blows rained upon it. A general lock-out of the builders in London had just imposed a further strain, which affected the Consolidated as a whole, though the brunt of it fell directly on the Builders' Union. Members were already flocking out of the Consolidated Union, and local Societies breaking away, almost as fast as they had flocked in a few months before. Owen realised that the Union had failed, and that the great strike was impracticable. But his resilient mind could not accept the idea of failure. Militant Trade Unionism and the general strike had made a temporary appeal to him because it appeared they could be made to serve as instruments of the great change. When he found that they could not, he speedily steered a new course. Calling a Congress of Owenite Societies, he persuaded it to resolve that the Consolidated Union should give place to the British and Foreign Consolidated Association of Industry, Humanity and Knowledge, and that "effective measures should be adopted to reconcile the masters and operatives throughout the kingdom."[1]

At the same time Owen wound up the *Crisis*, announcing that it had served its turn. The crisis,

[1] *Crisis*, August 23, 1834.

he said, was over; the old world would pass away "through a great moral revolution of the human mind, directed solely by truth, by charity, and by kindness." The sign of the change would be the issue of a new journal to replace the *Crisis*. It would be called the *New Moral World*, "in which Truth, Industry and Knowledge will ever reign triumphant."[1]

Previous writers[2] have expressed the view that the Congress of August 20 brought the Consolidated Union to an end. I do not agree with this view. Apart from one incident still to be mentioned, the Congress ended Owen's connection with the Union. But the Union itself, I think, staggered on for some months longer. Indeed, it seems clear that a delegate meeting of it was held as late as October 1, and that Owen tried again on that occasion to get in touch with it in order to make "an important communication." The delegates' reply, conveyed by the J. D. Styles who had been Secretary to the Co-operative Congress of 1832 and to numerous other Owenite bodies, was "that this meeting respectfully declines holding any conference with or receiving any communication from Mr. Owen, and that the Secretary be requested to communicate this resolution by letter."[3]

Behind this note evidently lies a quarrel, of which the particulars are lost. But it seems plausible to suppose that the Trade Union leaders, who had followed Owen as long as he appeared to be leading a militant Trade Union crusade, were

[1] *Crisis*, August 23, 1834.
[2] Podmore, Webb, Postgate.
[3] Owen's Correspondence, Co-operative Union, Manchester.

not prepared to have their organisation, tottering though it was, converted by him to what they regarded as a quite different use. It is also very probable that the growing difficulties on religious questions, which we have noted as the basis of Smith and Morrison's rupture with Owen, had undermined Owen's position as leader. The main body of the Trade Unionists were ready enough to follow him as a strike leader; they were probably not prepared to regard denunciation of all religions as a necessary qualification for Trade Union membership.

By the end of 1834, or thereabouts, the Consolidated Union was dead. This does not mean that Trade Unionism died with it, though it passed for the time into eclipse. The Builders' Union and the Leeds Union went down in 1835, and the Potters and the Spinners a little later. But fragments of these bodies, including the Stonemasons and the Carpenters and Joiners, held together, and many sections of the Consolidated survived as separate bodies, mostly reduced again to purely local action, and shorn of much of their membership. The Consolidated Union was bound to fail. The forces against it were too strong. In mere strike action the employers were certain to wear down the Unions; and if matters had come to revolution, all the forces were at the disposal of a Government whose strength and public backing had recently been renewed by the Reform Act. As usual, Owen attempted the impossible. What must be regarded as amazing is even the temporary success of his incursion into the industrial field. Trade Unionism reached a point which it certainly did not reach again for half a century. It captured the imaginations of the workers as it has never captured them since.

Why was this? The workers of 1834 were far more readily impressionable than their successors of the Victorian era. They were more miserable, less educated, and less used to accept the daily servitude of the factory as man's natural lot. The factory system was newer, and revolt against it more instinctive than it has been since. The workers, crushed down remorselessly by the new capitalism, turned readily in their despair to any new gospel that seemed to promise relief. Messiahs and religious fanatics, as well as political and industrial salvationists, found disciples easy to come by. Men were simpler-minded then than now. Owen's visions, backed by his sweet persuasiveness, captured their minds. They followed him to defeat; but they could not follow the abrupt change of course by which he met defeat. The ways of Owenism and Trade Unionism converged from 1830 to 1834; after 1834 they diverged sharply. Owen's brief leadership of the working-class movement came abruptly to an end. Chartism took the place of Co-operation as the dominant working-class gospel.

CHAPTER XVII

OLD AGE

In Owen's view, the "crisis" was over. The great attempt to use Trade Unionism as the instrument of Socialism had ended in disaster for the Trade Unions. The working class turned from industrial action to Chartism, building a new organisation to further the radical aims which the Reform Act of 1832 had failed to fulfil. The struggle against the new Poor Law of 1834, the attempt to conquer political power as a means to economic freedom, occupied the attention of the masses. Owenism was not quite forgotten; but it was pushed into a corner. New men assumed the leadership. Cobbett died in 1835, and Henry Hunt in the same year. Feargus O'Connor took their place as the outstanding popular leader. Working-class leaders like Lovett, Hetherington and Bronterre O'Brien, who had worked with Owen, even if they did not forget their Owenism, passed on into the Chartist movement. Many, indeed, of Owen's old followers stayed with him, and he and his views continued to win new disciples. But they were no longer in the main stream of working-class thought.

The Owenite movement assumed a new shape. Labour Exchanges, Trade Unions as the basis of Co-operative Societies or Guilds, even Co-operative Stores, ceased to play any considerable part in it. It was as if the years from 1830 to 1834 had never been. Owen himself returned to the preaching of his ideas about education and the influence of environment, and to working out, in ever-growing detail, the principles of the "New Moral World." He still went everywhere about the country lecturing; but now he addressed himself, not to the Trade Unions or to distinctively working-class audiences, but to all who would respond to his new moral gospel. His lectures dealt more and more with moral and religious, rather than political or industrial, questions. He preached again the ideal of Community, and urged the founding of Villages of Co-operation as the means of realising the new system. But primarily he was from this time engaged in a moral and religious crusade.

This was not a new departure, but a change of emphasis. Throughout the troubled years of the "crisis," the direct propaganda of Owenism as a social gospel went on side by side with the more spectacular adventures of Owenite Trade Unionism. The Owenite Societies up and down the country maintained their distinct existence, and enrolled many new members; and Owen's disciples in London worked under his direct auspices through the parent body, called at this time the "Association of the Industrious Classes." In July, 1832, a "Missionary Society,"[1] subsequently called the "Social Missionary and Tract Society," was formed as a subsidiary organisation for propaganda on a national scale; and another subsidiary, "The Social Reformers," meeting at Lovett's Coffee House, was formed in September, 1833, for social purposes.[2] Indeed, the movement was constantly

[1] *Crisis,* July 21, 1832.   [2] *Ibid.,* September 28, 1833.

throwing off new organisations, and changing the names of those already in being. This helps to make its complexities especially bewildering to follow in the casual references of contemporary journals.

When Owen parted company with the Trade Unions after their disaster, he had all this network of purely Owenite organisations to fall back upon. He did not need to make a new movement, but only to develop one which was already in lively existence, and apparently little affected by the collapse of his wider plans. He lost, indeed, the adherence of the great body of workers; but he retained to the full the loyalty of the bands of disciples who had definitely accepted Owenism as their social gospel. With his extraordinary buoyancy of mind, he seems to have been hardly conscious of the wreck from which only this small remnant had been saved. He set to work planning more grandiosely than ever for the great moral revolution that was to come swiftly by a change in men's minds and hearts.

His new journal, *The New Moral World*, plainly expressed this change of orientation on the part of Owen and his disciples. His new Society, the British and Foreign Association of Industry, Humanity and Knowledge, signified the same change. In 1835 it, with various other Owenite bodies, was reorganised as the Association of All Classes of All Nations, a name eloquent of the founder's departure from all thoughts of a struggle of classes as the means of achieving his ideal. At the same time the movement throughout the country was similarly reorganised. Owenite Societies were formed, or re-formed, in most of the important towns, and in 1837 these Societies threw off two further bodies—a new Social Missionary and Tract Society, which was to be the means of spreading Owenite propaganda throughout the country, and the National Community Friendly Society, which was to gather together funds for a new experiment in community-making. In the following year six paid Owenite missionaries—sometimes called the "Socialist Bishops"—were appointed, with their headquarters in the principal towns, to tour the country and preach the gospel to every creature. In 1839 the above Societies united to form the Universal Community Society of Rational Religionists, which three years later changed its name again, and became the Rational Society. Meanwhile, in 1840, Owen and some of his supporters had formed the Home Colonisation Society, yet another body designed to raise funds for the financing of Owenite Communities, and especially Queenwood, or Harmony Hall, the new Community which was actually started by the Owenite Societies in 1839.

During these years Owen was ceaselessly active in writing as well as speaking. The most important of his later works, *The Book of the New Moral World*, appeared in parts between 1836 and 1844.[1] In it he attempted to give a complete general statement of his views, dealing both with his educational, moral and religious theories, and with the structure and working of his proposed Communities. It is a clear statement, marred sometimes by the unbalanced prophetic fervour which grew on him with age, but in general only reaffirming his earlier views. *The*

[1] Part I., 1836; Parts II. and III., 1842; Parts IV.–VII., 1844.

Book of the New Moral World became the Bible of the Owenites; lessons from it were regularly read, as from the Scriptures, in the Owenite Halls and Institutes.

This was by far the most considerable of Owen's later books. But another, a reprint of a course of lectures delivered in 1835, caused a much greater sensation, and was used with great effect in controversy against him and his followers. This work, *The Marriages of the Priesthood of the Old Immoral World*,[1] was in effect a denunciation of the whole religious basis of marriage as a fatal obstacle to the dominion of reason and the establishment of the new social order. Owen did not advocate promiscuity; but he wanted marriage set free from all religious sanctions and made purely a civil and a terminable contract. His enemies, and the foes of Socialism, naturally fastened on this book, and denounced Owen and the Owenites as not only infidels and blasphemers, but also open advocates of sexual immorality. In 1838, in *The Marriage System of the New Moral World*, Owen restated his arguments on this matter more clearly and temperately; but the earlier volume, an uncorrected reprint of a course of public lectures, served better his opponents' ends, and continued to be their chief weapon against his sect. I use the word "sect" advisedly; for during these years the Owenites were really ceasing to be concerned mainly with Socialism or economic change, and developing into a sect apart with a social religion of their own. In all the towns where they were

[1] Marriages *of* the Priesthood here means marriages *by* the Priesthood—*i.e.* all marriages solemnised by religious observances.

strong, they erected their own buildings. At first these were often called "Social Institutions," in imitation of Owen's Institution in London; but soon the name "Hall of Science" came to be preferred, and the buildings became in effect "Rational Churches," forerunners of the Ethical Churches of more recent times. The change of name, from the "Universal Community Society of Rational Religionists" to the "Rational Society," marks one of the later stages of this transition. The Owenite missionaries, who began by using Owen's ethical doctrines as an argument for the making of Communities, ended by largely dropping the Communities, and concentrating on ethical and Secularist teaching. As Owenism, at an earlier stage, had thrown off the Co-operative movement as a by-product, it now created the organised movement of Secularism.

Owen and his missionaries were vindictively pursued. A number of rival preachers of more orthodox religious sects took the road in opposition to them, and denounced them as infidels and immoralists, quoting or misquoting Owen's views on religion and marriage before scandalised audiences, often getting the authorities to refuse them halls or urging the mob to break up their meetings. The building of the "Halls of Science" was largely the Owenite answer to exclusion from hired places of assembly. In some cases, debates were arranged between the Owenites and their orthodox critics. Owen himself debated with the Rev. J. H. Roebuck in 1837, with the Rev. W. Legg in 1839, and with J. Brindley in 1841. But he was no debater. He was far too intent on stating his own case, at inordinate length, to pay any attention to his opponents. He made a naïve comment after his discussion with Brindley, the coarsest and most foul-mouthed of his critics. "It would have been the loss of most precious moments for me to have attended to anything Mr. Brindley might say, instead of using them to tell the world what I wished it to learn from myself."[1] Owen regarded a debate simply as affording a platform from which he could repeat his unvarying version of the truth. He was a most persuasive lecturer when he had the platform to himself; but he was always worsted in debate.

The complete conversion of the Owenite movement into an ethical society did not come until after its last great venture in community-making had ended in disaster. Harmony Hall, or Queenwood, near East Tytherley, Hampshire, was acquired by the Owenites in 1839, and operations were at once begun for converting it into a model Village of Co-operation, based chiefly on agricultural production. Owen was offered the governorship of the Community; but he refused, considering that the resources available, which had been largely accumulated by subscriptions from the local Owenite bodies, were inadequate for the purpose. The Owenites, however, were determined to make a start, and John Finch of Liverpool was appointed Governor. Soon difficulties began. The buildings were inadequate for the number of residents, and there was no money to build more. The farming, done mostly by men who had been trained to quite different pursuits, could not be made to pay, though the agricultural director, Aldam, was an experienced farmer, and some

[1] *New Moral World*, vol. ix. p. 87.

hired labour was employed. In 1840 the number of the residents was drastically reduced, and in 1841 Owen, who had been raising fresh capital through the Home Colonisation Society formed the previous year, was appointed Governor with full powers.

As ever, Owen's plans were on the grand scale. With Hansom, formerly of the Builders' Guild, as architect, he began erecting palatial buildings, with the finest modern equipment and expensive fittings and furniture. He took leases of new farms, though those held already were not paying. True to his principles, he started a finely equipped school for the children, not only of the residents, but of Owenites throughout the country. Owen remained Governor of Queenwood for three years; and all the time he drained money away from the Owenite Societies as well as from rich sympathisers for the great experiment. The social missionaries had to be discharged, because there was no money to pay their salaries. One sympathiser, F. Bate, alone put over £12,000 into the Queenwood enterprise, and in all about £40,000 was spent upon it. Though Owen made Queenwood a show place, and the school was well managed, financially things went from bad to worse. The Owenite Societies, finding the strain too great, began at last to criticise the leader whom, till then, they had almost worshipped. At length, in 1844, in Owen's absence, the Congress of the Rational Society elected John Finch to the chair in his place, and passed a series of resolutions relating to the management of the Community. Owen had come to regard the presidency as his by right, and the election of Finch was recognised as a challenge to his authority. It was carried chiefly by the delegates of the Owenite Societies in the north of England, harder-headed perhaps and certainly less under Owen's personal spell than the Londoners.

Owen refused to accept the position. He resigned at once the presidency of the Rational Society and the governorship of Queenwood, saying that he would only hold office if his powers were unrestricted, and insisting that the resolutions passed by the Congress must be rescinded if he was to stay. The Congress refused to withdraw, and elected John Buxton, a workman from Manchester, as President and Governor in his place. Owen thereupon retired for the time from active connection with the movement and left England for a long visit to his sons in the United States. He was seventy years of age when he became Governor of Queenwood, and seventy-three when he resigned.

The Community itself, under its new management, struggled on for a year longer. Severe retrenchments were carried through; but, although the loss was reduced, it still remained, and of course no interest could be paid on the large amount of capital sunk in the enterprise. In 1845 the Congress of the Rational Society decided to wind it up. Queenwood closed its career as a Co-operative community in 1845, and became a school, which continued for many years afterwards to be conducted at least on semi-Owenite principles. The *New Moral World*, which had been the organ of the movement for more than ten years, was sold. James Hill, who bought it, carried it on as a semi-Owenite organ till the following year, and G. A. Fleming, who had been the editor, unsuccessfully started a new journal, *The Moral World*, which ran for a few months. The Rational Society itself lived on for a time; but before long it broke up into its constituent local bodies, and many of these died out. Owenism, as an organised popular movement, was at an end.

After the fall of Queenwood, the preaching of "Community" practically died away. When George Jacob Holyoake, the most energetic and devoted of the Owenite missionaries, started the *Reasoner* as the new organ of the movement in 1846, he announced that it would be "Communistic in Social Economy, Utilitarian in Morals, Republican in Politics, and Anti-theological in Religion." [1] But, in fact, not only did the Communism soon drop out of sight; it was rapidly discarded in favour of other doctrines. The *Reasoner* became primarily a Secularist paper, and the change was typical of the new standpoint of the surviving Owenite Societies.

Indeed, when the Owenites, such as Holyoake, returned to the preaching of Co-operative doctrines, it was of a new and essentially different Co-operative movement that they had to tell. Owen himself, after 1834, had lost all interest both in producers' Co-operative Societies and in consumers' Co-operative Stores for the sale of provisions and household goods. The former had practically died out, crushed in the defeat of the Trade Unions. For a revival, producers' Co-operation had to wait till the days of Kingsley and the Christian Socialists. But retail trading was easier to undertake, and it never wholly died out. In 1836 Owen expressed his surprise at finding several Co-

[1] *Reasoner*, vol. i. p. 142, quoted Podmore, p. 581.

operative Societies still in existence, and apparently
doing well, in Carlisle. "It is high time," he commented, "to put an end to the notion, very prevalent in the public mind, that this is the Social
System which we contemplate, or that it will form
any part of the arrangements in the New Moral
World."[1]

But if these were things too low for Owen's
vision of the new Society, still they went on, until
in 1844 the little body of Owenites, famous as the
"Rochdale Pioneers," opened their store in Toad
Lane. That the Pioneers were in principle orthodox Owenites at the start their language plainly
shows. They set out not only to sell goods to their
members, but "to commence the manufacture of
such articles as the Society may determine upon,
for the employment of such members as may be
without employment, or who may be suffering
in consequence of repeated reductions in their
wages." And they ordained "that as soon as
practicable the Society shall proceed to arrange the
powers of production, distribution, education, and
government; or, in other words, to establish a self-
supporting home-colony of united interests, or to
assist other Societies in establishing such colonies."

But, if in principle the Rochdale Pioneers were
Co-operators in the Owenite sense, they had meanwhile to make their new store a success. How they
did this is told in the histories of Co-operation; for
the little store in Toad Lane is generally regarded
as the beginning of the modern consumers' Co-
operative movement, and the "dividend on purchases" by which the Society attracted and held
the support of its members has been repeatedly

[1] *New Moral World*, vol. iii. p. 26, quoted Podmore, p. 453.

proclaimed as the foundation on which the movement has been built up. All this falls outside the scope of this book; for, though Co-operators pay tribute to Owen as the founder of their system, it is more than doubtful whether Owen, if he could revisit the earth, would recognise his progeny, or take more than a passing interest in its growth. Owenism led on to consumers' Co-operation as we know it almost by an accident; the interesting question is how far consumers' Co-operation in its further development will be led on to the reassertion of the Socialist principles from which it has sprung.

The Rochdale Pioneers and the new Co-operative movement come into this story only because they appealed to the Owenites, if they did not appeal to Owen himself. Holyoake, William Pare, and many others who had been active propagandists of Owenism, became later active workers for the Consumers' Co-operative movement, and thus in some degree remade their broken contacts with the working class. But the new Co-operation was no longer a gospel of revolt, much less of revolution. It took colour from its environment, and developed almost as the working-class equivalent of the joint stock company, a field for the investment of working-class savings as well as an expression of the Victorian ideals of thrift and self-help. Chartism, the last of the great working-class movements of revolt, was already in decline when the Rochdale Pioneers opened their store. Victorian Trade Unionism, as well as Victorian Co-operation, aimed at making its peace with the capitalist order even while it protected the workers against its worst abuses.

Owen himself had no part in these strange fruits

of his sowing. From 1844 to 1847 he was mostly in America, paying only short visits to England, and dividing his time between staying with his sons at New Harmony and lecture tours, amazing for a man of his years, about the United States. He had by this time spent all his money, the last of it having gone into the Queenwood experiment. He had sunk most of his fortune in New Harmony, and his sons, during that experiment, had transferred to him their entire holding of £20,000 in the New Lanark mills. This too went, and by 1844 Owen had nothing left. But his sons, who had taken over what was left of the property at New Harmony, had money, and they now arranged, after presenting him with what Podmore calls "an audaciously cooked account," to pay him an income of £360 a year for life—interest at 6 per cent. on an imaginary debt of £6,000. Owen's personal needs had always been small—as small as his power of spending capital on grandiose schemes was large—and on this modest income the once rich "Mr. Owen of New Lanark" contrived not only to live in adequate comfort for the rest of his days, but also to finance quite a number of publications and small enterprises of his decline.

For, old as he was, it was not in Owen's nature to retire from active work. In 1845 he called a "World Convention" in New York, and expounded again his familiar views. In 1846 he tried to settle the Oregon boundary dispute between Great Britain and America, and paid a special visit to England for this purpose. In 1847, after leaving America for good, he proposed to stand for Parliament, and issued a Radical election address as candidate for Marylebone, urging, among other reforms, a graduated property tax and the repeal of all other taxation, free trade with all the world, absolute religious freedom, national education for all, national employment for all who were out of work, and a reform of the currency which would enable the circulatory medium to be increased or decreased in correspondence with the quantity of wealth to be circulated. He did not go to the poll.

The next year, the year of Revolution, 1848, found him in Paris, assiduously issuing pamphlets and leaflets explaining his system, urging upon Louis Blanc, Lamartine and other leaders of the Revolution the need to use it as the means of establishing the new system in human affairs. In 1852, when he was already eighty-one, he proposed to stand for Oldham; but once more he withdrew before the day of the poll.

From 1844, when he left the *New Moral World*, to 1850, Owen had no periodical at his command. But after his return to England the itch for writing returned again upon him. In 1849 he published *The Revolution in the Mind and Practice of the Human Race*—a book in which he once more expounded his system. Next came *Weekly Letters to the Human Race* (1850), and *Robert Owen's Journal* (1851-2). Then the *Rational Quarterly Review*, which ran through 1853, and was followed by *The New Existence of Man upon the Earth*—a sort of autobiographical record in periodical form, including reports of many of Owen's earlier works and manifestos. This, the germ of his published *Autobiography*, appeared in 1854 and 1855. His last venture was *Robert Owen's Millennial Gazette*, which ran on from 1856 until his death in 1858.

It was not until 1853, when he was already

eighty-two years of age, that Owen became a convert to Spiritualism, and fell under the influence of
the new cult, then spreading from America to
Europe. His first references to this theme occur
in the *Rational Quarterly Review*, and thereafter
spiritualist phenomena become inextricably mingled in his mind with his moral and social doctrines.
Having outlived all his old associates, he evokes
their spirits at séances, and becomes the willing
dupe of mediums, and especially of a certain Mrs.
Hayden, who had come to England from the
United States. Jefferson, Benjamin Franklin,
Shakespeare, Shelley, Napoleon, the Duke of Wel-
lington, and the prophet Daniel became his
familiars; but the most frequent of all his spiritual
visitants was His Royal Highness the Duke of Kent,
whose steady support had meant much to Owen in
the early days of his crusade. "His whole spirit
proceeding with me," Owen wrote, "has been
most beautiful; making his own appointments;
meeting me on the day, hour, and minute he
named; and never in one instance (and these appointments were numerous as long as I had
mediums near me upon whom I could depend) has
this spirit not been punctual to the minute he had
named."[1]

The Owen of these last years makes a pathetic
figure. After his return from America in 1847 he
went to live at Cox's Hotel in Jermyn Street, where
he was looked after by Mr. Cox and his family, with
whom he was on terms of friendship. But in 1853
his friends felt that it would be better for him to
live in the country, and, under instructions from
his son, Robert Dale Owen, rooms were taken for

[1] *Life*, p. 316.

him at Park Farm, Sevenoaks. At the same time James Rigby, one of the original delegates of the Builders' Union and later a faithful Owenite missionary, went to live with him and took charge of his affairs.

Rigby's job was no sinecure. Through these last years Owen kept up a ceaseless, ineffective activity. He was for ever sending Memorials and Addresses to Queen Victoria and other crowned heads and ministers about his new system, journeying to London to interview promising mediums, and calling "Congresses of Advanced Minds," "Congresses of the Reformers of the World," and the like. Apparently none save a few of the faithful and a casual stranger here or there attended these Congresses, at which Owen read out papers and addresses in profusion, mingling sense with nonsense, his moral and economic views with the latest communications from departed spirits. Rigby often read his papers for him, and then led and stage-managed the perfunctory discussion. The curious may read the full reports in the *Millennial Gazette*.[1]

The strength of Owen's personal hold over his followers, and of their affection for him, is shown by the devotion with which they continued to do homage to him even in these last years. The centre of Owenite activities in London was at this time the Literary and Scientific Institution (note the further change of name) in John Street, and here, on Owen's birthday, a special celebration was always held in his honour. The leading Owenites spoke, and everything was done to make the old

[1] *E.g.* Report of Congress of Advanced Minds in the *Millennial Gazette*, August 1, 1857.

man feel that he was still the centre of a living movement. But, in fact, both Owen and Owenism had long been dead.

At least, one would have called him dead had he not, in 1857, in the eighty-seventh year of his life, published the liveliest and most readable of all his books, the first volume of his unfinished *Autobiography*. I have quoted from it freely earlier in this volume, and, I hope, given some idea of its simple excellence. Owen had planned the writing of his life in 1835, after his withdrawal from the Consolidated Union, and perhaps he had written much of it then. A good deal of it had actually appeared in *The New Existence of Man upon the Earth*, but this would only antedate it by a few years. Certainly the prefatory addresses and dialogues, which take up a good part of the volume published in 1857, read very differently from the *Life* itself. Of this there is but a fragment, telling his story up to the early eighteen twenties, and therefore not dealing at all either with New Harmony or with his incursion into the sphere of working-class agitation. Another volume, numbered "IA," appeared in 1858; but this consisted wholly of Appendices, in which Owen reprinted the most important of his earlier reports and other writings, including the *New View of Society* and the *Report to the County of Lanark*. Of the *Life* itself, presumably no more was ever written, though there are fragments of autobiography scattered through many of his later writings, and a brief *Life* covering a longer period appeared in *Robert Owen's Journal*.

The two volumes of the *Autobiography* were his last works. In 1857 he had been much excited by the news of the formation of the National Association for the Promotion of Social Science, largely promoted by his old and still faithful friend, Lord Brougham. He was not able to attend; but he sent five papers to the inaugural Conference of the Association, and two of these were read at its meetings in Birmingham.

The following year the Association met in Liverpool, and Owen insisted on attending, in order to deliver there in person his final message to the human race.[1] "This," he wrote after finishing his paper for the meeting, "I believe will be my last effort, and I intend it to be the crowning one. I am full of pain, more acute, I think."[2]

Despite his pain, Owen travelled to Liverpool, where he had to take to his bed. But on the day of the meeting he insisted on being dressed and taken to the hall. "Four policemen bore him to the platform. It is now a matter of public history, how kindly Lord Brougham, as soon as he saw his old friend, took him by the arm, led him forward and obtained a hearing for him. Then Mr. Owen, in his grand manner, proclaimed his ancient message of science, competence, and goodwill to the world. When he came to the conclusion of his first period, Lord Brougham, out of regard for his failing strength, terminated it. He clapped his hands, applauded his words, then said, 'Capital, very good, can't be better, Mr. Owen! There, that will do!' Then in an undertone, 'Here, Rigby,

[1] He had also attended and spoken, in favour of "the whole Charter," at the last Chartist Conference, held in London in February, 1858.
[2] Letter to Rigby, quoted Podmore, p. 625.

convey the old gentleman to his bed.' He was carried back. As soon as he reached his bed he became unconscious."[1]

Owen missed this chance of a dramatic exit from the world. After a fortnight in bed at Liverpool, he rallied. But, instead of returning to Sevenoaks, he had made up his mind to revisit the place of his birth. He went by train to Shrewsbury, and thence drove to Newtown. After visiting the house where he was born, and calling on an old friend who had been dead twenty years, he returned to Shrewsbury. But here he changed his mind, and wrote to a Mr. Thomas in Newtown, asking that a public meeting should be called, and promising to return to address it. He did actually return, and put up at the hotel. Rigby left him there, in the doctor's care, and went to fetch Robert Dale Owen, who was in London on a visit. In his absence, Owen sent for the Rector of Newtown, arranged for a series of public meetings, and drew up a plan for reorganising the education of the town. Rigby returned with Robert Dale to find him sinking, and on the following day, November 17, 1858, he "passed away as gently and quietly as if he had been falling asleep." His last words were, "Relief has come."[2]

Owen was buried next his parents, in the old churchyard at Newtown. His grave, with a memorial tablet and railing erected by the Co-operative movement in 1902, stands by the ruinous wall of the old church.

[1] Holyoake, *Life and Last Days of Robert Owen*, p. 7.
[2] Letter of R. D. Owen, quoted Podmore, p. 629.

CHAPTER XVIII

CONCLUSION

In most cases, a biography is best left to explain itself; and the biographer does well to keep his own views and interpretations in the background, or to express them only in his arrangement and selection of the facts. But I cannot quite leave Owen's life to explain itself in this way, because I have found so prevalent what seems to me a wrong view of him, or rather a view taken from a wrong angle of vision. Owen lived to be very old: he was eighty-seven when he died. His later years were years of dotage, and even long before his final adventure into Spiritualism the balance of his mind had gone. It is obviously unfair and misleading to judge him by what he did in old age, or to view him in the light of these latter dealings.

Yet this is precisely the image of Owen I have found most firmly fixed in men's minds. He is thought of as an old man, whose flashes of brilliant sanity were crossed and often obscured by mere maundering. If he had died in 1834, when he was already sixty-three years old, this vision of him could never have become established. It simply is not a true picture of Owen, or even a plausible caricature, until he had reached an age beyond the common span. We must judge him as he was, not in the long years of his decay, but in vigorous manhood.

312

There was, of course, even then something in him, besides genius, that was abnormal. He was "very positive," as David Dale said, or even fanatical, in his beliefs. He thought alone, and having worked out his conclusions for himself, he was not to be swayed, even in the smallest particular, by any argument that could be presented to him. He never argued; he only reiterated his views, and waited patiently and in all charity for his listeners to perceive the truth of what he said. His mind was closed early to influences from without—at least to any conscious learning from others. A self-made man in the fullest sense, he believed that his own experience had unlocked for him the gates of truth, and that he had no need of other guides. He could only live by his own light, and he made the mistake of regarding his own light as a sufficient light for others. For this reason, he could lead, but could not follow; could organise, but could never really co-operate. He demanded from all his associates an unquestioning obedience to his own inner light.

Whence came this light? He was fond of saying, in terms of his cherished theory of character, that it came solely from his own experience. His environment had taught him to think as he thought, and to grasp the truth while others were enmeshed in error. Yet clearly some of these others had much the same environment. Not every village lad who became a shop-boy and then a great manufacturer found himself irresistibly impelled to believe in Co-operation instead of competition, Rationalism instead of orthodox religion, education instead of repression of the poor and needy. Owen's own explanation of his character was clearly no explanation at all. It involved, moreover, a confusion, very common in

313

his thinking, between character and belief. Environment may have formed Owen's character: it certainly did not dictate, though of course it affected and conditioned, his beliefs.

How far did Owen borrow his ideas from others? How far was he even influenced by preceding thinkers and writers? We do not know, because he did not know himself. In early life he was a voluminous reader; but I think he never consciously borrowed an idea. He assimilated what he wanted in the books he read and the opinions of the people he met; but all that he took in came out somehow different, and appeared to him as the exclusive product of his own mind. Others doubtless set him thinking; but he always thought for himself.

It is, therefore, not very profitable to inquire how much Owen owed to earlier writers. There is obviously much in common between his educational ideas and Rousseau's; but it is a matter of conjecture whether he ever read *Emile*. He was a friend of William Godwin's, and in all probability he read *Political Justice*, which is in part an interpretation of Rousseauism to an English audience. Certainly he talked much with Godwin, and he may well have learnt a good deal from him. Certainly his thought is on many points closely akin to Godwin's; but it is equally certain that all his principal theories were fully developed in his mind long before he met Godwin. Again, he may have learnt from Pestalozzi, Fellenberg and other practical pioneers of education; but he had already set his own schools on foot at New Lanark before the visit to the Continent which brought him into direct contact with them. The *Report to the County of Lanark* recalls at some points Thomas Hodgskin's almost contemporary lectures on *Popular Political Economy* at the London Mechanics' Institute, and at others William Cobbett's *Paper against Gold*. He may have known both of these; but there is no evidence that, at this stage, he knew either.

Indeed, while it is obvious that no man does all his thinking by the unaided light of his own mind, close resemblances of thought are no evidence at all of intellectual borrowing. The same problems and situations suggest to different minds the same or closely similar ideas, and the credit of originality is often given on account of a mere accident of date. It is simply not worth while to discuss how far Owen picked the brains of others; it is enough to make plain that his thinking was not that of an isolated freak out of relation to his time, but bore close similarities to the thought of other original minds among his contemporaries. Like them, he was trying to solve the riddles of his time, and he often hit on the same, or kindred, solutions and ideas.

Owen, however, differed from most writers in that he was not at all an "intellectual," or a student in any ordinary sense. Thought was for him always an instrument, and never a self-sufficient exercise. He was careless of his debts to others, and unconscious of them, because he thought in terms of problems and not of persons. This was in part his strength; but it became also a source of weakness. Used to command in practical affairs, he was used also to isolation. He applied the same method to his thinking, and became also intellectually autocratic and isolated, losing that equal communication of minds which is a powerful stimulus to fresh discovery. He was sure he was right, and in his assurance he locked the door to new ideas.

That this confident shut-up-ness of his mind was the cause of his becoming mentally unbalanced in old age is obvious. No man is strong enough to live so utterly by his own illumination. It was also clearly a potent cause of failure as soon as he left New Lanark, where he could be the benevolent capitalist with full autocratic powers, and entered on fields of action which involved some form of democratic co-operation with others. Smith and Morrison were only two among many who found that Owen demanded not equal co-workers, but disciples and even devotees to do his bidding.

It is hard to say how far this attitude of mind was inborn in him, or how far it developed out of, or side by side with, his theories. From the first, he was extraordinarily self-reliant. His life, even before going to Manchester, and still more his career at Manchester show plainly that unquestioning faith in himself which went with him all his days. His theories, I think, arose out of this attitude of mind, though in a sense they are inconsistent with it. For his view of the paramount influence of environment on character, and his sweeping condemnation of the environment of the "old immoral world," led him to regard all men as children, to be saved, not by their own bemused kicking against the pricks, but by the action of some beneficent power that should change their environment for them. He was inconsistent only in thinking himself strong enough to be that beneficent power, and even this inconsistency he sought to explain away by saying that the illumination which had come to him was all the fruit of his own experience.

Sooner or later, those who tried to work with Owen were bound to discover that he thought of them as little children, and of himself as the chosen instrument of their enlightenment, to whom they must surrender their will and judgment for their own good. Strong men, like Smith and Morrison, rebelled against this tutelage: only weak men would submit to it. The most faithful Owenites were largely weak men, who were prepared to give up their wills to the stronger spirit.

This is true, and damaging. But if we see only this in Owen we make a great mistake. He had, despite this fatal fault, a quite extraordinary power of making men love him. This was not mainly due to his utter disinterestedness, to which even his enemies were bound to pay tribute; for disinterestedness alone is cold, and cannot create warmth. Owen inspired not merely cold praise or trust, but love.

Whence arose this power, which seems strange in a spirit so solitary and self-contained? It was felt, because Owen was not merely "benevolent," as he was so often called, but himself a person of warm affections. We have seen how the children at New Lanark loved him; and it is plain that, equally, he loved the children, not merely in the mass, but each for itself. Nor did he love only children. He had, at any rate in his earlier years, the rare quality of feeling not merely benevolence for all the human race, but affection for nearly everyone with whom he was brought into contact. Even to an audience at a meeting he could speak as if he loved it, not merely collectively, but as man to man. And it was because men felt this warmth of feeling in him that they loved him back, and gave him freely of the best that was in them.

J. E. Smith was not a mild man, and his judgments, particularly when he had quarrelled, were apt to be harsh. But even he, at the crisis of their quarrel in 1834, wrote to his brother that they remained "very good friends apparently for all that."[1] And years later, Smith wrote of Owen that "his good-nature has gained him as many friends as his doctrine."[2]

Morrison too, at the height of his anger with Owen over the deposition of the *Pioneer* from its status of official organ of the Consolidated Union— a check fatal to its circulation—wrote these penetrating sentences: "It gives us pain to write our free, untethered thought, for we do love the man, because he loves his species; and yet we fear him for that self-same love. The sweetest despotism is that of universal love, and this we yield to Mr. Owen; but even this has thorns and briers growing in its path, and, looking forward with boundless hope to lands of promise, would drag the human race through slough and bramble to a distant paradise, before the half of them are ready for the journey."[3] The tone is not at all of bitterness, but rather of disappointed affection.

Lovett was colder and more critical, especially of Owen's "anti-democratic" attitude.[4] But even he thinks "it is necessary to state that I entertain the highest respect for Mr. Owen's warm benevolence and generous intentions, however I may differ from many of his views."[5] And Lovett's friend Henry Hetherington, the Chartist editor of the *Poor Man's Guardian* and stalwart fighter for a free Press, remained a devout Owenite to the end, and in his

---

[1] *Life of Smith*, p. 113. [2] *Op. cit.*, p. 209.
[3] *Pioneer*, June 7, 1834. [4] Lovett, *Life and Struggles*, p. 48.
[5] *Ibid.*, p. 43.

will wrote that "grateful to Mr. Owen for the happiness I have experienced in contemplating the superiority of his system, I could not die happy without recommending my fellow-countrymen to study its principles and earnestly strive to establish them in practice." Earlier, he speaks of his "ardent attachment to the principles of the great and good man—Robert Owen."[1]

This is the testimony of supporters. That of opponents of Owenism is even more telling. We have quoted in an earlier chapter Francis Place's unusually warm commendation. Lord Brougham called him "one of the most humane, simple-minded, amiable men on earth," and said that he was "one of the most calm and candid men I have ever conversed with."[2] "As long," wrote Harriet Martineau, "as the name of Robert Owen continues to be heard of, there will be some to laugh at it, but there will be more to love and cherish it." Yet that she had a keen appreciation of Owen's faults the following passage shows: "At every moment, his plans were going to be tried in some country or other, which would bring over all other countries. Everybody who treated him with respect and interest was assumed to be his disciple; and those who openly opposed or quizzed him were regarded with a good-natured smile, and spoken of as people who had very good eyes, but who had accidentally got into a wood, where they could not see their way for the trees. He was the same placid, happy being into his old age, believing and expecting whatever he wished; always gentlemanly and

[1] Quoted in M. Beer, *History of British Socialism*, vol. ii. p. 7.
[2] Speech in House of Commons, December 16, 1819, quoted Podmore, p. 637.

courteous in his manners; always on the most endearing terms with his children, who loved to make him, as they said, 'the very happiest old man in the world'; always a gentle bore in regard to his dogmas and his expectations; always palpably right in his descriptions of human misery; always thinking he had proved a thing when he had asserted it in the force of his own conviction; and always really meaning something more rational than he had actually expressed." [1]

"Always a gentle bore." Macaulay, not fitted by temperament to be a sympathetic critic, remarked more brusquely that he "fled at the first sound of his discourse." [2] Sir Leslie Stephen, in his biography of Owen in the *Dictionary of National Biography*, called him one of those "bores who are the salt of the earth." That Owen was a bore is beyond dispute. All occasions were for him chances of expounding the truth. When Macaulay fled, Owen was engaged in expounding the "New System" to Sheil, the Irish M.P., at a fancy-dress ball. All times were alike to him, all persons worth conversion. And he was extremely long-winded. Yet he kept his friends, and they valued not only his friendship, but his conversation. Owen at least bored his friends charmingly. Southey called him "eloquent," and held that "there are few who speak better, or who write so well." [3] After all, there are worse things than being a bore, when one has something to say. Most men with a message are apt to be bores. But let us grant that Owen, espe-

[1] H. Martineau, *Biographical Sketches*, p. 313. See also p. 151 of this *Life*.

[2] Trevelyan, *Life of Macaulay*, vol. i. p. 220.

[3] Southey, *Sir Thomas More*, vol. i. p. 144.

cially in his later years, was a greater bore than most. Even for those he bored, the charm of his personality remained strong and compelling. Where he did not convince, he often pleased.

Still, our tolerance of bores depends largely, though not wholly, on our sense of the value of what they have to say. Owen had not many things to say, and he said them many times over; but the few things were of paramount importance. At a time when manufacturers and statesmen were ready to defend in the name of progress all the enormities of the Industrial Revolution, he, a great manufacturer, stood out against them, and preached the virtue and efficiency of good factory conditions and humane treatment. When all the other "practical men" were hymning the virtues of competitive capitalism, he saw not only its vices, but the vision of another system, based on co-operation and human fellowship. When the "monitorial system" was considered an advanced educational project, and the State still divested itself of all responsibility for the upbringing of its citizens, he not only preached universal free education, but gave practical demonstrations far in advance of his time in the practice of teaching. When the workers were sinking under the despair bred by evil factory conditions, his faith and hope raised them up to strike the first concerted blow for economic freedom. Not for nothing do many movements look back to him as their founder or source of first inspiration.

If in his later years he lost that practical grip and capacity for organisation which made New Lanark the model factory, the model school, and the model village of Europe, let us remember that he was already an old man when he plunged into the struggles most closely associated with his name. Even when he founded New Harmony, he was fifty-four. When he started the Labour Exchange he was sixty-one, and when he helped to found the Consolidated Union sixty-two or three. He was seventy when he became Governor of Queenwood, and eighty-two before his conversion to Spiritualism. Judge him, not by his old age, but by the works of his manhood. He will not be found wanting in that which passes for greatness. And he will appear, not only a great man, but a man, lovable and loved, whose faults were plain for all to see, but his virtues also plain and compelling. Place spoke of his "nonsensical notions." Well, "nonsensical notions," as well as bores, are oftentimes the salt of the earth.

APPENDICES

APPENDIX A

THE BUILDERS' GUILD, 1833

*Proposals for the Establishment of a National Association for Build-
ing, to be called "The Grand National Guild of Builders"; to
be composed of Architects and Surveyors, Masons, Carpenters and
Joiners, Bricklayers, Plasterers, Slaters, Plumbers, Glaziers and
Painters, Whitesmiths, Quarrymen and Brickmakers.*

OBJECTS OF THE UNION

1. The general improvement of all the individuals forming
the building class; ensuring regular employment for all.
2. To ensure fair remuneration for their services.
3. To fix a reasonable time for labour.
4. To educate both adults and children.
5. To have regular superior medical advice and assistance,
and to make provision for the comfortable and independent
retirement of the aged and infirm.
6. To regulate the operations of the whole in harmony, and
to produce a general fund sufficient to secure all these objects.
7. To ensure a superiority of building for the public at fair
and equitable prices.
8. To obtain good and comfortable dwellings for every
member of the Union; extensive and well-arranged workshops; places of depôt for building materials; halls for the
meetings of the Lodges and Central Committees; schools and
academies for the instruction of adults and children in morals
and the useful sciences.
9. And also the establishment of Builders' Banks in the
various districts in which the Grand District Lodges shall be
established.

MEANS OF EFFECTING THE OBJECTS OF THE UNION

*Capital at least £15,000, in one or more shares of 5s. from each
member of the Union, already sufficient in numbers to effect these
objects.*

1. Each class of the builders to be composed of men who
have served five years' apprenticeship, and are above eighteen
years of age.

2. Each Lodge to be governed by a president, vice-presidents, treasurer, secretary, and assistants, chosen from the Lodge. Each Lodge to elect a foreman to every ten men, and a general superintendent or clerk of works where necessary. The Lodges to meet weekly.

3. The *Local Lodges* to elect their Central Committee of local management. Each Local Committee to be composed of a president, vice-president, treasurer, secretary, and assistants, chosen from their own body.

The Central Local Committees to superintend the building business of their localities and to sit daily.

4. Ten Central Committees to constitute a DISTRICT. Two delegates from each Central Committee to form a District Committee.

Each District Committee to have its president, vice-president, treasurer, secretary and assistants elected from the delegates of the Central Committee[s].

The District Committees to meet quarterly, to receive the reports of the Local Central Committees, regulate the proceedings, and audit the accounts of the district.

5. Each *District Committee* to elect a delegate to form a GRAND NATIONAL COMMITTEE in London, and this Grand National Committee to elect their president, vice-president, and treasurer.

The Grand National Committee to meet annually, to deliberate and decide upon the general interests of the Union.

6. The president of the Grand National Committee to be elected for three years (but removable if cause be seen), with power to appoint his own assistants, all of whom shall form a permanent establishment to receive reports from the DISTRICT and CENTRAL COMMITTEES; and to communicate weekly, through the medium of a Builders' Gazette, every important fact connected with the building transactions of the kingdom.

7. The voting at all elections to be taken by ballot.

(Quoted from the *Pioneer*, September 21, 1833.)

APPENDIX B

FIRST DRAFT PLAN OF THE GRAND NATIONAL CONSOLIDATED TRADES UNION

THE following plan of a general organisation of the producing classes is submitted by the General Congress of Delegates of the Co-operatives and Trades Unions, held in the National Equitable Labour Exchange Buildings, commencing October 7, [1833] :—

That the National Moral Union of the Productive Classes shall have a national establishment in London; provincial establishments, to comprise several counties; district establishments of counties; and parochial establishments.

The members of the Parochial Union to consist of delegates from each general trade, manufacture and productive occupation carried on within the limits of the Parochial Union, that has formed itself into a regularly constituted Lodge, to superintend the general interest of such trade, manufacture, or occupation.

The members of the District Unions to consist of delegates from the Parochial Unions.

The members of the Provincial Unions to consist of delegates from the District Unions.

The members of the National Union Establishment to be formed of delegates from the Provincial Unions.

All delegates to be elected by ballot.

That all who are employed, or who are willing to be employed, in producing wealth, knowledge, or happiness, for their associates or the public, and who are willing to conform to the regulations and laws of the Union, shall be eligible to become a candidate for membership.

That a provincial [*sic*—? provisional] council be appointed to draw up the regulations and laws of the Union.

That the next Congress be held at Barnsley, Yorks, on Easter Monday, March 31, 1834, and that it be called the Grand National Moral Union of the Useful and Productive Classes of Great Britain and Ireland.

(From the *Crisis*, October 19, 1833.)

APPENDIX C

RULES OF THE CONSOLIDATED UNION

Rules and regulations of the Grand National Consolidated Trades Union of Great Britain and Ireland, instituted for the purpose of the more effectually enabling the working-classes to secure, protect and establish the rights of industry. [1834.]

I. Each Trade in this Consolidated Union shall have its Grand Lodge in that town or city most eligible for it; such Grand Lodge to be governed internally by a Grand Master, Deputy Grand Master, and Grand Secretary, and a Committee of Management.

II. Each Grand Lodge shall have its District Lodges, in any number, to be designated or named after the town or city in which the District Lodge is founded.

III. Each Grand Lodge shall be considered the head of its own particular trade, and to have certain exclusive powers accordingly; but in all other respects the Grand Lodges are to answer the same ends as the District Lodges.

IV. Each District Lodge shall embrace within itself all operatives of the same trade, living in smaller towns or villages adjacent to it; and shall be governed internally by a president, vice-president, secretary, and a committee of management.

V. Each District Lodge shall have (if necessary) its Branch Lodge or Lodges, numbered in rotation; such Branch Lodges to be under the control of the District Lodge from which they sprung.

VI. An unlimited number of the above-described Lodges shall form and constitute the Grand National Consolidated Trades Union of Great Britain and Ireland.

VII. Each District shall have its Central Committee, composed of a Deputy, or Deputies, from every District Lodge of the different trades in the district; such Central Committee shall meet once in every week to superintend and watch over the interests of the Consolidated Union in that District, transmitting a report of the same, monthly, to the Executive Coun-

328

cil in London, together with any suggestions of improvements they may think proper.

VIII. The General government of the G.N.C.T.U. shall be vested in a Grand Council of Delegates from each of the Central Committees of all the Districts in the Consolidated Union, to be holden every six months, at such places as shall be decided upon at the preceding Council; the next meeting of the Grand Council of the Consolidated Union to be held on the first day of September, 1834, and to continue its sitting so long as may be requisite.

IX. During the recess of the Grand Council of Delegates, the government of the Consolidated Union shall be vested in an Executive Council of five; which executive will in future be chosen at the Grand Delegate Council aforesaid.

X. All dispensations or grants for the formation of new Lodges shall come from the Grand Lodge of each particular trade, or from the Executive Council. Applications for dispensations to come through the Central Committee of the District or by memorial, signed by at least twenty operatives of the place where such new Lodge is proposed to be founded.

XI. The Executive Council shall act as trustees for all funds provided by the Consolidated Union, and for the adjustment of strikes, the purchasing or renting of land, establishing provision stores, workshops, etc.; or for any other purpose connected with the general benefit of the whole of the Union.

XII. All sums for the above purposes to be transmitted from the Lodges to the Executive Council through some safe and accredited medium.

XIII. District and Grand Lodges shall have the control of their own funds, subject to the levies imposed on them by the Executive Council.

XIV. The ordinary weekly subscription of members to be threepence each member.

XV. No strike or turn out for an *advance* of wages shall be made by the members of any Lodge in the Consolidated Union without the consent of the Executive Council; but in all cases of a *reduction* of wages the Central Committee of the District shall have the power of deciding whenever a strike shall or shall not take place; and should such Central Committee be necessitated to order a levy in support of such strike brought on by such reduction of wages, such order shall be made in all the Lodges; in the first instance, in the District in which such reduction hath taken place; and on advice being forwarded to the Executive they shall consider the case, and order accordingly.

XVI. No higher sum than 10s. per week each shall be paid to members during a strike or turn out.

XVII. All Lodges shall be divided into local sections of twenty men each, or as near that number as may be.

Miscellaneous and Auxiliary Lodges.

XVIII. In all cases where the number of operatives in a particular Trade, in any District, is too limited to allow of such Trade forming a Lodge of itself, the members of such Trade shall be permitted to become Unionists by joining the Lodge of any other Trade in the District. Should there be several trades in a District thus limited with respect to the number of their Operatives, they shall be allowed to form together a District Miscellaneous Lodge, with permission, in order to extend the sphere of the brotherhood, to hold out the hand of fellowship to all really useful labourers employed productively.

XIX. And, in order that all acknowledged friends to the productive classes may attach themselves to the Consolidated Union, an Auxiliary Lodge may be established in every city or town in the kingdom. The members of each Lodge shall conform to all the rules and regulations herein contained, and be bound in the same manner, and subject to all the laws of the G.N.C.T.U.; and shall not, in any manner, or at any time or place, speak or write *anything* in opposition to these laws or the interests of the Union aforesaid. The Auxiliary Lodge shall be liable to be dissolved according to Article XXII.

XX. Lodges of Industrious Females shall be instituted in every district where it may be practicable; such Lodges to be considered, in every respect, as part of, and belonging to, the G.N.C.T.U.

Employment of Turn Outs.

XXI. In all cases of strikes or turn outs, where it is practicable to employ members in the making or producing of such commodities or articles as are in demand among their brother Unionists, or any other operatives willing to purchase the same, each Lodge shall provide a work-room or shop in which such commodities and articles may be manufactured on account of that Lodge, which shall make proper arrangements for the supply of the necessary materials; over which arrangements the Central Committee of the District shall have the control, subject to the scrutiny of the Grand Lodge Committee of the Trade on strike.

XXII. The Grand Lodge of each Trade to have the power of dissolving any District Lodge, in that Trade, for any violation of these laws, any outrage upon the public peace, or for gross neglect of duty; all Branch, Miscellaneous or Auxiliary Lodges to be subject to the same control.

XXIII. The internal management and general concerns of each Grand or District Lodge are vested in a Committee of twenty-five members, each to be chosen by ballot, and elected by not having less than three-fourths of the votes of the members present, at the time of his election, in his favour. The whole of the Committee to go out of office quarterly, eligible, however, to re-election. The Grand Master, or President, and the Secretary, or Grand Secretary, of a Grand or a District Lodge, to be considered members of its Committee of Management by virtue of their offices.

XXIV. Each Grand Lodge, in this Consolidated Union, to be considered the centre of information regarding the general affairs of its particular Trade; each District Lodge to communicate with its Grand Lodge at the end of each month, and to give an account to it of the number of people Members in the District Lodge—the gross number of the hours of labour performed by them in that district—the state of its funds—and any local or general intelligence that may be considered of interest to the Grand Lodge.

XXV. The Committee of Management in each Lodge shall sit at least on one evening in every week for the despatch of business—and oftener if necessary.

XXVI. Each Grand or District Lodge to hold its meetings on one evening in every month; at which meeting a report of the Proceedings of the Committee, during the past month, shall be laid before the members, together with an abstract of the state of the funds, an account of the prospects of the Society, and any other propositions or by-laws which the Committee may have to suggest for adoption, and any other information or correspondence of interest to the members. All nomination of fresh officers to be made at the Lodge meetings, and all complaints of members to be considered and discussed therein.

XXVII. The Grand Master or Deputy Grand Master, President, or Vice-President, or both, shall preside at all meetings of Grand or District Lodges, to keep order, state or put questions according to the sense and intention of the members, give effect to the resolutions, and cause them to be put into force; and they shall be addressed by members, during Lodge hours, by their proper titles.

XXVIII. No subject which does not immediately concern the interest of the Trade shall be discussed at any meetings of Committees or Lodges; and no proposition shall be adopted in either without the consent of at least three-fourths of the members present at its proposal—the question to be decided by ballot if any member demand it. No less than five members of Committee of Management to constitute a Quorum, provided the rest have all been duly summoned: no Grand or District Lodge to be considered open unless at least thirty members be present.

XXIX. Each Grand or District Lodge shall have the power to appoint sub-committees to enquire into or manage any affair touching their interests, of which Committees the head officers of the Lodge are always to be considered members.

Of Secretaries.

XXX. The duties of a secretary to a Grand or District Lodge are:—To attend Lodge and Committee Meetings and take minutes of the proceedings, entering the same in a book to be kept for that purpose.

To conduct all the correspondence of the Society. To take down the names and addresses of parties desirous of being initiated into the Order; and upon receiving the initiation fee from each, and entering the amount into a book, he will give each party a card, by which they may be admitted into the place appointed for the ceremony.

To receive subscriptions of members, entering the same into a small account book, numbering the subscribers from No. 1, and following up the sequence in regulation order, giving to each subscriber a card, on which his contribution or payment shall be noted.

To enter all additional weekly payments and all levies into separate small books; all subscriptions and payments to be afterwards copied into a ledger, ruled expressly for the purpose.

The Secretary to be paid an adequate weekly salary; and to be allowed an assistant if the amount of business require it.

The Secretary of each Grand or District Lodge shall balance his books once every fortnight, and the Managing Committee shall audit them, going over each item of receipt and expenditure with strict attention, checking the same with scrupulous care; and if found correct, three of the Committee shall verify the same by affixing their signatures to the page on which the balance is struck.

Initiation.

XXXI. Any of the officers or members of a Lodge may be appointed by the Committee of Management to perform the Initiation Service; and to have charge of the Robes, etc., for that purpose; for which the Committee may allow him a reasonable remuneration.

Any party applying to be initiated must bring forward two witnesses as to character and the identity of his trade or occupation.

Of Branch Lodges.

XXXII. Branch Lodge Meetings shall be held on one evening in every week, in the respective localities; at which Lodges any motion, proposed by law, etc., may be discussed and considered by the members previous to its being finally submitted to the Grand or District Lodge Committee.

XXXIII. The members of each branch may elect a president to preside at the Branch Lodge, and a secretary to collect subscriptions or levies for their Grand or District Lodge; who shall also attend meetings of the Committee of Management, for instructions and information, and to submit suggestions, complaints, etc., from his Branch Lodge. No salaries or fees to be allowed to officers of Branch Lodges, unless by the unanimous consent of their members.

Wardens, etc.

XXXIV. In addition to the officers before mentioned in these regulations, there shall be, in each Grand and District Lodge, a Warden, an Inside Tyler, an Outside Tyler, and a Conductor, whose principal duties are to attend initiations, and to see that no improper persons be admitted into the meetings. These officers to be elected in the same manner, and at the same time, as other officers.

Miscellaneous Articles.

XXXV. Any member shall be liable to expulsion from the Lodges for any improper conduct therein; and shall be excluded from the benefits of the Society if his subscriptions be more than six months in arrear, unless the Committee of Management shall see cause to decide otherwise.

XXXVI. The *G.N.C.T.U. Gazette* to be considered the official organ of the Executive Council, and the general medium of intelligence on the affairs of the Union.

XXXVII. Each Lodge shall, as soon as possible, make arrangements for furnishing the means of instituting libraries or reading-rooms, or any other arrangements, affording them every facility for meeting together for friendly conversation, mutual instruction, and rational amusement or recreation.

XXXVIII. In all cases, where it be practicable, each Lodge shall establish within its locality one or more depôts for provisions and articles in general domestic use, in order that its members may be supplied with the best of such commodities at little above wholesale prices.

XXXIX. Each District and Grand Lodge shall endeavour to institute a fund for the support of sick and aged members, and for defraying the funeral expenses of deceased members, on a similar principle to that of Benefit Societies, such fund to be kept up by small monthly contributions from those Unionists who are willing to subscribe towards it.

XL. Each Grand or District Lodge to have the power of making its own by-laws for purposes not comprised in these regulations; but such by-laws or laws must not be in opposition to, or in counteraction of, any of the Articles herein specified.

XLI. No member can enter Lodge Meetings without giving the proper signs, and producing his card to prove his membership, and that he is not in arrears of subscription for more than one month, unless lenity has been granted by order of Committee.

XLII. That a separate treasurer be appointed for each £20 of the funds collected; and that such treasurers shall not suffer any money to be withdrawn from their hands without a written order, signed by at least three of the Managing Committee, and presented by the secretary, or one of the other officers of the Society.

XLIII. All sums under £30 shall be left in the hands of the secretary for current expenses; but no outlay shall be made by him without an express order from the Managing Committee, signed by at least three of its members.

XLIV. That every member of this Union do use his best endeavours, by fair and open argument, and the force of good example, and not by intimidation or violence, to induce his fellows to join the brotherhood, in order that no workmen may remain out of the Union to undersell them in the market of labour; as, while that is done, employers will be enabled to resist the demands of the Unionists, whereas, if no operatives remain out of union, employers will be compelled to keep up the price of labour.

XLV. That each member of the Consolidated Union pay a Registration Fee of 3*d.* to defray the general expenses; which fee is to be transmitted to the Executive once in every month.

XLVI. That, although the design of the Union is, in the first instance, to raise the wages of the workmen, or prevent any further reduction therein, and to diminish the hours of labour, the great and ultimate object of it must be to establish the paramount rights of Industry and Humanity, by instituting such measures as shall effectually prevent the ignorant, idle, and useless part of society from having that undue control over the fruits of our toil, which, through the agency of a vicious money system, they at present possess; and that, consequently, the Unionists should lose no opportunity of mutually encouraging and assisting each other in bringing about A DIFFERENT STATE OF THINGS, in which the really useful and intelligent part of society only shall have the direction of its affairs, and in which well-directed industry and virtue shall meet their just distinction and reward, and vicious idleness its merited contempt and destitution.

XLVII. All the rules and regulations herein contained be subject to the revision, alteration, or abrogation of the Grand Delegate Council.

(From a copy in the Goldsmiths' Library, University of London.)

APPENDIX D

NATIONAL COMMUNITY FRIENDLY SOCIETY, 1837

Preamble to Rules.

THE objects of this Society shall be to raise, from time to time, by subscription among the members thereof, or by voluntary contributions, or donations, or loans, various stocks or funds for the mutual assistance, maintenance, and education of their wives and husbands, children or nominees, in sickness, infancy, advanced age, or other natural state or contingency; which stocks or fund shall be applied as follows:—

First for the purchase or rental of land whereon to erect suitable dwellings and other buildings; or for the purchase or rental of dwellings or other buildings wherein the members shall, by united labour, support each other, under every vicissitude, including the establishment of schools for children, or any other purpose not unlawful; by these and every other means consistent with honesty and impartial justice to arrange the powers of production, distribution, consumption, and education, in order to produce among the members feelings of pure charity, and social affection for each other, and practically plant the standard of peace and good will on earth towards all men.

Second, an auxiliary fund for the payment of the current expenses of the Society, and for such other incidental charges as may be necessary to carry out its objects.

(From the Registered Rules of the Society, 1837.)

336

APPENDIX E

PRINCIPAL WRITINGS OF ROBERT OWEN

Books are printed in capitals, pamphlets in ordinary type. In order of publication; published in London unless a place is given. An excellent full bibliography of Owen's writings is published by the National Library of Wales.

APPENDIX F

BOOKS USEFUL FOR THE STUDY OF OWEN AND OWENISM

A. LIVES AND STUDIES

[*In order of publication, except the works of R. O. and R. D. O. Books in capitals, pamphlets in ordinary type. Published in London unless a place is given.*]

Robert Owen: THE LIFE OF ROBERT OWEN. Vol. I. [to about 1822, with some appendices]. 1857.

Robert Owen: THE LIFE OF ROBERT OWEN. Vol. IA. Appendices [covering the same period]. 1858.

[Vol. I. has been reprinted in Bohn's Popular Library, but without the prefatory matter or the appendices, which are important.]

Robert Owen: THE NEW EXISTENCE OF MAN UPON THE EARTH. 8 Parts [contains much autobiographical matter subsequently worked over in the *Life*]. 1854–5.

Robert Dale Owen: THREADING MY WAY [autobiography]. 1874.

"Robert": Robert Owen, Esq., the Unique. 1823.

J. Watts: Robert Owen the Visionary. Manchester, 1843.

M. R. L. Reybaud: In ÉTUDE SUR LES RÉFORMATEURS CONTEMPORAIRES. Paris, 1849.

G. J. Holyoake: Life and Last Days of Robert Owen. 1859.

W. L. Sargent: ROBERT OWEN AND HIS SOCIAL PHILOSOPHY. 1860.

Harriet Martineau: In BIOGRAPHICAL SKETCHES. 1869.

J. O. Wolbers: ROBERT OWEN [in Dutch]. Utrecht, 1878.

Charles Bradlaugh: In Five Dead Men Whom I Knew. 1884.

E. R. A. Seligman: Robert Owen and the Christian Socialists. Boston, 1886.

Lloyd Jones: LIFE, TIMES AND LABOURS OF ROBERT OWEN. 1889–90.

Leslie Stephen: In DICTIONARY OF NATIONAL BIOGRAPHY. Vol. 42. 1895.

339

ROBERT OWEN

A. Fabre: Un Socialiste Pratique: Robert Owen. Nîmes, 1896.

J. Glasse: Robert Owen and his Life Work. 1900.

Helène Simon: Robert Owen: Sein Leben und seine Bedeutung für die Gegenwurt. Jena, 1905.

E. Dolléans: Robert Owen. Paris, 1905.

F. Podmore: Robert Owen: a Biography. 1906.

R. E. Davies: The Life of Robert Owen. 1907.

Richard Roberts: Robert Owen [in Welsh]. Carnarvon, 1907.

G. R. S. Taylor: In Leaders of Socialism. 1908.

Joseph Clayton: Robert Owen: Pioneer of Social Reform. 1908.

B. L. Hutchins: Robert Owen: Social Reformer. 1912.

C. E. M. Joad: Robert Owen: Idealist. 1917.

Joseph McCabe: Robert Owen. 1920.

Of the above, Owen's *Autobiography* is invaluable for the earlier years. Robert Dale Owen is very useful for New Lanark and for Owen's private life. Some of his pamphlets also contain useful matter bearing on these points. The standard large-scale biography is Podmore's, which is very full about New Lanark, New Harmony, Queenwood, and the Labour Exchange, but very inadequate about the Trade Union events of 1834. Podmore, I think, got a wrong perspective by approaching Owen chiefly through his hostile interest in spiritualism, which caused him to think of Owen always as an old man and, within limits, an old fool. Podmore was, moreover, a congenital Fabian.

Of the rest, McCabe's short sketch is by far the best. Dolléans has some useful material bearing on Owen's connections with the French Revolution of 1848. Lloyd Jones is disappointing; though he was closely associated with Owen, he presents no intelligible picture of him. Harriet Martineau's sketch is excellent, and there is also good material in her *Autobiography*. Leslie Stephen's *D.N.B.* article is fair.

B. Other Works

Manchester.

Wheeler: History of Manchester. 1836.

Bruton: Short History of Manchester and Salford. Manchester, 1924.

APPENDICES

New Lanark.

A. Cullen: Adventures in Socialism. 1910.

R. Dale Owen: Outline of the System of Education at New Lanark. Glasgow, 1824.

"Robert": Robert Owen at New Lanark. Manchester, 1839.

E. Baines, etc.: Report of the Leeds Deputation to New Lanark. Leeds, 1819.

J. Griscom: A Year in Europe. Vol. II. New York, 1823.

Allen: The Life of William Allen.

H. G. Macnab: The New Views of Mr. Owen of Lanark, Impartially Considered. 1819.

New Harmony, Queenwood, Orbiston, etc.

A. Cullen: as above.

A. Combe: The Sphere of Joint Stock Companies [Orbiston]. Edinburgh, 1825.

A. Kent: Co-operative Communities in the United States. Washington, 1901.

C. Nordhoff: Communistic Societies of the United States. New York, 1874.

J. H. Noyes: History of American Socialisms. 1870.

M. K. E. Blake: Hearts Haven [N. H.]. Indianapolis, 1900.

P. Brown: Twelve Months in New Harmony. Cincinnati, 1827.

W. Herbert: A Visit to the Colony of Harmony. 1825.

R. D. Owen, etc.: New Harmony Gazette. 1825–9.

G. B. Lockwood: The New Harmony Movement. 1905.

E. T. Craig: The Story of Ralahine.

G. J. Holyoake: A Visit to Harmony Hall [Queenwood]. 1844.

A. Somerville: A Journey to Harmony Hall [Queenwood]. 1843.

M. Hennell: Social Systems and Communities founded on Co-operation. 1844.

W. Thompson: Practical Directions for the Establishment of Communities. 1830.

Labour Exchanges, Builders' Guild, the Trades Union.

S. and B. Webb: History of Trade Unionism [revised edition]. 1920.

R. W. Postgate: The Builders' History. 1923.

R. W. Postgate: Revolution [documents and notes]. 1920.

341

Max Beer: History of British Socialism. Vol. I. 1920.
W. A. Smith: Shepherd Smith the Universalist [J. E. Smith].
1892.
The Pioneer (edited by Morrison). 1833–4.
G. J. Holyoake: History of Co-operation. 1875–9.

Later Owenite Movements.

G. J. Holyoake: Sixty Years of an Agitator's Life. 1892.
J. McCabe: Life and Letters of G. J. Holyoake. 1908.

Add to the above a mass of contemporary pamphlets, prospectuses and other documents issued by the Owenite Societies and their opponents.

INDEX

343

INDEX

Canterbury, Archbishop of (Dr. Sutton), 137, 149, 151, 175, 186
Cartwright, Edward, 36
Major John, 171
Capitalism, growth of, 170
Carpenters and Joiners, General Union of, 291
Castlereagh, Lord, 215
Character, Owen's views on, 34, 98, 101, 107, Ch. VIII, 189, 208, 313
Charlotte St. Institution, 265 f., 277
Chartism, 11, 33, 232 f., 254, 292, 304
Child labour, 96 ff., 139 ff., 160 ff., 171, 207 f.
Chorlton Hall, 81
Chorlton Twist Co., 75, 80, 82, 88
Christian Socialism, 302
Cloncurry, Lord, 228
Clothiers' Union, 280
Cobbett, W., 25, 171, 198, 199, 201, 204, 223, 229 f., 241, 252, 286, 293, 315
Cochrane, Lord, 175
Coleridge, S. T., 55, 78, 241
Combination Acts, repeal of, 253, 267, 279
Communities. See Villages of Co-operation.
Communities, Society for Promoting, 242
Consolidated Union. See Trades Union
Co-operation, Villages of. See Villages of Co-operation.
Co-operative and Economical Society, 233
Community Fund Association, London, 234
Congresses, 261, 290
Knowledge, British Association for Promoting, 261
Movement (modern), 29, 32, 257, 303
Societies, 29, 232 f., 252 ff., 269 ff., 284, 293, 302 f.
Owen's views on, 260 f.
Society, Brighton, 234
London, 233
Co-operator, the, 234, 258

Copenhagen Fields, 286
Corn Law (1815), 162
Corresponding Societies, 118
Cotton Trade, Glasgow Board of Management, 123, 153
Cotton trade, growth of, 36, 56 ff., 123
Cox's Hotel, 307
Crespigny, Sir W. de, 218, 228
Crisis, the, 276, 282, 287 ff., 327
Crofters, 93, 95
Crompton, S., 36, 61
Currency reform, 223 f.
Cuvier, 214.

Dale, Anne Caroline. See Owen, Annie Caroline.
Dale, David, 83, 84 ff., 90, 93 ff., 102, 116 ff., 128, 313
James, 90
The Misses, 117 f.
Dalton, John, 76, 78, 79, 182
Daniel, John, 213
Defoe, Daniel, 46
Dennistoun, Mr., 109 f.
De Quincey, Thomas, 76, 82
Derby Turn-out, 285
" Document," the, 274, 286
Doherty, John, 203, 267, 270
Donne, James, 44
Dorchester labourers, 285
Committee, London, 285
Drinkwater, Miss, 73 f.
Mr., 67 ff., 91
Drunkenness, 68, 94, 107

Economist, the, 232
Edgeworth, Maria, 118, 210
Education at New Lanark, 95, 101, 107 f., 127 ff., 207 ff.
Education, Owen's ideas on, 14, 124, Ch. VIII, 207 ff., 226, 300, 311
Eight Hours' Day, 29, 270, 285
Enclosures, 30, 92
in Highlands, 93
Ethical Societies, 32

Factory Bill (1815–9), 140, 154 ff., 173, 207
reform, 16, 139 f., 153 f.
Family Herald, the, 277

344

INDEX

INDEX

349

INDEX

PRINTED IN GREAT BRITAIN BY R. CLAY & SONS LIMITED
Bungay, Suffolk